25 Essential Lessons for Employee Management

How to Protect Your Business

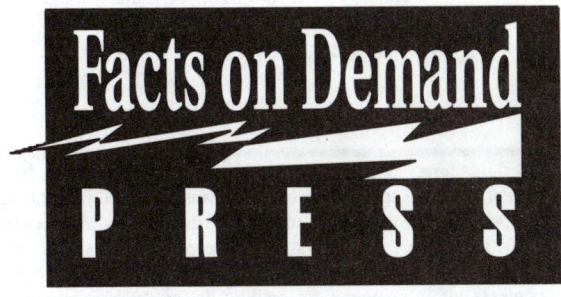

©2001 By Facts on Demand Press
PO Box 27869
Tempe, AZ 85285-7869
(800) 929-3811
www.brbpub.com

25 Essential Lessons for Employee Management
How to Protect Your Business

©2001 By Facts on Demand Press
PO Box 27869
Tempe, AZ 85285-7869
(800) 929-3811

ISBN 1-889150-25-8
Cover Design by Robin Fox & Associates

Cataloging-in-Publication Data

    DeMey, Dennis L.
       25 essential lessons for employee management : how to protect your business / Dennis L. DeMey with James R. Flowers Jr. and Michael L. Sankey.
      -- 1st ed.
      p. cm.
      Twenty-five essential lessons for employee management
      Includes index.
      ISBN: 1-889150-25-8

      1. Personnel management. 2. Supervision of employees. 3. Small business--Personnel management. I. Flowers, James R. (James Robert), 1973- II. Sankey, Michael L., 1949- III. Title. IV. Title: Twenty-five essential lessons for employee management

    HF5549.D46 2001   658.3'03
                               QBI01-200766

All rights reserved. Printed in the United States of America. No part of this book may be used or reproduced in any form or by any means, or stored in a database or retrieval system without the prior written permission of the publisher, except in the case of brief quotations embodied in critical articles or reviews. Making copies of any part of this book for any purpose other than your own personal use is a violation of United States copyright laws. Entering any of the contents into a computer for mailing list or database purposes is strictly prohibited unless written authorization is obtained from Facts on Demand Press.

This book is sold as is, without warranty of any kind, either express or implied, respecting the contents of this book, including but not limited to implied warranties for the book's quality, performance, merchantability, or fitness for any particular purpose. Neither the authors, the publisher nor its dealers or distributors shall be liable to the purchaser or any other person or entity with respect to any liability, loss, or damage caused or alleged to be caused directly or indirectly by this book.

~~~~~~

This book is dedicated to Mary, Big Charlie, Kathy, and Adam for their inspiration and support.

A special *thank you* to Mark, Pam, Derek, and Richard for all of their help, and especially Peter Weber who always makes me look good.

And last but not least, a special *thanks* to Ned Flanders for his inspirational support.

<div align="right">

Dennis L. DeMey
June 16th, 2001

</div>

~~~~~~

"You can't do the same things today as you did yesterday and expect different results."

– Albert Einstein

Contents

Introduction: 3

Section One: The Hiring Process 5

Lesson 1: How to Set the Foundation for a Proper Company Hiring Process 7
Problems With Today's Hiring Techniques.. 7
Prepare a Job Description 8
Define the "Type" of Employee 8
The Importance of Proper Documentation 9
Establish Proper Paperwork Policies 10

Lesson 2: Recruitment & Resumes 15
Why Sound Recruitment is Important 15
Before Looking for Candidates 16
Using Community & College Sources 18
Resumes 18
Tips on Analyzing Resumes 19

Lesson 3: The Importance of Job Descriptions 21
Defining Duties & Responsibilties 21
Defining Specifications & Requirements 23

Lesson 4: Make The Basic Application Form & Other Pre-Hiring Forms Work for You 25
Start with a Cover Sheet 25
The Importance of the Basic Application 27
Four Critical Items on the Application Form 27
Subject Areas to Avoid On the Application 29
Other Critical Pre-Hiring Forms 30

Lesson 5: Hiring & Discrimination 41

Discrimination Quiz 41
Occasions for Discrimination 42
The Major Federal Laws That Prohibit Hiring Discrimination 42
Compliance with the Fair Credit Reporting Act (FCRA) 43
Illegal Discrimination Definitions per EEOC 44
More About Disability Discrimination 45
The Do's & Don't List - What You Can & Cannot Ask Prior to Hiring 46

Lesson 6: Pre-Employment Screening Policy 49

No Screening is the Worst Policy 50
The Components of a Pre-Employment Background Check 50
Formulating a Proper Company Screening Policy 51
Pre-Employment Screening Vendors 54
Be Aware of the Potential of Identity Theft 54

Lesson 7: Background Checks 57

Obligations of Employers and the Fair Credit Reporting Act (FCRA) 57
How to Verify Social Security Numbers 58
How to Utilize Credit Report Data 63
How to Verify Employment History 65
How to Verify Personal References 72
How to Check Criminal History 73
Local Police Record Request 78
How to Verify Educational Background 80
How to Confirm Professional Licenses & Registrations 83
How to Verify Military Service 86
How to Obtain Motor Vehicle Reports 89
How to Search for Civil Records 93

Lesson 8: Pre-Employment Screening Firms 99

Components of a Quality Screening Vendor 101
Where to Find a Vendor or Screening Company 105

Lesson 9: Pre-Employment Testing 107

Psychological & Aptitude Testing 107
Skills Tests 109
Drug & Medical Testing 110
Importance of Drug Testing to Business Today 110
How to Establish a Drug Testing Policy 111
The Other Side — Beating the Drug Tests 115
A Few Words About Lie Detector Tests 115

Lesson 10: Conducting The Interview 117

"Before the Interview" Checklist 117
Interview Procedures 118
A Guide to Proper Questioning 119
Avoid Improper Interview Questions 121
After the Interview 123
Applicant/Resume Evaluation Form 124
Computer-Assisted Interviewing 125

Lesson 11: Making the Job Offer — The Proper Sequence 127

1. The Acknowledgement 127
2. Complete All Requisite Forms 128
3. Verify, Verify, Verify 137

Lesson 12: How to Properly Reject Candidates 139

Options Not Recommended 139
Options Recommended 139
What to Tell a Rejected Candidate 140

Section One: Pop Quiz 143

Section Two: Bringing The New Employee On Board 147

Lesson 13: The New Employee Orientation Process 149

Creating an Orientation Program & Schedule 149

Lesson 14: The Employee Handbook 153

Hours of Employment 153
Salary Issues 153
Benefits 154
Sick Leave 154
Holidays, Vacations & Job Attendance 154
Conduct of the Employee 154
A Few Words of Caution 155

Lesson 15: Probationary Employment, Temporary Help, & Subcontractors 157

Use of Probationary Employment 157
Using Temporary Help (Temps) 159
Using Subcontractors 160
Leasing Employees or Using a PEO (Professional Employment Organization) 164

Lesson 16: Retention Efforts 167

Recognition and Encouragement 167
Open Communication 168
Competitive Salary 168
Benefits Package 169
Ongoing Education 169
Out-of-the-Ordinary Perks 169
Make It Fun to Come to Work 170

Lesson 17: Using Performance Reviews 173

When Should Reviews be Conducted 173
Designing a Performance Review Form 174
Summary of Performance and Call For Action 176

Section Three: When Problems Arise... 181

Lesson 18: How to Deal With Unsatisfactory Employees 183

Recognizing the Root of the Problem 183
Disciplinary Measures Vs. Corrective Actions 184
A Motivational Approach to Discipline 186
How to Conduct Corrective Interviews 186

Lesson 19: How to Handle a Complaint, Grievance or Potential Litigation 191

Treatment of Complaints 191
Treatment of Grievances 192
Treatment of Litigation 193
Consider Arbitration Agreements 194

Lesson 20: How to Handle Workers' Compensation Issues 195

Set Company Safety Policies 196
Guidelines to Reduce Fraud 196
How to Spot Signs of Potential Fraud 197
Suggested Remedies to Control Abuse 198
Tie It Al Together 203

Lesson 21: Termination Procedures 205

Legitimate Reasons for Dismissal 205
Act Swiftly 206
Is the Termination is Legal? 206
Employment At-Will 207

Lesson 22: Exit Interviews, Packages, & Termination Meetings 211

Exit Interviews 211
Exit Packages 212
Termination Meetings 212

Section Four: Abiding By The Law 217

Lesson 23: How to Comply with State Discrimination Laws 219

Laws Defined by Number or Type of Employees 219
State Specific Discriminatory Laws 219
An Overview of Certain State Law Topics 220
#1 - Reasons for Terminating Employees 220
#2 - Obtaining Criminal Record Checks for Employment Purposes 221
#3 - Alcohol and Drug Testing 222
#4 - Former Employer Immunity for Reference Checks 222
#5 - Workers' Compensation 224

Lesson 24: How to Comply with Federal Discrimination Laws 227

Important Federal Discrimination Laws 228
Other Topics of Employer Concern Administered by the US Department of Labor 236
Quick Guide Federal Law Chart 240

Lesson 25: Answers on How to Comply with Other Legal Issues 243

Sexual Harassment 243
Hiring the Handicapped 244
Age, Race, Ethnic Background, Religion, Pregnancy 245
Retention of Employee Records 245
Employers Monitoring Employees 245
Hours of Employment 247
Dealing with AIDS 248

Appendices:

I.	Fair Credit Reporting Act	249
II.	The Social Security Number Check	257
III.	Employer Forms	269
IV.	Summary of Recommended Web Sites & Other Resources	299
V.	State Agency Public Record Restrictions Table	309

Introduction

If you're like most employers, your valuable time is spent on increasing your profits and pleasing your customers. Protecting yourself against the dozens of employee/employer pitfalls may be at the bottom of your priority list, add to that keeping up with the big and small labor laws that seem to change at least every other year. Regardless of where your priorities are, if you are not prepared to handle your employee-related challenges, it can cost you dearly and unnecessarily.

Which of these "funds" does your company unwillingly contribute to:

- $200 billion is lost annually to Workers' Compensation fraud - says The U.S. Department of Labor.
- $55 million in wages and 1.8 million workdays are lost annually due to Workplace Violence - says The US Bureau of Justice.
- $200 billion is lost annually due to employee theft - estimates the Professional Investigative Consultants.
- $85.8 billion annually is lost due to alcohol abuse - says The National Council on Alcoholism and Drug Dependence.
- $21,263 is what the average crime-related claim costs - says The National Council on Compensation Insurance.
- $25,000 to $30,000 to replace a middle management employee, $5,000 for a clerical position - says Labor Arbitrator Michael Berzansky.

That's just the start. The average jury award for Employment Claims has almost doubled from approximately $168,000 in 1990 to $300,000 by 1996. Now, more than ten percent of all awards for discrimination and wrongful termination are in excess of $1,000,000.

We do not have to resign ourselves to these economic facts of life says author Dennis DeMey, who, for decades, has assisted companies in reducing these losses. Dennis' priceless advice on how to protect your business and retain good employees comprises the pages of *The 25 Essential Lessons*.

Introduction

There is so much you need to know.

- Does your company have a written, fair, and bombproof policy for every phase of employment management? For every issue, positive or negative?
- Do your hiring practices comply with all federal and state laws?
- Do you have the right company policies in place for bonuses, sick days, promotions, tracking employee performance – and do your rules fit the guidelines of the discrimination laws?
- How can you reduce your Workers' Compensation costs?
- If ever you find yourself in court, on the witness stand, how will you answer this question: "So, why didn't you check?"

Section One walks you through the important steps of the Hiring Process. Here you will learn how to properly gather information, verify it, and make an offer of employment. Section Two helps you bring that employee on board. Here you will also find advice on retention efforts and what should be in your employee handbook. When problems arise, refer to Section Three. Section Four explains the laws and regulations we all must live with. For your convenience and to augment each lesson, at its end we present a list of useful sources available on the Internet. We recommend that you visit these web pages. The Appendix contains a myriad of useful information, including 22 employment forms that you are free to copy and use for your business.

Use *The 25 Essential Lessons* whenever an employee-related problem develops. Use *The 25 Essential Lessons* before they develop. Know the rules. Find the solutions here. This is your human resource **Consultant–on–a–Shelf!**

No contents of this book are intended as legal advice, and should not be used as such. For legal advice consult an attorney. The laws and rules reproduced herein are gathered from official sources, but they may have been paraphrased, or may have changed due to recent legislation. For updates and full-text versions, please consult the source.

Section 1
The Hiring Process

Finding the Perfect Candidate is Never Easy

People are complex, and there seems to be no clear-cut method of appraising them. It shouldn't surprise you when we say that success in recruiting and hiring qualified individuals will take time and effort. It will, but all of the lessons presented here will make the task less of a chore – and you will avoid some serious mistakes.

Much has been written about how to train and develop employees effectively, and these activities are important. However, if the wrong employee is selected to begin with, **no training program or motivational techniques will compensate for the hiring error.**

A contention of this section is that a company's hiring policy, whether that company is large or small, MUST extend beyond the "old standard" of merely reading resumes and conducting interviews. Since the chances of discovering the major problems employees bring with them to the workplace are slim, there is a clear need to rely on simple, inexpensive methods of testing the accuracy and honesty of the applicant's statements and claims.

On the pages in the eleven lessons to follow, you will learn that the hiring process consists of three critical stages:

1. Gathering Information
2. Verifying Information
3. The Offer of Employment

The proper implementation of each of these stages will provide the employer a strong measure of protection from civil litigation based on negligent hiring practices.

Once the ground rules are established, the hiring process will become automatic and easy to follow. In fact, your efforts now will seem like a very good investment when compared to the long-term benefits later.

1 Hiring Policy
How to Set the Foundation for a Proper Company Hiring Policy

Problems With Today's Hiring Techniques

The hiring techniques used by a great number of businesses do not and have not worked for many years. Most personnel departments and department managers spend much of the pre-employment process simply reviewing applications and conducting interviews. These actions are just scratching the surface. With resume mills and interview coaching, anyone can look good on paper and devise impressive answers to questions about his or her strengths and weaknesses.

If you don't believe it, consider these findings about job applicants, as compiled over a one-year period by the author's company, Adam Safeguard, Inc.

16%	Lied about their criminal record
14%	Lied about their Workers' Compensation claims
28%	Misrepresented their education history
24%	Misrepresented their prior employment history
17%	Used multiple names
29%	Lived at addresses not listed on their applications
14%	Had serious motor vehicle violations
5%	Supplied false Social Security Numbers

Scary, isn't it?

💡 **KEY POINT:** Ideally, the employee selection process must be a sequential system for selecting only the best applicants and maintaining employee quality. Unfortunately, in today's atmosphere of litigation activity, this entire process must be approached with an attitude of self-defense. The foundation for such a system rests upon using *proper documentation to gather and verify information.*

Prepare a Job Description

A key first step in the hiring process is creating a job position description. A job description will detail the duties and responsibilities expected of the new employee.

Also, the job description will assist you to:

- Evaluate whether you need a full-time or part-time employee
- Write media advertisements for the position
- Later, evaluate if the employee has met the expected duties and responsibilities

Job Descriptions are covered in Lesson 3.

Job Requirements

If the job position requires certain physical and/or mental capabilities, or if certain schooling and training is required, this must be quantified and established. Using a Job Requirements data sheet will further establish the position description assist in creating employment ads.

Define the "Type" of Employee

Will the new person be a seasonal temp, an independent contractor, a union member, or an "employment at will" employee?

Employment at Will

Per the *Society for the Advancement of Education*, Employment at Will "...refers to the legal rule that presumes that an employer can fire workers without just cause, if the employer and employee do not enter into a separate legal contract during the hiring process." Companies who hire without a promise of continued employment (or collective bargaining agreement) usually fall into this category. In fact, the majority of employers are covered under this doctrine without being aware of it or the implications. Essentially, employment at will means either an employee or an employer can terminate their relationship at any time for any reason

While some companies inform candidates of employment at will during the application process, it is not always advisable to do so. In workplace environments where employees come and go routinely, this notice seems to fit well without generating negative feelings. Most employers would desire long-term associations with employees, as long as they are productive. The value here is to be aware of what issues keep the relationship "at will" without being offensive.

This doctrine does not lessen or remove any requirements of federal or state laws governing employees. In fact, the "at will doctrine" is in effect in all states. Note:

Public employees are protected by civil service rules and are not considered at will employees.

By indicating the type of employment during the application process, an employer makes the future relationship very clear and removes any guesswork from an employees' mind.

For more information regarding probationary or temporary employment and independent contractors, refer to Lesson 15.

The Importance of Proper Documentation

Today, many companies strive to reduce personnel paperwork to a bare minimum. Yet, the information absent from an employee's personnel file may later cost the employer thousands of dollars for what occurs during the term of employment.

Proper Documentation Helps Avoid Discrimination Lawsuits

Lack of paperwork has impacted litigation based on equal pay, civil rights, workers' compensation and more. Hundreds of thousands of dollars have been awarded because vital information was missing or not obtained prior to employing an individual. For example, what if an employer is not careful in verifying the Social Security Number provided during the payroll process, and an employee's benefits are assigned to someone with a similar number?

If a legal action involves wage and hourly claims, discrimination or class action suits, then government agencies and the courts can compel an employer to produce related personnel records. Judges and arbitrators have ruled against employers who are not able to produce proof to support their actions.

Discrimination laws exist at both the Federal and State government levels. Historically, these laws have led to class action suits that originated from groups of current employees, former employees, or applicants. The ever-present possibility of such suits makes it imperative that employers document their actions from the time of hire to the time of termination.

In reviewing their company's personnel practices, employers should always keep in mind the goal of protecting against judicial imposition. However, defensive personnel policies alone will not prevent unfair discharge litigation or union grievances. Still, if the employer focuses on maintaining good internal relations with employees, he or she can help eliminate many of the major sources of potential problems.

In contemporary employee selection, paperwork is your foundation for success and may be your best defense against challenges. If you are an employer and haven't taken time to formally examine and design the employment paperwork used by your company, it is imperative that you make time to do so. There may be questions on your forms that are illegal, essential items may be missing, or something simple, like more room to write, may be necessary.

Establish Proper Paperwork Policies

KEY POINT: Employers must establish firm policies regarding what paperwork and procedures they will use during the recruiting process, through the application and hiring process, and beyond.

Policies must be in writing and kept current to be effective and avoid ambiguity. Once established, these policies should be strictly adhered to.

> **Oops, I Forgot**
>
> Suppose ABC Company's policies state "...any applicant who is caught omitting a past employer on his or her application must be rejected." Mr. Horvath, ABC Company's personnel manager, interviews a promising candidate named Mr. Bartiromo. However, Mr. Horvath learns during the screening process that Mr. Bartiromo excluded a past employer from his application. Adhering to company policy, Mr. Horvath decides not to hire Mr. Bartiromo and follows it up with detailed documentation, including a copy of the interview with the past employer.

In the above example, Mr. Horvath performs several actions that are beneficial to ABC Company. Firstl, he sticks to company policy, helping to establish positive expectations within the community and the workforce. Secondly, Mr. Horvath protects ABC Company by documenting his actions. Were Mr. Bartiromo to pursue litigation, Mr. Horvath would *not* have to rely on his memory to recount the steps he took. In other words, the case would not boil down to the word of Mr. Horvath versus the word of Mr. Bartiromo. Mr. Horvath would have evidence to support his claims.

Require that All Forms Be Completed

It is important to insist that all blanks on forms be completed. At the top of the forms, or on a separate instruction sheet, include some text to explain that applications not completed in full will not be accepted. For example,

> "All blanks on this form must be filled in completely or it will not be processed. If an item does not pertain to you, write 'N/A' in the blank provided. Additional or explanatory information may be included on the reverse or on separate sheets."

Large companies sometimes designate an "intake person" to review the application for completeness. Any blank items are marked and returned to the applicant for completion.

Items that are often left blank include the names of former supervisors, as well as the addresses and telephone numbers of past employers. These pieces of information are important to the verification process and, if the applicant does not provide them, it will cost additional time and money to complete the process. The cost to verify information without full details is usually higher, especially when a background screening service is used.

The idea of using proper forms is to transfer the effort from the employer to the applicant. Let the applicant "look up" phone numbers, addresses and other details essential for verifying "their" claims or statements.

For example:

> **Know the License Number**
>
> A screening company in New Jersey charges $12.00 to verify a registered nurses license validation and status, when the license number is provided. When a license number is not provided, the same service is available but incurs a $20.00 statutory fee and extra effort on the part of the screening company.

How to Interpret Incomplete Forms

First, is there some logical reason for information to be neglected on the application form? Maybe the applicant failed to mention that the information was on the resume, or perhaps the applicant was nervous, or just plain forgot.

The truth is, an incomplete application may be an indicator of the applicant's worthiness. Perhaps the applicant is careless or does not pay enough attention to detail. Or worse, he or she may be trying to hide something, something that may cost your company severely.

> **KEY POINT:** If the applicant "forgets" to provide his or her signature, doubt should be raised. The absence of a signature makes the documents worthless, and therefore may be a deliberate attempt to deny responsibility for questionable actions he or she might commit in the future.

If the company requires that all portions of the application be complete, a surprising number of applicants will find a reason to leave without having finished the paperwork. Depending on the text of the forms they are asked to sign, they might realize that the employer is going to do a criminal history check or verify their educational background. If an applicant leaves at this point in the process, it may not be clear what the "problem" was, but rest assured that one just went away.

The Consistency of Forms Rules

A company's hiring policy should always include the following rules—

1. Consistently require the same set of forms for every applicant. Failure to do so could be viewed as negligence or even discrimination.
2. Include *all* the forms that will be required in the *initial* application packet. Why? Chances are, if the applicant has a reason for not wanting to submit to a criminal check, education verification, drug test or some other procedure, he or she will not return with the completed paperwork. Thus, the employer has saved the time and the $25-150 involved in the verification process simply by demonstrating how extensive it is from day one.

For example:

> **Lies — Where There's One, There May Be More**
>
> Sally fills out an application for employment, but chooses not to include a local bank as one of her previous employers. Her prospective employer discovers her deception and requests employment verification from the bank. The bank reports that Sally worked there for three months and had poor attendance during that time. She quit without notice.
>
> When confronted with this information, Sally admits that she'd been untruthful. She explains that, at the time of her employment at the bank, she was going through a divorce. She had two children, one of whom was pre-school age, and since her family was not in the area, she had a great deal of difficulty with childcare. The stress and demands of being a single mother made it impossible to work full time, and she had been unable to find a part-time position. Thus, she took the job at the bank and performed poorly. Ultimately, she moved closer to her family, hoping to reorganize her life. She was embarrassed about the situation and remains so.

There is an emotional appeal to Sally's story. One can understand the difficulty of raising children alone and making ends meet.

However, what if what Sally said was yet another attempt at deception? Perhaps Sally, in concert with others, actually defrauded the bank through a phony loan scheme and had been caught. In the end, she agreed to resignation and repayment and therefore wasn't prosecuted. In this version of the scenario, the bank might be contractually obligated to keep Sally's actions under wraps, and a criminal history check might not reveal this information.

Excusing Sally's deception based on the emotions her confession elicited could cost your company in the long run. If you find yourself in this situation, think logically.

Lesson 1 - Hiring Policy

Don't feel sorry for someone to the extent that you let that person get away with something they shouldn't. If you are about to hire someone and you've already had a situation where you've had to give him or her the benefit of a doubt, that person isn't being chosen logically. At least check out their story first. Applicants know that must make a good impression, and that everything said or done during the application process can be a "strike" against them. Chances are, if Sally were rejected a deception had been discovered, she would know why.

Here is another example of form inconsistency:

> **Check the Details**
>
> Everything about Jack's application checks out except the address on his driver's license is in a different county than the one in which he has claimed that he has lived. During a discussion about the discovery, Jack explains that he is single and has often moved about, so he uses his parents' address for his license and registration rather than notify the DMV every time he moves.

Satisfactory explanation? Maybe.

What if a Motor Vehicle Report (MVR) on Jack disclosed that his driving privileges had been suspended for numerous violations, including a conviction for Driving While Intoxicated? Later, a closer look at a copy of his driver's license shows that his date of birth is off by twenty-five years. It turns out that the driver's license number given is actually that of his father, Jack Sr.

Without sound, consistent hiring procedures in place, these Jack and Sally examples would not have been brought to the attention of the employer.

A well-documented, consistently applied pre-employment application process will go a long way in eliminating poor hiring decisions and/or future litigation. The bottom line? Proper paperwork policies can lead to a more effective, efficient organization that is staffed with the best possible candidates.

Lesson Summary:

- The employee selection process must be a sequential system for selecting only the best applicants and maintaining employee quality. Unfortunately, in today's litigious atmosphere, this entire process must be approached with an attitude of self-defense. The foundation for your hiring system rests upon using Proper Documentation to Gather and Verify Information.

- A key first step in the hiring process is creating a job description. A job description will detail the duties and responsibilities expected of the new employee.

- Employers must establish firm policies regarding what paperwork and procedures they will use during the recruiting process, through the application and hiring process, and beyond. Policies must be in writing and kept current to be effective and avoid ambiguity. Once established, these policies should be strictly adhered to.
- Require that all forms be completed. If the subject "forgets" to provide his or her signature on an application, doubt should be raised. The absence of signatures makes documents worthless.

Recommended Resources:

http://csi.toolkit.cch.com

This site provides an excellent array of downloadable checklists, model employment-related business plans, forms and other documents.

http://www.hrtools.com/frames.asp

HRTOOLS.com is an excellent, comprehensive site that is focused on attracting, maintaining, and managing the workforce. Here are lots of good "tool kits" to browse.

2 Recruitment and Resumes
A Few Words on Recruitment and Using Resumes

Why Sound Recruitment is Important

In recent years, the cost of hiring employees has risen substantially. According to Michael Berzanksy, a federal and state labor arbitrator, the average cost to replace a clerk is about $5000, and the normal cost to replace a middle management employee is between $25,000 and $30,000. Typically, these turnover costs include severance pay, searching for a replacement, training, and lost money spent on benefits including retirement.

Yet there are other costs that are not as easily identified. The additional costs most commonly ignored are those that are incurred *before* termination. Few companies understand and have calculated these *hidden costs*. Consider how much time and money is spent on the following prior to termination:

- Progressive discipline.
- Theft and/or fraudulent workers' compensation claims.
- A decrease in the quality of the employee's work, especially if he or she suspects that termination is *imminent*.
- Disruption and chaos caused in the interim between the onset of problems and the termination.
- Repairing customer ill will that is generated by problem employees.

Likewise, a vacant position can lead to the following costs, some of which may occur on a company-wide level, depending on the position:
- Lost production
- A decrease in overall company efficiency
- Potential loss of valuable accounts

These costs, combined with the standard expenses of placing advertisements, screening and interviewing, add up. Some companies must also consider the cost of out-placement services and unemployment insurance.

A well-developed hiring process that puts the right person in the right job can diminish these costs significantly. Examining and adjusting your company's hiring policies ultimately may be more cost effective than maintaining the status quo.

Before Looking for Candidates

Before advertising a vacancy, carefully re-examine the position. If ever there is a time to restructure, eliminate and/or enhance a position, it is prior to filling it.

Examine a job vacancy with the following questions, before placing an ad—
- Is the position a necessary one? Is it redundant, integral or in-between?
- Is the position in the right department?
- How does the position relate to the other jobs within the company? Is it closely related to other positions or is it one that is pretty much a stand-alone job?
- How frequently has this position been vacant? If the answer is "often," address why. Reducing turnover always saves time and money.
- Is the position supervisory in nature? Should it be?
- Should the position be split into one or more jobs?
- Should more than one person be hired with the same title?
- Does the job description need updating?

Taking the time to examine the position prior to seeking applicants can reduce turnover and confusion that results from making changes *after* hiring someone.

Using Classified Ads

Here are some tips for using classified ads to advertise job openings:

Try other sources in addition to the local paper.

- Consider trade magazines, trade association newsletters, and/or newspapers that might better reach applicants with experience or education in your industry.

Beware of politically incorrect language.
- Be aware of raising a red flag for bias or implied discrimination. For example, using use the phrase "salesman needed." Use "salesperson."

Be careful not to exaggerate benefits and/or the position itself.
- When the position is exaggerated, applicants may either start the application process without completing it, thereby wasting your time and theirs. Or they will get the job and then be disappointed when they wind up doing something else.

Include list of requirements if appropriate.
- Doing so will prevent people who are incapable of meeting these requirements from applying.

Specify the job duties.
- If there are tasks that may be unpleasant and must be performed frequently, be sure to include them. If you include that the person must be able to answer sixteen phone lines, this can weed out those who can't or won't.
- When listing duties, be specific when possible. It is important that the applicant understand what is involved. Also, refrain from listing the obvious, i.e., in an ad for a "hair stylist" do not list "styling hair" as a job requirement. Listings costs for most advertisements are based on the number of words or lines.

Consider whether to include the company's name.
- Do you work for a well-known company? If so, including your company name may attract candidates who are only interested in the prestige and/or security that come from working for a well-known organization. This can be good or bad. If the position is related to research and development, inclusion of the company's name might give your competition a clue as to what new products are being developed or the direction the company is taking.

Ask an outsider to read a preliminary copy of the ad.
- If you are new at writing ads, ask a family members or friend to read the job ad and give an interpretation of it. These people are likely to point out items that have been neglected or areas that are unclear, such as abbreviations or vague statements. In addition, it is important to understand the perception that the ad conveys. Almost any assistance can help.

Using Community & College Sources

Be careful not to underestimate your community's potential, especially its educational institutions. Contact local high schools and vocational schools, and establish a relationship with them. The students can be an excellent source for augmenting your staff, especially with part-time employees and interns.

These institutions are excellent places from which to recruit employees. Many students appreciate the opportunity to gain experience while completing their education. In some cases, students can attend school for a portion of the day and then work for the remainder.

Twenty years ago, these students might have only been capable of filing tasks. Now, they are capable of much more, especially when it comes to operating computers.

Student work programs are very popular because of their success rate. Interested businesses should contact their local board of education to learn the specifics on the programs available.

In addition, there are many cooperative and internship programs available on the college level. These programs are available for many industries. Typically, the students work for a business for a semester, then the employer and the assigned professor determine the student's grade. Students in these programs are highly motivated given that the opportunity provides work experience and affects their grades. The benefits of these programs are mutual. The students get experience and possibly college credit whereas the businesses get qualified help.

Once your company has established a relationship with educational facilities, you can use the connection as an ongoing resource. In fact, you may develop a reputation within the university or school that makes their best and brightest want to work for you.

Resumes

Many times, resumes are the first contact an employer has with an applicant. They can be used as a yardstick to measure a recruitment program.

Track the Resumes

Monitoring the responses from ads will give insight to the ad's suitability and value. For example, if an ad generates an inordinate amount of resumes without the education or work experience needed, perhaps the ad did not properly outline the job requirements. Monitoring the responses from different ads can be quite useful for large companies that hire quite frequently.

Tips on Analyzing Resumes

The benefits are self-evident when reading the education, training, experience, accomplishments, skills, honors, etc. that appear on a resume. Indeed, reading a resume is the first filter in the employment screening process.

In addition to providing talking points for interviews, there are other aspects of a resume that should be examined before a decision is made to bring in an applicant for an interview. Consider the items below:

Proper English

Do you find spelling mistakes or punctuation errors? Do you find that tenses are switched in the same sentence? Are all proper nouns capitalized? Of course, not all applicants are hired for their English skills, but you do want someone who makes an effort to do things right.

Gaps in Time

Look at the prior employment history and observe if there are long (six months or more) periods of time between jobs. Of course, not everyone is hired immediately when they become unemployed. But gaps in time may be an indicator that the applicant is not truthful about all of his or her previous employers. The same principle applies if the candidate was attending a school, but left and showed no work experience over an extended time period, then returned to school. There may be a plausible explanation, so, if the candidate is interviewed, be certain to ask.

Pattern of Short Tenure

Look at the length of time an applicant has held previous positions and see if there are a number of short job durations. Usually, a short duration is explained on the resume, such as moved, company went out of business, etc. However, if a pattern of frequent occurrence is observed, this can be an indicator of an inability to get along with others, or of someone who is always looking for a "better deal."

Pattern of No Growth

Also, observe if the applicant has been taking on more responsibility, or are they doing basically the same job over and over. If so, they may be leaving prior to termination action.

Resumes - A Few Words of Caution

There are many resume writing services available that do a professional job of writing resumes. Literally hundreds can be found using Internet search engines. There is nothing wrong with applicants using these services to present their credentials in the best possible manner. However, some of these services, which we call *spin doctors*, will take the content and enhance one's expertise. Their concern is getting the applicant to the interview stage, regardless if they have to amplify the facts.

The bottom line is do not use the resume as the sole basis for hiring. The resume is merely an indicator, and, hopefully, it is truthful. The wise employer will not stop the hiring process upon finding the perfect resume.

Lesson Summary:

- Without applicants, one cannot hire an employee. However, one can have a lot of applicants with no real candidates. Recruiting applicants properly can make the rest of the process go much smoother.
- Before advertising a vacancy, carefully re-examine the position. If ever there is a time to restructure, eliminate or enhance a position, it is prior to filling it.
- An employer should periodically take time out to examine recruitment policies before moving forward in the hiring process.
- Resumes should be evaluated for not only candidates' credentials and experience, but also for the effectiveness of your ads and recruitment efforts.
- Be sure to evaluate resumes for proper use of English, gaps in time, history of short job tenure, and no growth in assuming responsibilities.

Recommended Resources:

www.looksmart.com

This search engine gives excellent results if you search using these key words—recruitment articles for human resource professionals.

http://www.tsbj.com/editorial/03030407.htm

This site contains an excellent article entitled *Recruiting Employees Can Be A Difficult Task* written by Gary M. Brown

http:// www.amanet.org

The American Management Association is a worldwide leader in management development. With over 7,000 corporate and 225,000 individual members, their web page has many materials oriented toward recruitment.

Winning the Talent Wars, by Bruce Tulgan

A great book if you are looking to change your recruitment methods. Mr. Tulgan offers a myriad of innovative techniques that can be applied almost immediately at little or no cost.

Competing for Talent: Key Recruitment and Retention Strategies for Becoming an Employer of Choice, by Nancy S. Ahlrichs

Ms. Ahlrichs advocates becoming an Employer of Choice, or EOC, which charts "new strategic directions that put people in the profit equation." Interesting reading.

3 Job Descriptions
The Importance of Job Descriptions

The object of the job description is to create a realistic portrait of the job's scope and requirements.

Use the following lists to establish the two parts of a job description: "Duties & Responsibilities" and "Specifications & Requirements."

Defining Duties & Responsibilities

The following text, while not necessarily applicable for all positions, outlines nine categories used to define duties and responsibilities.

Physical Environment & Working Conditions
- Will the job be performed in an office, warehouse, factory or outdoors?
- Will it be hot or cold?
- Will there be hazards, such as dust, fumes, etc.?
- Are there any unusual physical or environmental factors associated with the job?

Equipment, Machinery & Tools
- What equipment, machinery and tools will the employee be working with?
- Will the employee be using any special devices, instruments or gauges?

Extent of Authority & Responsibility
- How difficult is the job? Is it fairly simple, or is it complex or very difficult?
- What is the intent and nature of the responsibility inherent in the position?
- How much authority will the employee be expected to exercise?
- What will the employee be "accountable" for?

Contact With Others
- What is the nature and type of contact the person will have with other employees?
- Will there be contact with the general public and/or government officials?
- Will there be contact with customers or clients?
- If there will be contact, what will be the extent of that contact, and what are the possible ramifications of such?

Access to Information
- Will the employee be working with confidential and/or competitive information?
- What is the degree of discretion the person will be expected to exercise with regard to privileged information?

Independent Judgment, Initiative & Supervision
- Are the duties of the employee standardized and routine?
- To what degree will the person be supervised on the job?
- Will the person be expected to make decisions on his/her own? If so, how often, and what will the nature of those decisions be?

Job Structure
- Is the job fairly structured with little variability?
- Is there a high degree of uncertainty involved so much so that one cannot always rely on precedent or company policy for guidance?
- What is the nature and extent of the pressure and stress related to the job?

Terms of Employment
- What is the amount and manner of compensation?
- What are the hours of work?
- Is there shift work, work on weekends and/or work at night?
- Is there travel involved or even possible relocation?

Special Features
- Are there any special aspects or features of the job that would be important for an accurate and complete job description?
- Who are the new employee's supervisors, subordinates and peers?

Defining Specifications & Requirements

Level of Education

- How much education is really necessary for this position?
- Will a high school education suffice? Is a college degree essential? Is post-graduate work crucial?
- In what field or course of study should the person have specialized? Is a specific major preferred or required?
- Is any level of certification required or desired?

Prior Work Experience

- What type of work experience should the employee possess?
- How much experience is required? Years?
- What level of managerial or supervisory experience should the employee possess?

Specialized Skills

- Should the employee have specialized or technical skills?
- Must the employee be computer literate and/or able to type?
- What software should the employee be familiar with?
- Are there any license requirements the employee must meet?
- What level of speaking, writing and reading is required?

Personality Traits

Are certain personality traits desirable or undesirable for the position (e.g. an outgoing personality being an excellent trait for a receptionist)?

> **Front Room vs. Back Room**
>
> Ms. Mulford could make any computer program hum and was hired as a customer service troubleshooter. Face to face with her supervisor, she was exuberant. The only problem was that she could not answer the telephone properly. She became very self-conscious and terribly perplexed when asked a simple question. Ultimately, her supervisor learned that she was a "back-room" employee and not a "front-room" employee. In other words, a review of her work experience revealed that Ms. Mulford had always worked with computers in a closed environment and had never experienced the front-end of any business. The job description used when she applied for the job did not define the personality traits needed for the position. Ultimately, Ms. Mulford was moved to a different position within the company.

Job Requirement Data Sheet

If the job position requires certain physical and/or mental capabilities, or if certain schooling and training is required, this must be quantified and established. Consider outlining the specific job requirements in writing to further establish the position description.

Remember—Proper Job Descriptions Prevent Possible Problems

Since job descriptions define the duties and requirements for a particular position they can be used to eliminate a host of problems. When a new employee is provided with a clearly written job description, this person cannot deny knowledge of the position's responsibilities. Furthermore, how can someone live up to the expectations of his or her position, if the duties and responsibilities haven't been explained?

A proper and functional job description can, also, be an important first step should an employer be faced with a hiring discrimination suit. This is covered in Lesson 5.

Lesson Summary:

- The first step when creating a job description is to gather all the pertinent information that is available regarding the position.
- Use the lists of questions found under "Duties & Responsibilities" and "Specifications & Requirements" to establish the components of a proper job description.
- A properly written job description can prevent possible problems or misunderstanding down the road regarding the duties and responsibilities of a specific job position.

Recommended Resources:

www.wave.net/upg/immigration/dot_index.html

The National Academy of Sciences, Committee on Occupational Classification and Analysis has created the *Dictionary of Occupational Titles* (DOT). Job Descriptions for everything from an abalone diver to a wrong-address clerk are included. Thankfully, the full text of the DOT is available on the Web. By visiting this site, one can access the full-text of the dictionary at no cost and download a searchable version.

4 The Basic Application
Make the Basic Application Form & Other Critical Pre-Hiring Forms Work for You

Forms, forms, forms. Nobody likes them. We don't like filling them out and we especially don't like inventing them, handing them out, reading them or filing them. Yet nothing in this entire process is more important than a consistent paperwork trail.

However, if there is one part of the process that deserves special attention, it is the design and use of the Basic Application Form. Why? The application is the first and most important step in establishing an honest and productive working relationship.

If an applicant is willing to deceive a prospective employer on the application itself, imagine what he or she will lie about later. A good, basic application form will let you close the loopholes that may lead to the hiring of a candidate that will later be regretted.

Start with a Cover Sheet

An applicant verification cover sheet is designed to limit time and money wasted on candidates who would not wish to comply with a series of employers requests. By setting the tone that a company takes the hiring process seriously, an employer can minimize a number of applicants they talk to and the amount of paperwork to be reviewed. A serious job seeker will not be dissuaded by this cover sheet. But, that sharpie who already handed over his "customized" résumé doesn't want to get caught.

When the application process itself is professional, the integrity of the business is instantly perceived as "above board." The "people" can be friendly and congenial, but the paperwork is dead serious. In other words, this is a great place to work but we don't mess around.

A Sample Applicant Cover Sheet Could Include...

Opening Text:

"The employer is pleased to consider all qualified applicants. In an effort to protect our business, customers, clients, and to provide a safe work environment, we have a strict acceptance process and pre-employment screening procedures.

"The forms listed below are required to be completed and the background elements listed will be conducted. Please review them to insure your written permission will be granted prior to starting the application process."

- "The Application must have all entries completed, indicating 'n/a' where not applicable. Incomplete forms will be rejected without further consideration.
- "The Applicant Waiver Form grants permission to the employer to verify answers on the application and resume submitted. This form must receive an original signature and be witnessed by the employer or their representative.
- "The I-9 Form (Federal Employment Eligibility Form) must be completed. Identity documents (i.e. driver's license, Social Security card, birth certificate, alien registration card, etc.) must be presented in the original form."

Detail the Forms to be Signed and Checks to be Performed:

The employer will:

- Obtain a Social Security Number verification and/or a consumer credit report.
- Order a motor vehicle report.
- Conduct criminal history searches with appropriate state or county agencies.
- Verify all education, attendance and degrees.
- Verify any professional license, trade or certificate claimed whether or not it is required for the position.
- Verify all prior employment reference checks.
- Conduct personal reference checks.

Successful applicants are required to complete and sign the following:

- New employee record chart.
- Confidentiality Agreement describing areas of the business an employee may have access to which are considered confidential by the employer.
- Non-compete agreement.
- Employee induction form. This form details pay rate, job function, benefits and work rules of the employer.
- W-4 tax withholding form.

Companies that conduct medical, drug or psychological tests should indicate so here.

The Importance of the Basic Application

Since the Basic Application provides the opportunity to stop problems before they start, it is important to examine its functions. The purposes of the application are:

- To obtain information required by law and essential to government reporting.
- To secure the information necessary to participate in employee benefit programs.
- To provide the employer with contact information for regular communication and emergency situations.
- To supply information, such as a Social Security Number, that will enable verification of the applicant's statements and credentials.
- To furnish information about skills and qualifications that will assist in choosing the right candidate for the job.

Ask yourself, "Does my company's application(s) meet these objectives?" A full size version of the Basic Application Form is available in the forms section of the Appendix.

Four Critical Items on the Application Form

Of course, all items on the application are important, but four areas as crucial. And, for information on what NOT to include on an application, turn to Lesson 5.

1. Include a Place for the Social Security Number

Social Security Numbers dramatically enhance your capability to evaluate potential employees. Always include a prominent position for them on your application, and make sure there is sufficient space to insure it is legible.

Much of the critical information found on typical applications can be verified by running a Social Security Number search or by requesting a credit report on the applicant.

The Social Security Number

Also, running an applicant's Social Security Number through a credit bureau's verification system reveals a great deal. Statistics compiled from 500 recent background investigations performed by ADAM Safeguard revealed that 17% of the applicants used additional names not shown on the application. 29% had an address other than the one they listed. In addition, 4.9% supplied Social Security Numbers that were not theirs! Some numbers belonged to deceased individuals!

Yet, in the same group of applicants, prior employers were identified and easily contacted in 72% of the cases.

Crucial employment information such as the name, address and Social Security Number can and should be verified in this manner (see Lesson 7).

On occasion, a Social Security Number verification or credit report can identify employers that were not listed on the applicant's resume or application. Very often, the failure to include former employers is an attempt to cover a problematic background. Therefore, these former employers should always be included on the list of prior employers to verify. Also, one should ask the applicant why they left that particular employer off the application.

There are many pre-employment companies that can authenticate this information for you. Shop around. Find out how extensive their verifications are and, if applicable, check for volume discounts. For more about using a pre-employment screening company, see Lesson 8.

2. Education and Credentials

Ask not only for the name of the school attended, but also if the person has graduated and if a degree was granted. It is okay to ask about organizations the applicant if affiliated with, as long as no inquiry is made about organizations based on race, ancestry, religion, and politics.

3. Previous Employment

Regarding previous employment, these items should be included on the application include:

    Company name, address, telephone number, nature of the business

    Position(s) held, name of supervisor

    Dates of employment

    Ending salary

    Reason for leaving

4. The Signature Line

An application should always include the applicant's signature and the date signed.

Immediately above where the signature is recorded, there should be some wording that indicates that all information provided must be true and that any attempt to deceive is reason for rejection or dismissal. Here is a sample statement that may be used:

> "I agree that any omission, falsification, or misrepresentation is cause for immediate termination at any time during my employment."

Additional wording should release from liability those who provide information about the applicant:

"I hereby authorize investigation of all statements at this time with no liability arising therefrom."

Many employers neglect to have the applicant's signature witnessed. Do not make this mistake. Should litigation arise, the witnessing of the signature and date or lack thereof could impact the case.

Hint—Ample Space vs. Additional Forms

Space on the Basic Application is precious. Before an application is put into use, fill out a sample application for yourself and see if there is truly enough room.

All applicants should be encouraged to list previous employers and former places of residence. How many years to go back is the up to the employer. Ten years is reasonable, but sometimes fifteen to twenty years is asked. As such, ample room for such information must be made available. If the current application is not adequate, one option is to use supplemental forms to record this information. If additional pages are used, make sure that each page is identified with the applicant's name *and* firmly attached to the application.

Subject Areas to Avoid On the Application

There is no standard format or prescribed list of questions for an application form that has been established by legislation. However, in recent years, state and federal EEOC legislation has outlawed or restricted questions about topics (see Lesson 5) that were previously included in most applications. Title VII of the Civil Rights Act of 1964 prohibits discrimination on the basis of race, color, age, sex and national origin. Questions pertaining to areas covered by the Equal Employment Opportunity Commission (EEOC) are hazardous because they can lead to unlawful use (e.g. discrimination). However, the areas covered by the Civil Rights Act of 1964 or EEOC are not the only ones that should be avoided.

Lesson 5 outlines what is considered discriminatory, i.e. what questions you can or you cannot ask. For detailed information on state and federal discrimination laws, turn to Lessons 23 and 24.

A full size version of the Basic Application Form is available in the forms section of the Appendix in the back of this book.

Other Critical Pre-Hiring Forms

In addition to the Basic Application Form, a number of other forms should be used during the pre-employment process. And, there are additional forms that should be used *after* hiring. These forms are discussed later in the book.

Employment Eligibility Verification - The I-9 Form

The Immigration Reform and Control Act (IRCA) of 1986 obligates every employer to verify, within three days of hire, the identity and employment authorization of every employee hired. To adhere to the directives of this act, employers must use the Employment Eligibility Verification Form, commonly known as the I-9 Form.

The purposes of the IRCA are to prohibit employment of illegal aliens, offer amnesty to qualified illegal aliens, and expand the scope of federal anti-discrimination laws. Per the ICRA, employers of four or more employees are forbidden from discriminating on the basis of national origin, citizenship or "intending citizenship" i.e. whether someone has the intention of becoming a citizen. However, the act does not exclude the preference of a citizen over an equally-qualified legal alien.

According to a back issue of *You and the Law*, "the appeals court held that [Section 1981 of the Civil Rights Act of 1991] does prohibit discrimination based on citizenship." *You and the Law* also advises that you not "use citizenship to disqualify anyone from a position at your company, except in those very narrow circumstances where . . . citizenship is a bona fide occupational qualification" such as "positions involving national security."

Using the I-9 Form as a Tool

Although the I-9 Form is not necessarily required to be completed until the applicant has been hired, it is an excellent tool to use as part of the pre-employment procedure. To complete this form, employers need to see proper identification from the applicant.

Obtaining copies of applicant identity documents is a benefit, since the documents will help immediately in the verification process. If the applicant refuses to disclose proper ID, then there is no reason to continue considering him or her for employment.

> **KEY POINT:** In addition to the mandatory use of the I-9 form, employers are required to *maintain* proof of the applicant's identity. In other words, the employer must retain copies of the items presented for verification. Passports, drivers' licenses, Social Security cards, birth certificates and alien registration cards are some of the documents typically used to comply with the ICRA.

Lesson 4 - The Basic Application

Also, retention of these documents can be very important after hiring. Consider the following example—

> **Who was he?**
>
> John was hired for a management position. He was foreign born and had allegedly immigrated to the US some time ago. While preparing the information necessary to ensure that John received his company benefits, a clerk noticed that the date of birth on his I-9 Form did not match that of his alien registration card. John was informed and a copy of his birth certificate was requested but never produced. John's supervisor gave him time to comply, but ultimately John became irritated with the repeated requests and began to claim discrimination and that he was being harassed due to his foreign origin. Suspicions grew further when it was discovered that the date of birth on his driver's license did not match either of the other documents. Confronted with these inconsistencies, John abruptly left the building without explanation and never returned. A report along with copies of the documents was given to the local immigration office.

In the above example, the documents should have been shown to be inconsistent prior to hiring. Nonetheless, the maintenance of them allowed for the situation to be rectified, thus re-establishing the company's compliance with the ICRA.

A copy of the I-9 Form can be viewed on the next page.

Lesson 4 - The Basic Application

A closer look at the I-9 Form

A larger version of the form is available in the Appendix.

This section must be completed by the *employee* upon being hired, but should be completed during the application process.

The signature is critical if someone other than the applicant completes the form.

The *employer* must complete this section, and include date and signature.

EMPLOYMENT ELIGIBILITY VERIFICATION (I-9)

SECTION I. EMPLOYEE INFORMATION AND VERIFICATION: (To be completed and signed by employee)

NAME: _____
   Last   First   Middle   Maiden

ADDRESS: _____
   Street number and name   City   State   Zip

DATE OF BIRTH: _____   SOCIAL SECURITY NUMBER: _____

I attest, under penalty of perjury, that I am (check one):
- ___ A citizen or national of the United States
- ___ An alien lawfully admitted for permanent residence (Alien #A_____).
- ___ An alien authorized by the Immigration and Naturalization Service to work in the U.S.(Alien #A_____). or Admission Number _____. Expiration of employment authorization, if any _____.

I attest, under penalty of perjury, the documents that I have presented as evidence of identity and employment eligibility are genuine and relate to me. I am aware that federal law provides for imprisonment and/or fine for any false statement or use of false documents in connection with this certificate.

SIGNATURE: _____ DATE: _____

PREPARER/TRANSLATOR CERTIFICATION (if prepared by other than the individual). I attest, under penalty of perjury, that the above was prepared by me at the request of the named individual and is based on all information of which I have any knowledge.

SIGNATURE: _____ NAME (print or type): _____
ADDRESS: _____
   Street number and name   City   State   Zip

SECTION II. EMPLOYER REVIEW AND VERIFICATION: (To be completed and signed by employer)
Examine one document from those in List A and check the correct box, *or* examine one document from List B *and* one from List C and check the correct boxes. Provide the *Document Identification Number* and *Expiration Date*, for the document checked in that column.

List A Identity and Employment Eligibility	List B Identity	List C and Employment
___ United States Passport ___ Certificate of U.S. Citizenship ___ Certificate of Naturalization ___ Unexpired foreign passport with attached Employment Authorization ___ Alien registration Card with photograph	___ A State issued drivers license or I.D. card with a photograph, or information, including name, sex, date of birth, height, weight, and color of eyes. ___ U.S. Military Card ___ Other (Specify document and issuing authority)	___ Original Social Security Number Card (other than a card stating it is not valid for employment) ___ A birth certificate issued by State, county, or municipal authority bearing a seal or other certification ___ Unexpired INS Employment Authorization. Specify form.

Document I.D.# _____   Document I.D.# _____   Document I.D.# _____
Exp. Date _____   Exp. Date _____   Exp. Date _____

CERTIFICATION: I attest, under penalty of perjury, that I have examined the documents presented by the above individual, that they appear to be genuine, relate to the individual named, and that the individual, to the best of my knowledge, is authorized to work in the United States.

SIGNATURE: _____ NAME (print of type): _____ TITLE: _____
EMPLOYER: _____
   Name   Address   Date

32

Applicant Waiver Form

The Applicant Waiver Form is a means to certify the accuracy of an application and to grant permission to check references, employment history and verify other information given by the applicant.

From the applicant's perspective, experience indicates that falsification, distortion and error are reduced if the applicant knows that the data he or she gives in the interview and on the application will be checked for accuracy. Using the Applicant Waiver Form is an easy way to make the intention to verify information clear from the start.

Applicant Waiver Form

(To be signed by all job applicants along with application form.)

1. I agree and understand that all the information and statements on my application are correct and no attempt has been made to conceal or withhold pertinent information. I agree that any omission, falsification, or misrepresentation is cause for my immediate termination at any time during my employment.

2. In connection with this request, I authorize all corporations, companies, credit agencies, persons, educational institutions, law enforcement agencies and former employers to release information they may have about me, and release them from any liability and responsibility from doing so; further, I authorize the procurement of an investigative consumer report and understand that such report may contain information as to my background, mode of living, character and personal reputation. This authorization, in original and copy form, shall be valid for this and any future reports that may be requested. Further information may be made available upon written request from _____

3. I hereby authorize investigation of all statements at this time with no liability arising therefrom.

_____   _____
Signature   Date

_____   _____
Signature of Company Representative   Date

* * *

STATE of:_____   This Instrument was acknowledged before me this _____ day of
COUNTY of:_____   _____, 19____, by _____
My commission will expire: _____ AS WITNESS.

_____
                                   Notary Public   No.

This statement reiterates the policy that all information provided must be true, and that deception is cause for denial or termination.

This paragraph authorizes the prospective employer to verify the information.

The General Release Form

Either a General Release Form or a series of subject-specific release forms should be incorporated into the application and screening process. While the General Release Form may be sufficient for many types of job hiring, in more-complex hiring scenarios a selection of the various subject-specific release forms should be used. These subject-specific release forms focus on all of the items an employer intends to verify for the records they will be obtaining.

> **KEY POINT:** In *some* states, a signed release is *required* prior to conducting a criminal background check or a driving record request. In *all* states, a written release is *required* for any report used for employment, if the report is obtained from a Consumer Reporting Agency. For more information, see the Fair Credit Reporting Act section in the Appendix.

As in the sample General Release Form, there should be wording to exonerate all persons, agents, employers or third party vendors supplying information.

General Release Form

In connection with my application for employment (including contract for service) with you, I understand that investigative inquiries are to be made on me including consumer credit, criminal convictions, motor vehicle, and other reports. These reports will include information as to my character, work, habits, performance and experience along with reasons for termination of past employment from previous employers. Further, I understand that you will be requesting information from various Federal, State, and other agencies that maintain records concerning my past activities relating to my driving, credit, criminal, civil, education, and other experiences.

I authorize without reservation any party or agency contacted by this employer to furnish the above-mentioned information.

I hereby consent to your obtaining the above information from _____ and/or any of their licensed agents. I understand to aid in the proper identification of my file or records, the following personal identifiers, as well as other information, is necessary.

Print Name _____

Social Security Number _____-____-_____

Date of Birth _____ Sex _____ Race_____

Current Address _____

City/State/Zip Code+4_____

Former Address _____

Applicant Signature _____ Date_____

Prospective Employer _____

If obtaining a credit report, driving record and criminal history is intended, then that should be specifically identified in the release. While one may utilize specific release forms for education and credit, the all-encompassing General Release Form will be of great benefit because is says you have permission to gather information from employers and anyone else who may have knowledge about the applicant.

A larger version of the General Release Form is available in the forms section in the Appendix.

A Few Hints About Release Forms and Former Employers

As mentioned previously, it can be very difficult to obtain information from previous employers. Anti-discrimination regulations and the drastic increase of labor-related litigation have made employers uncertain as to what can be revealed about past employees. Almost everyone is afraid of being sued, and so it seems safer to say little or nothing at all. One way to address this problem is to include a copy of the Applicant Waiver Form or the General Release Form in queries to former employers. You will find that many former employers will not release any information on a current or past employee without a signed release from that employee.

A signed copy of the form(s) should be sent with any written inquires. To eliminate any doubt as to the validity of the request as well as to expedite it, you should include the following with any verification request:

- A notarized copy of the request. Although not required, it is recommended that the waiver be notarized. Notarization will increase the response rate.
- Include the signature of a company executive.
- Enclose a business card. Use of letterhead is also advised.
- Include a self-addressed, stamped envelope.

One additional last caution is to be aware that forty-one states have laws that regulate the content of references from former employers. But, more about that in Lesson 23.

Lesson 4 - The Basic Application   36

Specific Release Forms

Sometime a specific release form is needed due to requirements by certain state agencies. It is useful if an applicant has resided in a state with which the employer is unfamiliar. For example, many states require a notarized release, but don't require a specific release form to be used — in which case, this form will suffice.

Here is an example of a "specific release form."

Criminal Release Form

**Criminal Background Check
Release Form**

NAME _____
      Last   First   Middle   Maiden

ADDRESS _____
      Street   City   State

ALIASES OR OTHER NAMES USED _____

DATE OF BIRTH _____ AGE ___ RACE _____ SEX ___

SOCIAL SECURITY # _____

DRIVER'S LICENSE # _____ STATE _____

* * *

I hereby authorize _____ of _____
                     Name   Name of Company

_____
           Company Address/City/State/Zip

to conduct a criminal background check on myself through the

_____ .
        Name of State and Police Agency

X _____
    Applicant Signature

* * *

STATE of: _____ This Instrument was acknowledged before me this _____ day of

COUNTY of: _____ _____, 19 ___, by _____

My commission will expire: _____ AS WITNESS.

_____
                                          Notary Public   No.

A larger version of this Criminal Release Form is available in the Appendix.

Requesting Driving Records is more complex than requests for other types of records because many states have their own forms that requestors must use. Although rules vary from state to state, as a general rule, employers *can* access these records. The key is that the states *require* verification and signature(s) from the employer.

Substance Abuse Test Consent

Government agencies are emphasizing health, safety and accident prevention in the workplace, and so should you. This fact, coupled with the spiraling costs of fringe benefits, has made drug screening a common component of the Verifying the Information stage. However, the act of presenting a Drug Abuse Test Consent form for completion as part of the initial paperwork, regardless of whether a test will actually be conducted, can act as a deterrent against substance abuses.

> For more information about each state's driving records access and procedures, we recommend *The MVR Book* by BRB Publications, 800-929-3811 or www.brbpub.com. The book outlines in detail the individual states' requirements for acquiring driving records. This informative book is well-written and surprisingly inexpensive.

Many applicants look good on paper, pass the typical test and make a great impression during the interview. Then, when the Drug Abuse Test Consent is presented, suddenly the job they wanted so badly isn't so desirable. An excuse is given and they leave without filling out the form. The time and money spent for the actual test have been saved.

Government sources have indicated that alcohol and drug abuse cost businesses billions of dollars in additional healthcare coverage, accident coverage, and loss of productivity. In the workplace, substance abuse can lead to a high degree of employee absenteeism, higher medical costs and an increase in on-the-job accidents. Thus, it is simply cost effective and liability conscious to institute and adhere to substance abuse testing procedures.

A Substance Abuse Test Consent Form is presented in the Appendix.

Applicant/Resume Evaluation Form

It's bad enough that some employees are taking frivolous legal actions, but a wave of litigation is coming from those who are *not* hired.

Lesson 4 - The Basic Application

> 💡 **KEY POINT:** An Applicant Evaluation Form that clearly indicates the reasons why the applicant was not employed should always accompany the company copy of a rejected application. If the reason for rejection was based on an established company policy, the documentation will be further supported by the existence of such policies.

The rejection and acceptance of candidates is a step that must be recorded. As such, the Applicant/Resume Evaluation Form is a handy tool for documenting the review of applications.

This form complies with non-discrimination guidelines and ensures that the basis for hire or rejection are documented and job-related. An employer should never have to rely on memory to recall the specifics, if questioned later. Remember, many of the lawsuits filed against an employer are not filed by current employees, but by applicants who were rejected. These cases present a circumstance where there is very limited knowledge available about the plaintiff. This gives the plaintiff an advantage and puts you at a disadvantage. It is not always easy to understand the motivations or background of an applicant given that the company's relationship with him or her is typically short-lived.

Please note that the Application Evaluation Form is an internal form used by the employer, and does not require a signature from the applicant.

This form is shown on the next page. A larger size version of the Applicant/Resume Evaluation Form is available in the Appendix.

Applicant/Resume Evaluation Form

> **APPLICANT/RESUME EVALUATION**
>
> *Completion of this form assists compliance with non-discrimination guidelines and ensures the basis for hire and reject decisions are documented and job related.*
>
> Name of Applicant: _____
>
> Date Application/Resume Received: _____
>
> Position Available: _____
>
> Will Applicant be Interviewed: _____ Yes   Date of Interview: _____
>
> _____ No   Reason for Rejection: _____
>   Code Number(s)
>
> Will Job be extended: _____ Yes Title: _____ Salary: _____
>
> _____ No
>
> Job-Related Reason Applicant is Best Qualified: _____
> _____
>
> If No, Reason for Rejection: _____
>   Code Number(s)
>
> _____
> Signature Interviewer/Evaluator   Position/Department   Date
>
> *You have the right to hire qualified individuals and to reject unqualified individuals. Selection and rejection decisions must be based on valid job-related criteria that are consistently applied to all applicants. The following are acceptable reasons for rejection provided the same statement could not be applied to the selected candidate. If numbers 1-8 do not apply, please complete 9 with a job-related reason.*
>
>   1. *Does not meet minimum job requirements*
>   2. *Meets minimum requirements but not best qualified*
>   3. *Cannot work required hours/schedule*
>   4. *Cannot perform physical requirements of job*
>   5. *Prior experience unrelated*
>   6. *Less related experience than person selected*
>   7. *Less related education/training than person selected*
>   8. *Lower skill level than person selected*
>   9. *Other (specify)_____*

These codes allow for very specific descriptions as to why an applicant was rejected. Combined with a copy of the submitted application and/or resume, this information can be crucial to winning a court case.

Lesson Summary:

- Start with cover sheet that accompanies the various application and release forms. This will limit time and money wasted on candidates who would not wish to comply with a series of employer's requests.

Lesson 4 - The Basic Application

- The purposes of the application are:
    1. To obtain information required by law and essential to government reporting.
    2. To secure the information necessary to participate in employee benefit programs.
    3. To provide the employer with contact information for regular communication and emergency situations.
    4. To supply information, such as a Social Security Number, that will enable verification of the applicant's statements and credentials.
    5. To furnish information that will assist in choosing the right candidate for the job.
- In addition to the mandatory use of the I-9 form, employers are required to *maintain* proof of the applicant's identity. In other words, the employer must retain copies of the items presented for verification. Passports, drivers' licenses, Social Security cards, birth certificates and alien registration cards are some of the documents typically used to comply with the ICRA.
- Either a General Release Form or a series of subject-specific release forms should be incorporated into the application and screening process. While the General Release Form may be sufficient for many types of job hiring, in more-complex hiring scenarios a selection of the various subject-specific release forms should be used.
- In *some* states, a signed release is *required* prior to conducting a criminal background check or a driving record request. In *all* states, a written release is *required* for any report used for employment if the report is obtained from a Consumer Reporting Agency.
- An Applicant Evaluation Form that clearly indicates the reasons why the applicant was not employed should always accompany the company copy of a rejected application. This documentation will support the reason for rejection, when the rejection is based on an established company policy.

Recommended Resources:

www.brbpub.com/forms

From this site you can download all of the forms shown in this book.

www.e-zlegal.com

Look for their book entitled *Personnel Director*. It contains over 100 useful personnel forms.

5 Hiring & Discrimination
Avoid Negligent Hiring & Job Discrimination

Discrimination Quiz

Below is a list of possible questions that could be asked on an application form or during an interview. Some are legal, some are not.

Which ones would you consider "safe" today?

1. Have you ever used a different name while employed?
2. What is your maiden name?
3. How old are you?
4. Are you married or single?
5. Do you have children?
6. Do you feel the job will be difficult because you are a woman?
7. Are you a US citizen?
8. Have you ever been arrested?
9. What social clubs do you belong to?
10. What is your address?

The correct answers are on the next page.

An extensive list of sample questions detailing what you can or cannot ask prior to hiring appears at the end of this lesson.

Lesson 5 - Hiring & Discrimination 42

Occasions for Discrimination

There are four distinct occasions when employers must be wary of discrimination challenges:

1. Pre-employment inquiry

    Applications, interviews, testing

2. Making the job offer to the applicant (see Lesson 11)

    Testing, medical exams

3. During term of employment (see Lessons 16-19)

    Evaluations, promotions, training, compensation and benefits, disciplinary action, compliance with job description

4. Termination or exit (see Lessons 21-22)

    Firing, lay off

While much of this lesson examines the first occasion, all the above-mentioned occasions are affected by laws that are examined in Lessons 23-25.

> By the way, the "safe questions" in the Discrimination Quiz are numbers 1, 7 and 10.

The Major Federal Laws That Prohibit Hiring Discrimination

There is a myriad of state and federal laws influencing what the employer can or cannot do. While these laws are covered in detail in Lessons 23-25, the following seven major laws directly affect pre-employment inquiry.

The Fair Credit Reporting Act (FCRA)

Prohibits improper access to consumer reports such as credit reports, criminal histories, and reports on one's character and general reputation. Defines the responsibilities and liabilities of businesses that provide such information.

Title VII of the Civil Rights Act of 1964 (Title VII)

Prohibits employment discrimination based on race, color, religion, sex, or national origin.

The Equal Pay Act of 1963 (EPA)

Protects men and women who perform substantially equal work in the same establishment from sex-based wage discrimination.

The Age Discrimination in Employment Act of 1967 (ADEA)

Protects individuals who are 40 years of age or older.

Title I of the Americans with Disabilities Act of 1990 (ADA)

Prohibits employment discrimination against qualified individuals with disabilities in the private sector, and in state and local governments.

Section 501 of the Rehabilitation Act of 1973

Prohibits discrimination against qualified individuals with disabilities who work in the federal government.

The Civil Rights Act of 1991

Provides monetary damages in cases of intentional employment discrimination.

Enforcement

The entity responsible for enforcement of the first six above-mentioned laws is The Equal Employment Opportunity Commission (EEOC). The EEOC also provides oversight and coordination of all federal equal employment opportunity regulations, practices, and policies. The enforcement of the FCRA falls on the Federal Trade Commission (FTC).

The next several sections of this lesson outline key portions of the FCRA and ADA as they apply to pre-employment.

Compliance with the Fair Credit Reporting Act (FCRA)

As mentioned above, the FCRA does not only pertain to, and this is crucial. The act defines the term "consumer report" as—

"...any written, oral, or other communication of any information by a consumer reporting agency bearing on a consumer's credit worthiness, credit standing, credit capacity, character, general reputation. Personal characteristics, or mode of living which is used or expected to be used or collected in whole or in part for the purpose of serving in establishing the consumer's eligibility for

a) credit or insurance to be primarily used for personal, family, or household service;

b) employment purposes; or

c) any other purpose authorized under section 604 [#1681b]"

The Act makes it illegal to obtain the needed background checks used for pre-employment purposes without first having authorization from the candidate. This is why the proper use of pre-employment forms is so essential.

FCRA and State Criminal Records

One of the most important pieces of information obtained in pre-employment screening is the criminal record. The FCRA disallows the use of arrest records over seven years from the date of arrest or until the state governing statute of limitations has expired. There is an exception; if the candidate is applying for a position that has a salary paying over $75,000 annually, then this limitation is removed.

> **KEY POINT:** The employer must be aware that if a negative hiring decision is made based on an arrest record with an arrest date that is older than seven years, this may be illegal. It depends on the state where the criminal record resides and the salary of the position the candidate is applying for.

Illegal Discrimination Definitions per EEOC

Listed below are definitions of what constitutes illegal discrimination, as provided by the EEOC—

Individual with a Disability

An individual with a disability under the ADA is a person who has a physical or mental impairment that substantially limits one or more major life activities, has a record of such an impairment, or is regarded as having such an impairment. Major life activities are activities that an average person can perform with little or no difficulty such as walking, breathing, seeing, hearing, speaking, learning, and working.

Qualified Individual with a Disability

A qualified employee or applicant with a disability is someone who satisfies skill, experience, education, and other job-related requirements of the position held or desired, and who, with or without reasonable accommodation, can perform the essential functions of that position.

Reasonable Accommodation

Reasonable accommodation may include, but is not limited to—

- making existing facilities used by employees readily accessible to and usable by persons with disabilities
- job restructuring
- modification of work schedules
- providing additional unpaid leave
- reassignment to a vacant position
- acquiring or modifying equipment or devices
- adjusting or modifying examinations, training materials, or policies

Lesson 5 - Hiring & Discrimination

- providing qualified readers or interpreters.
- perform job functions
- enjoy same benefits and privileges enjoyed by people without disabilities.

An employer is not required to lower production standards to make an accommodation. An employer generally is not obligated to provide personal use items such as eyeglasses or hearing aids.

Undue Hardship

An employer is required to make a reasonable accommodation to a qualified individual with a disability unless doing so would impose an undue hardship on the operation of the employer's business. Undue hardship means an action that requires significant difficulty or expense when considered in relation a business' size, financial resources, and the nature and structure of its operation.

Drug and Alcohol Use

Employees and applicants currently engaging in the illegal use of drugs are not protected by the ADA, when an employer acts on the basis of such use. Tests for illegal use of drugs are not considered medical examinations and, therefore, are not subject to the ADA's restrictions on medical examinations. Employers may hold individuals who are illegally using drugs and individuals with alcoholism to the same standards of performance as other employees.

More About Disability Discrimination

As mentioned previously, Title I of the Americans with Disabilities Act (ADA) prohibits discrimination on the basis of disability in all employment practices.

💡 **KEY POINT:** Be aware that the ADA only applies to employers who have fifteen or more employees. However, all states have employment laws, many that prohibit some of the same discrimination practices covered by ADA, regardless of the number of employees.

An employer may not make a pre-employment inquiry on an application form or in an interview as to whether, or to what extent, an individual is disabled. The employer may ask a job applicant whether he or she can perform particular job functions. If the applicant has a disability known to the employer, the employer may ask how he or she can perform job functions that the employer considers difficult or impossible to perform because of the disability, and whether an accommodation would be needed.

A job offer may be conditioned on the results of a medical examination, provided that the examination is required for all entering employees in the same job category regardless of disability, and that information obtained is handled according to confidentiality requirements specified in the Act. After an applicant begins work, all medical examinations and inquiries must be job related and necessary for the conduct of the employer's business. These provisions of the law are intended to prevent the employer from basing hiring and employment decisions on unfounded assumptions about the effects of a disability.

The Do's and Don'ts List

What You Can and Cannot Ask Prior to Hiring

Personal Data	What You Cannot Ask	What You Can Ask
Name	What is your maiden name? What is your spouse's maiden name?	Have you ever used a different name while employed? Do you have a spouse employed here?
Address	Do you own your own home?	What is your current address?
Date of Birth Birthplace	How old are you? What is your date of birth? Where were you born? When did you graduate from high school?	Are you 18 years of age or older (or the legal age for employment in this state)? Do you have a work permit?
Height, Weight	How tall are you? How much do you weigh?	n/a
Race, Color	What is your race? What is your color? What is your parent's race or color?	Do you voluntarily wish to be identified as a minority (to help employer meet affirmative action)?
Picture	Please submit a photograph of yourself.	n/a
Marital Status	Are you married or single? Do you have any children? Is your spouse employed?	Are you married to someone working at this company?

Lesson 5 - Hiring & Discrimination

Personal Data	What You Cannot Ask	What You Can Ask
Gender Related	Do you plan to become pregnant? Do you have child care? Do you feel the job will be difficult because you are a woman?	Do you voluntarily wish to be identified as a female (to help employer meet affirmative action standards)?
Citizenship (Note - many questions cannot be asked, except as provided on the I-9 Form.)	In what country are you a citizen? What is your nationality? What is your native language?	Are you a US citizen? If not, do you intend to become a US citizen?

Background Data	What you Cannot Ask	What You Can Ask
Education	n/a	Inquiry of attendance and degrees for schools or occupational training is legal.
Experience	n/a	You may ask about an applicant's previous work experience.
Criminal Record	Have you ever been arrested?	Have you ever been convicted of a crime? If so, what were the charges? Do you have criminal charges pending against you within the last seven years?
Religion	All questions regarding the applicant's religious denomination, including church or religious holidays observed, are forbidden.	n/a
Memberships or Organizations	What social or religious clubs or organizations do you belong to? Questions regarding memberships in organizations based on race, color, origin, ancestry, or religion must be excluded.	What relevant trade organizations do you belong to? What relevant professional groups or associations are you a member of?

Lesson Summary:

- Pre-employment inquiry, which includes the application, interview, and testing, is one of distinct occasions when employers must be wary of discrimination challenges.

- While a myriad of state and federal laws influence what an employer can or cannot do, there are seven major federal laws that directly affect pre-employment inquiry.

- Although the American with Disabilities Act only applies to employers who have 15 or more employees, many states have laws that prohibit some of the same discrimination practices regardless of the number of employees.

- Be sure your application form and interview inquiry list abides by the *What You Can and Cannot Ask Prior to Hiring* list.

Recommended Resources:

www.eeoc.gov

This is the web site is for the US Equal Employment Opportunity Commission, which administers many of the federal discrimination laws.

www.ftc.gov

The web site for the Federal Trade Commission, which oversees the Fair Credit Reporting Act. This site is filled with useful information about rights and compliance.

http://www.shrm.org/channels

The Society for Human Resource Management site has excellent free access articles. Click on the Compliance Channel.

http://www.nolo.com

Nolo Press is a leading publisher of legal "self-help" books. Their site is filled with great information regarding employment law and compliance.

6 Pre-Employment Screening Policy
How to Develop a Company Pre-Employment Screening Policy

Assume the applicant has filled out all the requisite paperwork. The information they have provided is complete. Basically, everything looks good. The applicant is willing to start now and help is needed. What is next, hiring or screening?

Unsure? Consider this true story:

> **A Great First Day**
>
> A local gas station needed to hire a new cashier quickly. The third applicant that filled out their application form looked good. He passed the interview stage with flying colors and was hired. On the first day of employment, he walked away with a large amount of cash that belonged to the station. The police ran a background check based on information on his application and discovered that the name, address and personal identifiers were all fictitious.

It is obvious in the above example that even a basic background check would have uncovered the crook before he got to the cash. This would have not happened had the employer went directly from the application process to hiring without verifying any information.

An important step was skipped. That step is screening.

KEY POINT: Over 25% of all applications contain misrepresentations! Whether intentional or not, these misrepresentations should be discovered before a final hiring decision is made.

Once you have the various application forms signed and resume from the applicant, it is important to verify the contents of those documents. In other words, you must screen your applicants. This process of verification is generally known as a "Pre-Employment Check" or "Background Investigation."

💡 **KEY POINT:** The purpose of a pre-employment check is to develop a picture of the background and character of an applicant. Essentially, the results of an effective check should provide an accurate assessment of the applicant's reputation, reliability, truthfulness and qualifications.

No Screening is the Worst Policy

As with all other aspects of the pre- and ongoing employment process, employers should establish and adhere to strict policies regarding background screening. Regardless of the details of such polices, without fail there should be a specified minimum amount of screening that is accomplished for each applicant considered. Failure to follow the policy in every case can be the basis for litigation and can result in the hiring of unqualified or troublesome employees.

When pre-employment paperwork and screening are handled haphazardly, the risk of discrimination charges increases. Even if an applicant is a friend's relative or long acquaintance, the same rules should apply.

> **Nepotism**
>
> Several applicants for a position complete the required paperwork, and screening confirms that each is telling the truth. Then, Mr. Whalen, fresh from college and a relative of a current employee, expresses an interest in the position. The employer likes Mr. Whalen and hires him on the spot. Ultimately, one applicant inquiries as to why she did not get the job. Feeling slighted, she files a complaint under the Americans with Disabilities Act via the Equal Employment Opportunity Commission (EEOC). One of these agencies investigates the matter and determines that although the other applicants were put through screening, the one hired was not. In this case, discrimination can be assumed.

As an employer, do not needlessly expose your company to this type of litigation. It is imperative to stick to a regimented company policy, regardless of who is being considered for employment.

The Components of a Pre-Employment Background Check

Traditionally, the main sources used by employers for obtaining background information are prior employers and character references. And now, typically, companies also obtain credit reports, verify education and in some cases even request a criminal history search and driving record check. Even though these traditional means might seem comprehensive enough, they are often inadequate and incomplete.

In reality, there are nine possible searches, or "research components" that encompass a pre-employment background check. The type of position, policies of the company and availability of the information usually are major factors in determining the extent of the check.

The nine searches are:

- Social Security Number Verification
- Criminal History Check
- Credit History Check
- Employment History Verification
- Motor Vehicle Report—Driving Record
- Verification of Educational Background
- Confirmation of Professional License or Registration
- Civil Litigation Record Search
- Military Service Records Check

Lesson 7 deals with how to perform each of these searches. In this lesson, you must determine which searches are applicable and who is going to do them.

Formulating a Proper Company Screening Policy

There are four components that must be considered when developing a company screening policy.

1. Match the Screening Options to Job Description

The type of position, policies of the company and availability of the information will usually determine the extent of the check. The table below lists the recommended screening options every employer should consider. Of course, this assumes that the applicant has signed the proper release forms (see Lesson 4).

Not every option applies to every screening applicant, as the table indicates. For example, if the position does not require special skill for which a college degree is a typical requirement, then verification of college or professional licensing credentials may not be necessary.

Lesson 6 - Pre-Employment Screening Policy   52

The options layout shown in the table below is a great starting point to set your company's screening policy.

Screening Options Table

	All Applicants	Management	When Claimed or Required
Social Security Number Verification	•	•	
Credit History Check		•	
Employment History Verification	•	•	•
Criminal History Check	•	•	•
Verification of Educational Background		•	•
Confirmation of Professional Licenses & Registrations			•
Military Service Records Check			•
Motor Vehicle Report	•	•	•
Civil Record Searches		•	

2. Document, Document, Document

Each component must be documented throughout the entire process. There should be a separate file devoted specifically to each applicant. Each file should contain documentation of each verification attempt. You should include the date, the name of the person/organization with whom you spoke, and some general notes about the outcome. Even if you are unable to reach a particular employer or reference, document the *attempt*. If later, the worst-case scenario develops—a lawsuit—then your detailed documentation can jog your memory and help win the case.

The employer should keep track of every record request that is made. Copies of the letters should be maintained as well as a recording of the details as to when and to whom the request was mailed. In some cases, the employer may not receive a response at all or may be told to check another source. Thus, retention of copies of the original request serves as proof that an attempt has been made.

3. Decide Who Will Perform Each Screening Option

Now that we have discussed what needs to be screened, it is important to address the following question: who will do the screening? There are three possible answers—you can do it yourself, hire someone, or do some of it yourself and hire someone for the balance.

When employers understand the components involved with the screening process, they can make more of an informed decision whether to do the screening in-house or to hire a company or a combination thereof.

Readers who want to do their own screening will find the proper techniques within these pages. All the forms and tools to provide complete verifications are contained between the covers of this book.

However, for many businesses, time is a premium. Many companies would rather leave the screening process to the "experts." For a relatively small expense, employers can hire a pre-employment screening company to handle the task.

Regardless of whether the employer does the screening or if a vendor is hired to do so, the proper application forms and waivers must be filled out and signed by the prospective employee. Your familiarity with the issues discussed in these pages will enhance the effectiveness and interpretation of the results.

4. Know the Geographic Boundaries of the Search

Regardless who does the screening function, it is important to know what geographic area is covered by a particular government agency housing the public records you need. For example, we recommend both a local county search and a statewide search for criminal history information. You can visit your local courthouse for the local county search and write to the state agency for a statewide search. But you may find that statewide screening may also be done from your local court, meaning that a statewide database system is available at your local courthouse. If you require a statewide criminal record search, but the applicant is from a state that has no such search available (CA, MS, NC, TN, UT and VT), be prepared to do searching at the county court level. Budget permitting, a criminal search in the applicant's home county and all counties within a fifty-mile radius of a listed residence on the application is recommended. Regarding driver history records, you will have to check all the states of residence listed on the application.

Pre-Employment Screening Vendors

These companies can be found in telephone directories, advertisements or by calling the local police department for a recommendation. Business groups and trade associations may also offer contacts that have good reputations. Many private investigation firms offer pre-employment screening as a service. The Internet is also a good resource for finding screening companies. Using a search engine, type "pre-employment," "background info" or "screening" and the results will be more than sufficient. A good source that gives unbiased information about screening companies is BRB Publications' National Directory of Public Record Vendors. This source is also available on the Internet at www.publicrecordsources.com.

Vendors and Compliance with the Fair Credit Reporting Act (FCRA)

The FCRA terms a pre-employment screening vendor as a *Consumer Reporting Agency* (CRA). The FCRA terms the name of reports found on the Screening Option Table, provided by these companies, as *Consumer Reports*. There are inherent protections for an employer when they use a CRA because a good CRA will make sure that the employer is in compliance with the FCRA.

For example, an employer may decide not to hire an applicant based upon adverse information found in on a criminal record report provided by a CRA. Denying employment or promotion based on a consumer report is called an "adverse action" by the FCRA. This is fine; an employer has a perfect right to decide whom he wants to hire. But, per the FCRA, the employer must provide a copy of the report to the applicant as well as the summary of the applicant's rights. The CRA knows this because Section 604(b)(1)(B) of the FCRA requires CRAs to provide a copy of the summary with each consumer report obtained for employment purposes. Please refer to the FCRA section in the Appendix for more information regarding how CRAs and adverse actions affect employers.

To know more about screening vendors and how to choose the right vendor for your needs, turn to Lesson 8.

Be Aware of the Potential of Identity Theft

An alarming problem for employers has been the increasing number of job applicants providing phony identification and documents. This trend has gone far beyond embellishing a resume or covering suspicious gaps of employment. The reasons why vary from being an illegal alien, to hiding a criminal background, to debtors trying to evade collection.

The key point here is that employers are responsible and subject to fines if they fail to properly identify an employee. It is a good idea to have the "intake person" make copies of the identifying documents presented and not permit an applicant to simply fill in a Social Security Number or drivers' license number without adequate proof. These extra steps eliminate the potential for an applicant to claim that an "error" must have been made in transcribing his or her identification numbers. Plus, the employer will have proof on file that the numbers on the application match those on the supporting documents.

The identification verification sections in this book will help you discover fraudulent details before you perform a background check. When the information appears to be within the proper criteria, then a background check can begin. But remember — just because the information conforms to the charts, a match doesn't prove that it belongs to the applicant.

Fake Ids For sale

To further complicate the identity problem, there are now many sources that supply false identification for a price. In fact, a number of books have been written just for this purpose. One example, titled *ID For Sale in the Mail*, covers everything from birth certificates to college diplomas. But, one doesn't have to go to the library or a bookstore. A quick search of the Internet for "fake ID" provides everything you can imagine without leaving home, including how-to books and fake identification packages. Sophisticated manufacturing facilities have been found in homes, offices, hotel rooms and even vehicles.

The use, possession and manufacture of fake or counterfeit documents is illegal. Law enforcement agencies on all levels work jointly to discover and dismantle counterfeiting operations. The US Secret Service is the lead agency involved in the investigation and prosecution of those who are caught participating in such activities. Anyone who encounters counterfeit forms of identification should contact the local Secret Service office. They will notify the appropriate agency in the area. Do not be afraid to alert the government – private sector cooperation is essential in combating this form of illegal activity.

Lesson Summary:

- The purpose of a pre-employment check is to develop a picture of the background and character of an applicant. Essentially, the results of an effective check should provide an accurate assessment of the applicant's reputation, reliability, truthfulness and qualifications.
- Over 25% of all employment applications contain misrepresentations. Whether intentional or not, these misrepresentations should be discovered before a final hiring decision is made.

- Without fail, there should be a specified minimum amount of screening that is accomplished for each applicant. Failure to follow the policy in every case can be the basis for litigation, or can result in the hiring of unqualified or troublesome employees.
- There are four main components that must be considered when developing a company screening policy: deciding which screening options are applicable for the job in question; determining what is the geographic boundary of the public record searches; deciding who is going to perform each option of the screen; and document, document, document.

Recommended Resources:

www.publicrecordsources.com

This site profiles over 200 of the nation's leading pre-employment screening agencies. Many firms listed have links to their home pages, some filled with screening tips.

http://www.shrm.org

The Society for Human Resource Management (SHRM) is the world's largest human resource management association. SHRM provides education and information services, conferences and seminars, government and media representation, online services and publications to more than 160,000 professional and student members throughout the world. The web site is filled with articles and resources that can help in all phases of employee management.

7 Background Checks
How to do a Proper Background Check

In the previous Lesson 6, we examined the framework of a pre-employment screening policy. Lesson 7 takes a very detailed approach to the "how-to side" of performing all of the components of the background check. Regardless if you do all or portions of the check yourself or hire a professional, it is important to know and understand what is involved and the correct procedures.

Rather than summarize the process here and place the nitty-gritty details in the Appendix, we have included all of the procedural details in this one lesson.

The screening components examined are:

Social Security Number Verification
Credit History Check
Employment History Verification
Criminal History Check
Verification of Educational Background
Confirmation of Professional Licenses & Registrations
Military Service Records Check
Motor Vehicle Report
Civil Record Searches

Obligations of Employers and the Fair Credit Reporting Act (FCRA)

As mentioned in Lesson 6, if information from a CRA or consumer reporting agency is used for employment purposes, the FCRA regulations are in effect. The employer has specific duties, which are set forth in Section 604(b) of the FCRA. The employer must:

- Make a clear and conspicuous written disclosure to the applicant before the report is obtained, in a document that consists solely of the disclosure, that a consumer report may be obtained.
- Obtain prior written authorization from the applicant.
- Certify to the CRA that the above steps have been followed, that the information being obtained will not be used in violation of any federal or state equal opportunity law or regulation, and that, if any adverse action is to be taken based on the consumer report, a copy of the report and a summary of the applicant's rights will be provided to the applicant.
- Before taking an adverse action, such as denying employment or promotion, provide a copy of the report to the applicant as well as the summary of the applicant's rights. The employer should receive this summary from the CRA, because Section 604(b)(1)(B) of the FCRA requires CRAs to provide a copy of the summary with each consumer report obtained for employment purposes.

Employers who use the proper application and release forms, as shown in this book, will comply with the first two bulleted items above. All reputable screening companies (CRAs) will assist employers with the last two items.

For more information about the FCRA, employers' obligations, and the text of the summary, turn to the FCRA Section in the Appendix.

How to Verify Social Security Numbers

The applicant's Social Security Number should appear on the I-9 form. If the a[pplicant has signed one or more of the release forms, the employer now has permission to verify the accuracy of the number. The verification is performed to answer these key questions:

- Is the number an actual Social Security Number?
- Does the number truly belong to the applicant?

	All Applicants	Management	When Claimed or Required
Social Security Number Verification	•	•	

Social Security Number verification is often one of the most important steps in the screening process. More than any other item, the Social Security Number acts as a personal identifier. Social Security Number verification is the best means by which to ensure that those who are hired are, indeed, who they say they are. If an applicant is not who he or she claims, they shouldn't be hired. The Social Security Number should match on the Application Form and on the I-9 Form.

What if an applicant gave the Social Security Number of Britney Spears, Dave Letterman's date of birth and the name John Smith? Sounds easy to spot, doesn't it? The fact is, if this information were included as part of a criminal history search without fingerprints, no record would be found, making it seem as though the applicant had no criminal past. On the other hand, a Social Security Number check would instantly reveal the attempt at deception. So, remember: identity can be easily falsified and remain undetected unless a Social Security Number Verification is performed.

> **SSN Discrepancies**
>
> Ms. Reisen worked for an employer who had not performed a Social Security Number verification as part of the hiring process. One day, she went to the personnel department to report a recent marriage. During the discussion, Ms. Reisen indicated that she need to change her name to Mrs. Sharneck, and stated that she also had a new Social Security Number. Perplexed, the personnel department decided to have the matter investigated.
>
> The original number had never been issued. The new one was a recent issue that belonged to someone else on the other side of the country. When confronted with these discrepancies, Ms. Reisen admitted that she had supplied a fake Social Security Card twice, but refused to say why. The discussion was witnessed and therefore Ms. Reisen was terminated for providing false information. The real tragedy is that Ms. Reisen had been employed there for five years! During that time, she may have committed many other forms of deception and put the company at risk.

Where to Verify

Conducting a Social Security Number (SSN) verification can be accomplished through the utilization of one of the credit bureaus—Trans Union, Equifax or Experian. Some Internet sites offer a free verification (see Recommended Sources at the end of this lesson). For information on how Social Security Numbers are allocated and how to verify the validity of a number free through the Social Security Administration, turn to Appendix in this book or visit the Social Security Administration web site at www.ssa.gov.

The data that comprises the results of a Social Security Number verification supplied by a credit bureau is known as "header information." This header information can contain any or all of the following:

- The state of and approximate year of issue of the Social Security Number.
- Status as an invalid, non-issued or misused Social Security Number.
- Status as a Social Security Number that has been used to file a death claim.
- Address(es) of the Social Security Number user.
- Employer(s) of the user.
- The year of birth or age of the user.
- Additional or multiple users of the number, if any.

When an individual applies for credit, he or she must provide the header information to the potential credit lender. Lenders work in conjunction with the bureaus when deciding whether or not to extend credit. During the process, the information obtained by the lenders is used to upgrade the records of the credit bureaus.

Each time, new information is provided to the credit agencies, it is logged into the report by date. Every time an individual applies for credit, the exact spelling and format on the application is reported to the credit bureau. Hence the credit or the credit header will report all name variations and addresses an applicant has used. Updated information is also obtained through collection activity. If collection agencies receive any new information on a subject, they report it through the credit bureau's system.

KEY POINT: Keep in mind that there may be unintentional errors. Also, different credit bureaus can have different information. One credit bureau may have extensive information on the subject whereas another may have very little. Lenders do not necessarily utilize or communicate with every bureau. One bureau may be more up-to-date than another in a specific geographic region. In instances where such a search is crucial, it is wise to verify using more than one bureau.

What to Look for in the Results

Does the Social Security Number provided match the subject?

If not, verify that the number provided was entered correctly by the credit bureau as well as by your company staff.

Also, ask the applicant to provide proof of the Social Security Number.

Does the name in the results match that of the subject?

The middle name/initial and suffix are important for proper identification, especially if the subject has a relatively common name.

The subject may have the same name as a relative, with only a suffix to distinguish between them, i.e. Jr. (junior), Sr. (senior) or I (the first), II (the second), etc.

An individual's proper name may be George David Smith, but the subject prefers to go by the name David Smith. He or she may also have used a shortened version of his or her name as a matter of convenience, and that will show here.

Have additional names been revealed?

Perhaps a maiden name has been identified, but was not provided by the subject. If the subject is recently married, most of that person's information may appear under the maiden name, suggesting an additional search is necessary.

Also, the subject may have divorced and resumed the use of her maiden name. The subject may have even had another name from a previous marriage.

Regardless, to enable proper identification and facilitate subsequent searches it is important to determine why variations of the name exist.

Has the number been issued by the Social Security Administration?

When faking an identity, people frequently use numbers that have not yet been issued by the Social Security Administration. To see if a number has been truly issued, check the Social Security Number Allocations Section in the Appendix.

If the results of the verification indicate that the number has not been issued, ask the applicant to provide proof of his or her Social Security Number.

Was the number used to file a death claim?

Numbers used to file a death claim are also utilized to falsify an identity. If the results indicate that the numbers are shown on a death claim, ask for proof that the applicant is truly entitled to the use of that number.

Be aware that it may appear that someone is using the Social Security Number of a deceased person, when in reality he or she has only collected Social Security benefits as a relative of the deceased person.

In what state was the number issued?

It is entirely possible that the number was issued in a state other than the state in which the applicant now resides, and is not, in itself, cause for alarm.

However, such information can indicate other areas of the application that should be reviewed. Perhaps it hasn't been that long since the applicant moved from the state of origin, in which case he or she should have listed the previous addresses from that state.

In what year was the number issued?

First of all, compare the year of issue to the applicant's date of birth as shown on the I-9 Form or General Release Form.

Around 1984, it became mandatory to obtain a Social Security Number for a child at birth. Prior to this, there was no time limitation. However, most individuals acquired a Social Security Number at a fairly early age, generally no later than the time they entered the work force. If your applicant has an employment history of ten years with US companies, but his number was issued five years ago, it's time for some further investigation.

Immigrants should obtain a Social Security Number upon accepting employment in the US.

Do the addresses (and the corresponding time frames) provided by the subject concur with those obtained from the verification?

If the SSN information does not match or addresses other than those provided by the subject, the employer should question the applicant about these findings. The omission of addresses may be intentional, and therefore, further investigation may be warranted.

However, the absence of an address may merely be an oversight. The subject may have resided at the location for only a short time or may have used the address of a friend or relative while between residences. Many individuals, particularly those who are single, will use a parent's address as their permanent address rather than their actual place of residence, which is more likely to fluctuate.

Do the past employers (and the corresponding time frames) given by the subject coincide with those revealed by the SSN verification?

If additional employers are identified, they should be contacted to verify the validity of previous employment. At the same time, if the Request for Information (see page 57) is used, a review of the applicant's performance can be obtained. Regardless of the responses received, the applicant should be questioned about the omission of previous employers.

Is the subject using and/or associated with more than one Social Security Number?

All additional Social Security Numbers should be examined. However, the extra numbers may actually be very similar to that of the subject and potentially the result of a typographical error. Also, the number may belong to a spouse, relative or friend who applied for credit jointly with the subject.

Are additional individuals using the same Social Security Number?

Doing a record header search may reveal more than one individual is using the same SSN. There are several legitimate reasons why.

The additional individual may be a friend or relative who has applied for joint credit with the applicant. There may have been a typographical error if the additional individual happens to have a Social Security Number that is very similar to that of the applicant.

If the applicant claims to have no knowledge of the additional individuals, he or she should be advised to contact the credit bureau from which the information was obtained. It may be necessary for the applicant to have his or her credit report corrected to eliminate future problems.

It is possible that the applicant is entirely unaware of the additional individual. He or she may be the victim of someone who is using his or her SSN for dubious purposes. Do not assume that the applicant is up to something.

If the Social Security Number is Invalid

In each of the instances described above the applicant should be questioned and given the opportunity to explain the mismatch. There is either a legitimate mistake or the applicant's information is fraudulent. There is no legal reason to change one's Social Security Number. If a person is identified as using more than one number and states that he or she "changed it," he or she is not to be trusted.

If the Applicant is a Victim of Social Security Number or Identity Fraud

If your applicant appears to be a victim of identity theft, this should be immediately reported to the police as well as appropriate banks and credit card companies. Also, the applicant should immediately contact the fraud units of the credit bureaus.

If it appears that there is a case of misuse of an applicant's Social Security Number, the applicant should immediately call the Social Security Administration's (SSA) fraud hotline 800-269-0271. If a SSN has been misused by someone to obtain credit, don't call the SSA. They cannot fix anyone's credit record. That has to be done through the credit card companies and credit bureaus.

How to Utilize Credit Report Data

	All Applicants	Management	When Claimed or Required
Credit History Checks		•	

Similar to the verification of Social Security Numbers, credit reports can validate some of the information contained in the Basic Application. Credit reports can also reveal an applicant's outstanding debts, liens, judgments and bankruptcies as well as addresses and employer information. These reports are most often obtained for management positions and for those who will have access to money on the job.

The overall credit report can be a very useful tool for evaluating the background and character of an applicant. The report indicates delinquencies, accounts paid on time or as agreed to, which can go a long way to showing the responsibility of the candidate. If a candidate keeps his or her personal life in order, they may be apt to keep their business life in order.

The Credit Bureaus

There are three major consumer credit bureaus in the US. Here are the companies as well as their web addresses and phone numbers, which can be used to order reports and/or dispute them:

Equifax
www.equifax.com
800-685-1111

Experian
www.experian.com
800-682-7654

Trans Union
www.transunion.com
800-916-8800

These bureaus obtain information on a daily basis from private enterprises and government agencies. The private sources are primarily credit grantors, such as banks, department stores and credit card companies. The bureaus also collect data on judgments, liens and records from all levels of government for the purpose of updating their credit reports and the corresponding header information.

The three bureaus have more than 2,000 affiliated local bureaus across the country. Some are franchises while others are independent affiliates.

In addition, there are numerous agencies that may enter information into the credit system as they check credit for legitimate business purposes. Each entry, including the applicant's address, is required. Every time a consumer fills out a credit application for any purpose—credit card, store credit, mortgages, auto purchase, apartment rentals, etc.— the information supplied by the consumer is provided to the "Big Three" credit bureaus.

Credit Reports and the Fair Credit Reporting Act (FCRA)

Prior to obtaining a credit report, the employee must be informed in writing of the company's intention to do so, and a signature from the applicant agreeing to allow access to the information must be obtained. Further, a summary of the applicant's rights must be given to the candidate prior to taking any adverse action as a result of the credit check. This summary includes a full list of agencies, telephone numbers and places for an applicant to question or complain about items contained in their personal credit report. The candidate is entitled to see a copy of the adverse report.

If a friendly merchant offers to provide a credit report as a favor or for very little money and an employer accepts the offer, both are in serious violation of the FCRA. It is imperative that companies adhere to the FCRA rules. For more information on the act and its relationship with employers, see the Appendix.

How to Verify Employment History

	All Applicants	Management	When Claimed or Required
Employment History Verification	•	•	•

Although verifying past employment can be frustrating because it is often difficult to get a response from a former employer, it is crucial that the attempt be made and documented. If, for some reason, a discrimination suit is filed, there is a possibility that a jury member might think, "Why didn't you contact their last employer before hiring them?"

State Immunity Laws and Former Employer References

There are forty-one states with employment laws that deal with former employers. These states provide immunity to a former employer who provides information in good faith to a prospective employer. For additional information about the specific states, refer to Lesson 23.

If you are talking with a former employer who is in a state that has an immunity law, it may be prudent to notify them that as long as they are telling you the truth, they are protected by law from liability.

When someone provides written material that is derogatory or states that proof will be made available, feel free to use that information and refer to its source. However, in all cases, only provide the applicant with information that is totally necessary, and only if it is the basis for rejection.

Telephone or In Writing?

There are two primary ways to verify previous employment—by phone and in writing. Information that would not be committed to in writing is often revealed in a phone conversation. During the course of a phone conversation, you may learn that the applicant was slow, lazy or argumentative in the workplace. Such characteristics are not easy to prove, and as such, the previous employer may not have any documentation to support these claims. Nonetheless, he or she might mention such traits during a verification by phone.

Although verifying by phone can be the best method to learn the truth, be aware that off-the-record comments are of no use in court. Also, consider that the person providing the information may have had a personality conflict with the applicant, and therefore provides false information in order to bring harm to the applicant.

Verifying information in writing can be helpful for proving written documentation of one's efforts. However, only basic information, such as the dates of employment, is usually provided by mail.

Verifying Employment by Phone

If, as an employer, you are lucky enough to make contact with a prior employer via phone, ask to speak with the applicant's immediate supervisor. The former supervisor is more likely to provide in-depth and personal knowledge about the candidate, whereas the human resources department is most often limited to merely verifying dates of employment and payroll information. Even the most cooperative

Verifications and the Fair Credit Reporting Act (FCRA)

As reported in Lesson 6, if an employer obtains adverse information from a vendor a.k.a. Consumer Reporting Agency (CRA), provisions of the FCRA are in effect. If you use the report "in whole or part" and deny employment or promotion, the report itself along with a summary of rights must be given to the applicant.

However, if the employer, not a CRA, obtains the prior employment verification, the FCRA regulations do not apply.

representative of the previous employer may only relate information that is documented in personnel files.

The extent of the documentation of phone verifications varies depending on the person making the call. Some take copious notes while others merely jot down keywords. Regardless, the Pre-Employment Check by Phone is designed to maximize the results of a telephone verification. The questions on the form are designed to relate the information obtained to specific requirements of the job.

How to Handle Off-The-Record Comments

As mentioned previously, in some cases a person will discuss an issue over the phone that he or she would not commit to in response to a written request. Sometimes a prior employer will tell of problems or suspicions in confidence. Sometimes the person you speak with will accidentally blurt out something relevant. This situation requires the utmost caution. In almost all cases, you will not be able to quote or use these comments. They serve only as collaboration for re-enforcement of other reasons not to hire. If you believe the information provided is serious enough to make you not want to hire that applicant, then go back through your process and find another reason not to bring the person on.

If someone gives you positive information about the candidate, but off-the-record, send the former employer a form on which to write these positive comments. Always assure them that their off-the-record comments will be maintained as confidential.

KEY POINT: Making a decision based on an undocumented discussion by phone is extremely risky. A rejection that is based on a phone conversation that does not have supporting documentation is unlikely to hold up in a court of law.

A closer look at the Pre-Employment Check by Phone

A full size Pre-Employment Check Form may be found in Appendix III.

Pre-Employment Check by Phone

Name of Applicant: _____

Name of Company Contacted: _____

Name and Title of Reference: _____ Telephone: _____

INSTRUCTIONS:
Contact the reference, preferably the applicant's immediate supervisor. Identify yourself and state that you are "calling to verify some of the information given to _____ by _____ who we are considering for a position."

What were the dates of his/her employment with you? From _____ To _____

What was the nature of his/her job? _____

What did you think of his/her work? _____

How would you describe his/her performance in comparison with other people? _____

What job progress did he/she make? _____

What were his/her earnings? _____ Bonus? _____

Why did he/she leave your Company? _____

Would you re-employ? _____

What are his/her strong points? _____

What are his/her limitations? _____

How did he/she get along with other people? _____

Could you comment on his/her:
(a) attendance
(b) dependability
(c) ability to take on responsibility
(d) potential for advancement
(e) degree of supervision needed
(f) overall attitude _____

Did he/she have any personal difficulties that interfered with his/her work? _____

Is there anything else of significance that we should know? _____

SIGNATURE: _____ DATE: _____

Start with a check of the dates of tenure – though approximate, compare this with what is represented on the application.

Compare the information here with the applicant's representation of his or her previous earnings.

Verifying Employment by Mail

When a former employer is reluctant or unavailable to provide information about a previous employee over the phone, a request should be mailed.

Always make your request official. Use company letterhead with an officer's signature or a raised corporate seal. There should be no doubt as to the validity of your request.

One way to control the information you receive is to use the Request for Information Form shown on the next page. Also, be sure to enclose a self-addressed stamped envelope to expedite the response. Overall, do whatever you can to make your written request appealing and easy to respond to.

Along with the Request for Information, a copy of the signed Applicant Waiver Form (see Lesson 4) should be mailed to that previous employer. Both of these forms have proven to be effective at maximizing the responses received and providing useful information.

KEY POINT: Keep in mind, when commonly used letters and forms ask for a *detailed* evaluation, these efforts normally prove fruitless. The more detailed the request is, the more likely it will be ignored.

If the information supplied by the applicant is correct, all that is required of the previous employer is to signify the accuracy with a single check mark, sign and return the request.

Employers may want to produce the Request for Information in duplicate so that the former employer may maintain a record of your request in their files. Doing so gives them the opportunity to protect themselves should it become necessary to have documented proof of their actions regarding the matter. The inclusion of a copy of the signed Applicant Waiver should alleviate any liability concerns that the previous employer may have about providing that information.

In some cases, it is not practical to wait for the results of the employment history verification prior to hiring the applicant. If this is the case, simply indicate on the request that your company has already employed the applicant. It is not absolutely necessary that a response is received, but it is important to show that you have made an effort and support it with documentation.

How to Handle Derogatory Material

Remember, if someone provides written material that is derogatory or states that proof will be made available, feel free to use the information in the decision making process. But keep in mind, negative items must be provided to the rejected applicant upon request. It is therefore wise and less offensive to let an applicant know that the reason for rejection is the simplest item developed, thus other derogatory information or documents may not be required and would be used at a later date only if necessary. An example is if an applicant failed to list a prior employer and filled in a two-year gap to cover that problem. This same applicant may have a nasty credit report, which might also add to the rejection process. However, that credit report could be the source of disputes between the applicant and various credit bureaus. By using the credit report in conjunction with any other issue could raise a lot of unnecessary questions by the applicant, and merely cause more headaches for an employer.

A Closer Look at Written Request for Information Form

A larger version of this form is found in the Appendix.

DATE _____

REQUEST FOR INFORMATION

To Whom It May Concern:

Mr./Ms. _____ has applied for a position as a _____ and states that he/she was employed by you as a _____ from _____ to _____.

Will you kindly reply to this inquiry and return this sheet in the enclosed self-addressed envelope. Your reply will be held in strict confidence and will in no way involve you in any responsibility.

Sincerely,

Signature: _____

Name (print/type): _____ Title: _____

Company: _____ Telephone: _____

****

Is employment record correct as stated above?   Yes _____ No _____
What were this employee's duties? _____
Did he/she have custody of money or valuables?   Yes _____ No _____
Were his accounts properly kept?   Yes _____ No _____
Was his/her conduct satisfactory?   Yes _____ No _____
Do you recommend him/her for rehire?   Yes _____ No _____

He/she was: Discharged _____ Laid Off _____ Resigned _____

Please list any Workers Compensation Claims: _____

	EXCELLENT	GOOD	FAIR	POOR
Quality of work				
Cooperation				
Safety Habits				
Personal Habits				
Attendance				

REMARKS: _____
_____

Company Name: _____

Person Completing Form: _____ Title: _____

Date: _____

Typical Problems with Verifying Prior Employment

When you fill out an application or prepare your resume, do you include every single past employer? More than likely, you don't. It is safe to assume that most applicants selectively record the details of their previous employment.

KEY POINT: Applicants leave out information concerning employers with whom they have had a bad work experience. Likewise, employers do not always reveal negatives truth about former employees.

Short of a full-scale investigation, there is little hope of uncovering the names of employers that the applicant chooses not to list. Thus, a problematic work history and other key information crucial to employment decisions may go undiscovered.

The employers that the applicant *does* include may be a source of trouble as well. There are few laws that *require* a former employer to respond to a pre-employment inquiry, and if they do respond, there is no guarantee that they are going to be truthful. In some cases, employers will "rewrite" history to simply get rid of a problem employee.

Even if the employer wants to tell the truth, he or she may choose not to because of liability concerns. The number of US lawsuits filed against former employers has steadily increased the past ten years. Even if a past employer tells the truth, he or she might be sued. However, as mentioned previously, many states have prior employer immunity laws that remove liability from employers who pass along truthful information.

However, according to Derek Hinton, author of *The Criminal Records Book*, there is a developing legal doctrine called "negligent referral." This refers to an instance when a former employer is sued for failure to provide employment history information on an applicant who does the inquiring employer harm after hire.

> **To Catch A Thief**
>
> Suppose an employer named Mr. Citta suspected his assistant, Miss Miller of theft. Later, Citta fired Miller due to her inability to meet deadlines. Then Citta observed that the theft ceased at the same time Miller was terminated. Citta might have believed that the culprit was Miller, but can't prove it. Without proof and with a high degree of liability involved, Mr. Citta does not reveal his suspicions to those seeking details of Miller's past employment. If he were to do so, he would certainly be putting himself and the company at risk for a lawsuit.

With the time and financial costs involved in such litigation, companies have become wary of giving detailed information about a past employee's performance. Again, this is why many companies provide only a minimal response or none at all. Almost all former employers require a written request and then respond with only basic information about the applicant. With or without the proper paperwork, the prior employer may still not disclose that the applicant is a source of friction, i.e. "the office troublemaker") or practices poor hygiene, resulting in the loss of customers who have observed it.

> **KEY POINT:** Often, applicants are aware of what is likely to be revealed by former employers. Some are even savvy enough to have friends call pretending to be a prospective employer so that they can find out precisely what will be said.

Those applicants that have gotten into trouble are not likely to admit it, and many know that their past employers will not discuss it either because of liability issues. Given that past bad behavior is not likely to be revealed by previous employers, applicants have virtually nothing to lose. Moving from job to job, they repeat their transgressions, costing companies dearly.

So what can be done? Employers must abide by the law as well as institute and follow proper procedures. Essentially, employers must do the best that they can to verify all the details about the applicant. Even if the efforts are fruitless, the proof of the attempt follows an old standard that a jury would look for and understand.

Limited Access Companies

There has been a growing situation with major companies using an outside service as the point of contact for previous employment verification. Usually the way to only reach these vendors is via a 900 dial-up number, a fee is involved, and information given is limited to a "name, rank and serial number" response. Unfortunately, this may be the only way that some companies will give out information on prior employees. In this case, every attempt should be made to conduct a telephone conversation with an appropriate department head within the former employer company.

How to Verify Personal References

We've discussed the unreliability of past employers, but what about personal references? Once again, the applicant selects whom to list. Applicants purposefully choose individuals whom they believe will provide a good reference. Often those listed are best friends, close neighbors or other casual acquaintances. They are people who are going to say "good things."

If you do check references, listen for specifics. Take your time and ask probing questions. Think about the following:

- Does the person referenced seem professional?
- What is the reference's relationship (i.e. former employer, co-worker, etc.) to the applicant?
- Does he or she provide details about the applicant?

- If the reference says that the applicant "is hard-working," ask for an example. If he or she can't provide one, it may be an indication that the person is not being truthful.
- Ask the personal reference to identify the applicant's current and last known prior employer.

If the reference truly knows the applicant, the reference should be able to answer the question about past employers. If the given answer does not match the information on the application, you have made prudent use of the reference and uncovered a red flag.

A friend or acquaintance probably won't say that the applicant gets half drunk every night and keeps losing jobs. The fact that an applicant is a great worker, but only works long enough to collect unemployment or has a side business so he won't be staying long is probably not going to be revealed.

How to Check Criminal History

	All Applicants	Management	When Claimed or Required
Criminal History Checks	•	•	•

Every employee is entrusted with some form of responsibility, be it large or small. Whether someone is a government official, a business professional or in-home caretaker, he or she is given responsibilities. As such, it is important to feel confident that one's employees will not take advantage of your trust and commit crimes on the job. One way to achieve such confidence is to have criminal background checks performed for prospective employees.

Yet, investigation into the criminal history of an applicant has become a controversial subject. Consider:

- How far should employers go to protect themselves from hiring the wrong person?
- What justifies the need for a criminal background check?
- Who should be allowed to conduct such a search?

The news media is constantly reporting on employees who commit serious crimes. These reports have no real common denominator. Perpetrators can range from high-level figures to local volunteers, and the crimes run the gamut from theft to sexual assault, even murder.

> **Example**
>
> In 1997, a Stafford Township, NJ karate instructor admitted to committing sexual acts with seven pre-teen boys and one five-year-old girl. The subject was on parole from the State of Texas after found guily of similar charges. The resulting investigation uncovered that the subject used several names and was a suspect in similar crimes in four additional states.

A criminal history background check combined with a Social Security Number verification would have prevented the subject from obtaining a position that facilitated the commission of his crimes.

Business owners need to consider the possibility that one of their employees may commit a serious crime, and that the company itself could be liable. Employers should ask these questions:

- Can the company withstand the negative publicity that would result from such an unfortunate incident?
- Are such incidents covered by the company's current insurance policies?
- From where would the funds to pay the legal bills originate?
- Are personal assets protected by the corporate structure?
- How much business is likely to be lost?

Thankfully, federal and state legislatures have been responding to these issues by passing laws that require criminal background checks. For example, New Jersey requires criminal history checks for real estate appraisers, those who work with the institutionalized elderly, healthcare workers, childcare workers and sports volunteers. Similarly, the State of New York approved a law allowing parents to investigate nannies and au pairs.

Where to Perform a Criminal History Search

Criminal record searching is perhaps the most complicated and inconclusive part of the screening process. A criminal event is recorded on file at the courthouse, where a jurisdiction can be a city, county, state or federal court. These records then may *or may not* be forwarded to a state agency overseeing criminal records, or even to the FBI.

However, there is no national database available to employers or the general public. FBI records are only available to government law enforcement officials.

💡 **KEY POINT:** Beware of vendors promising to look up a record in their "national database of criminal records." There is no such all-encompassing database in existence that is available to the public.

All states but one (MS) have a central state agency that collects criminal record information from state police and the court system. Additionally, five state agencies deny access (CA, NC, TN, UT, VT) to most employers. Of the remaining 45 states, 22 states have severely restrictive policies and require extensive forms or the use of fingerprints. Thus, an extended delay in the return of criminal record checks is often experienced.

Also, there is no consistency in record disposition in instances where people have been arrested for a crime, but the trial has dragged out as much as a year without a decision as to quilt. The reality is, the applicant who looks good on paper may be awaiting disposition on a major felony that occurred months ago.

So, in those states where records are unavailable, checking criminal records at the county level is a must. But there are pitfalls you should be aware of. This can get costly if multiple counties are searched, but may still be worth the expense. If an applicant lives in close proximity to the border of another county and an employer does not check the records from both counties, there is a chance a criminal record will go unnoticed.

Commercial vendors of criminal records or pre-employment screening firms offer a strong alternative to accessing the records yourself. They are professionals and know the ins and outs of accessing records at state agencies and county courts.

The Arrest Records Vs. Conviction Records Dilemma

There is no uniform reporting system in place for the government agencies that report criminal records. Some go back seven years, some ten, some more than that. Some agencies report all arrests, with or without pending convictions. Some only report actions if there is a conviction. Some report arrest without dispositions, only if the arrest is more than one year old; others only if the arrest is less than one year old.

Per FCRA, information about criminal convictions obtained from a CRA may be reported without any time limitation. Also, per FCRA, any arrests that have not evolved—still pending—after seven years cannot be reported.

To further complicate the situation, ten states prohibit an employer from reviewing arrest information not associated with a conviction, except for a pending charge with regard to the applicant. These ten states are CA, HI, IL, MA, MI, NY, PA, RI, VA and WI. (One wonders, does this apply to the home state of the employer or the applicant, or both?)

You could, as an employer, receive a criminal record with information printed on it that you cannot legally use. A reputable CRA should filter the report before it is delivered to the employer, thus not putting the employer at risk. But, what if the applicant has been arrested for embezzlement, is awaiting trail, and applies for a bookkeeping job with your company? Do you want the CRA to tell you the complete information? {Yes you do because it is a pending charge.} If the employer reads about the arrest in the paper, he can use that information in the hiring decision without breaking the law? {Yes} What if the applicant is eventually found innocent? {At that point, the applicant may again be considered for employment} It is a confusing situation.

For those of you who would like to know more about the regulations and restrictions for using criminal records, we strongly urge you to obtain a copy of *The Criminal Records Book* by Derek Hinton, published by Facts on Demand Press.

A Checklist to Criminal Record Searching

What levels should be checked?

Criminal history checks should be done statewide in those states that provide for such a search. When statewide searches are not available, at a minimum the county of residence should be checked. It is not a bad idea to check the surrounding counties also, especially if a large city is nearby. If the applicant has lived in four different counties, or lived in one county but worked in another, those counties should be checked individually.

Federal searches are not part of typical screening procedures. However, certain positions, such as that of a worker in a nuclear facility, require a search via the National Crime Information Center (NCIC). If such a search is mandated, fingerprints and cooperation with the FBI is required.

What is needed from the applicant?

Most states and all counties do *not* require fingerprints for a statewide search. Normally, state agencies require the name, date of birth, Social Security Number, range of years to check, and any additional names that are used by the subject. County checks are by name, date of birth and Social Security Number. County courts are more apt to charge for additional name searches. Many jurisdictions require signed release forms. In some states, the applicant's signature must be notarized.

In a case where a candidate has used multiple names, even for legitimate reasons, it is recommended that each of those names be searched in a criminal system. A legitimate reason includes women who have been married or divorced, or those people who use a professional name. Most venues consider each name an additional search and therefore an additional fee would be incurred.

What are the typical costs and turnaround times for the searches?

Purchasing criminal checks directly from the courts normally costs between $5.00 and $10.00. The typical turnaround time at the county level is three to thirty days.

Statewide criminal history searches range in cost from $10.00 to $25.00 depending upon the venue. The turnaround time can be as short as three days in states such as Florida and New Jersey or as long as thirty days in states like Pennsylvania and Washington. When accompanied by a fingerprint card, the fee is typically $25.00 and receiving the results takes considerably longer.

Professional vendors typically charge between $18.00 and $20.00 for a county search with any statutory fees being additional. It is difficult for a vendor to provide a list of all 3,500 plus counties in the USA because the fees can change on daily. Many counties who did not have a charge yesterday will have one tomorrow.

What information will be found in the report?

The information received normally provides details on convictions for seven years or more. Beyond that, the response is not uniform. Some entities release information on pending cases, if a waiver or fingerprints are presented. Some states will list pending cases without dispositions, if the disposition is less than one year old. For example, the New Jersey State Police provide all convictions and all cases that appear to be open without disposition. They do not provide any case where there has been acquittal or "not guilty" verdict.

A Few Comments on Negative Findings

The presence of a criminal history should not always result in automatic rejection, especially if the applicant has admitted that he or she has a criminal record. Federal and state human resource personnel are required to consider the following factors in determining whether a criminal record is reason for rejection:

- The nature and seriousness of the crime
- The circumstances under which the crime occurred
- The date of the crime and the age of the applicant when the crime was committed
- Whether the crime was an isolated event
- Evidence of rehabilitation

There are also specific rules regarding job disqualification. For example, a person may be denied examination, eligibility or appointment when he or she has made a false statement of any material fact or attempted any deception or fraud in any part of the selection or appointment process.

In short, any applicant who lies during the application process should not take the required tests, much less get the job.

Local Police Record Request

Once in a while you may find it necessary to request information about an applicant from the local police. You may do this because you want to go the extra mile and not take a chance that a criminal record action may not yet appear on a state agency or county court database. Sometimes the local police may have knowledge not available to the court system or state police.

To facilitate the need to obtain police record information, this book includes a letter that has proven effective. The letter, referred to as the Local Police Record Request, is straightforward, requires very little customization and takes only a minute to read. To make the letter even more effective, have it printed on company letterhead, and include a raised seal by a Notary Public and an original signature, not one that has been stamped on the page. Following these techniques will remove questions of authenticity so that the police department may begin processing the request without further delay.

The results of a Police Record Request can reveal surprising and important information.

> **Example**
>
> Mr. Hill applies for a job working for a pharmacy. The employer initiates the verification process and at first, everything appears normal. However, there seems to be a severe absence of any credit information, also, an expired driver's license and a several year gap in employment. His resume explains these discrepancies. Supposedly, Mr. Hill had spent his time "participating in social work with the poor in Afghanistan." Then, the results of a Police Record Request arrive. Although the local police department had no contact with Mr. Hill, they did receive an international police agency memo that indicated he had been recently released from prison in Afghanistan. Apparently, he had attempted to smuggle cocaine into the United States.
>
> Mr. Hill is certainly not someone one would want working in a pharmacy! As in this example, a Police Record Request can answer lingering questions and make the hiring decision clear-cut.

Local Police Record Request

Using the example below, recreate this letter on your company's stationary. Replace all information contained within parenthesis with the appropriate information for your company.

Lesson 7 - Background Checks

A full size Local Police Record Request Form may be found in Appendix III.

TO BE PRINTED ON YOUR LETTERHEAD

(DATE)

(NAME OF POLICE DEPARTMENT)
Att: Records
(STREET ADDRESS)
CITY, STATE, ZIP)

Re: (NAME OF EMPLOYEE)

Dear Sir/Madam:

Our medical facility is conducting a background check on the above-captioned prospective employee. I am writing to obtain local criminal history and/or character information from your Department. Enclosed please find a consent form with original signature, which has been notarized, authorizing the release of this information. Please indicate on the form the results of your record check, or lack thereof, and return it to us in the self-addressed stamped envelope provided.

Please advise us if there are any additional requirements, fees, etc. necessary to obtain this information.

Thank you for your assistance in this matter.

Sincerely,

(NAME - TYPED)
(TITLE - TYPED)

How to Verify Educational Background

	All Applicants	Management	When Claimed or Required
Verification of Educational Background		•	•

Educational background encompasses high school diplomas, GEDs, college/university degrees, trade school completion and extension courses. Since the educational accomplishments of an applicant tend to enhance his or her status as a viable candidate for a position, there is a temptation to falsify one's educational background in order to appear more qualified. Applicants may claim successful completion of a degree or program without actually having earned it.

💡 **KEY POINT:** A recent study by Adam Safeguard Inc. found that 29% of applicants misrepresented their educational background.

Educational claims should always be verified, *even* if the degree listed is not one required for the position. Keep in mind, many professional and trade schools go out of business every year, and frequently the records of their graduates are no longer available.

Unfortunately, employers do not always confirm education claims because they don't know how. As with many areas of pre-employment, the "how" seems to be a mystery! Fortunately, educational claims are very easy to verify, if you have the phone number. Attendance and completion can often be confirmed with a single phone call. The key is to call the institution's Registrar's (or similarly named) Office, identify yourself, and state the purpose of your call. Educational institutions are normally quite receptive to helping former students obtain employment.

If an employer requires a transcript or written verification, the process takes longer and usually involves a signed release for the subject for that purpose.

> **A Learned Colleague**
>
> An applicant mentions on his application that he received a "BA Degree from Remington College in Lafayette, Louisiana." A phone call to the Registrar's Office for Remington reveals that Remington *only* grants an Associate Degree.

In this case, the applicant is caught in a lie.

Obtain the Necessary Information First

The Request for Education Verification on the next page places the burden of information gathering on the applicant. He or she must provide the details of education accomplishments in the spaces provided. The Request for Education Verification shows the employer's intent to verify educational background, and the applicant's signature confirms the applicant's awareness of this fact. Copies of this statement and signature may be sent to any educational institution that requires a written request for verification.

More important is the idea that with these statements clearly present on the Basic Application, applicants will be wary of making false educational claims. If the applicant has prepared a glowing resume laced with phony or over-stated achievements, he or she will quickly become aware that the deception has a good chance at being discovered.

Keep in mind that people say, "What's the big deal if someone 'gussies-up' their resume?" Think about it. If applicants "gussy-up" their resumes, maybe they will "gussy-up" their expense account reports.

Do You Do the Educational Verifications Yourself or Use a Vendor?

The answer to this question depends on your time and the ongoing need. Pre-employment screening firms regularly conduct these verifications. They have excellent book and media references that detail how to access the 4,000+ accredited learning institutions. In fact, there are several vendors who specifically offer educational verification and nothing more.

Below is a list of education resources:

www.studentclearinghouse.com

The National Student Clearinghouse will perform educational verifications for a moderate fee. This can be accomplished over the Internet.

www.publicrecordsources.com

This web site lists vendors who specialize in educational verification (under the Search Firms button). There also over 200 pre-employment screening firms profiled under the Screening Firms button.

The HR departments at many companies, as well as many screening vendors, use the *Public Record Research System* by BRB Publications. This CD or web-based product lists over 4,300 institutions and state GED offices, detailing the location, phone number, types of degrees offered, and procedures to verify or obtain copies of records.

Request For Education Verification Form

This is the form that should be used to confirm higher education issues – whether the applicant merely attended a college or university, or earned a degree. Have the applicant sign it early as part of the application process. This will weed out applicants who would otherwise falsify their education background.

A full size Request For Education Verification form may be found in Appendix III.

Date_____

REQUEST FOR EDUCATION VERIFICATION

Registrar's Office:

The applicant identified below has applied for a position with our organization. He/she has claimed attendance, credits and/or degree as denoted herein. Would you kindly verify this information and return this form in the enclosed self addressed stamped envelope. Please note, the applicant has signed for the release of this request.

NAME OF FACILITY

ADDRESS   CITY   STATE   ZIP

ATTENDANCE: FROM_____ TO _____
                 MO.   YR.   MO.   YR.

CREDITS
RECEIVED: _____   GRADUATE: YES   NO   _____
          TOTAL   AWARDS-LEVEL

DEGREE: YES NO _____ DATE _____
                 DEGREE RECEIVED

I hearby authorize the release to certify my records as stated above.

Signature _____
Name(print) _____
Address _____
City/State/Zip _____
Date of Birth _____
SS# _____

— Pay close attention to verifying the dates attended.

— Check degree claimed against types of degrees granted by the school.

How to Confirm Professional Licenses & Registrations

	All Applicants	Management	Whenever Claimed or Required
Confirmation of Professional Licenses & Registrations			•

Depending on the profession or industry, individuals (or businesses) may very likely need to have a license, possess a permit or be registered to legally practice or operate. Note the distinction between licensing and registration: unlike licensing, registration is *not* necessarily an indication of competency.

Types of Licensing, Registration & Certification

Private Licensing and Certification—requires a proven level of minimum competence before a license is granted. These professional licenses separate the true "professions" from the third category below. In many of these professions, the certification body, such as the American Institute of Certified Public Accountants, is a private association. A licensing body, such as the New York State Education Department, is the licensing agency. Also, many professions may provide additional certifications in specialty areas.

State Licensing and Certification—requires certification through an examination or other requirements supervised directly by the state rather than by a private association.

Individual Registration—required if an individual intends to offer specified products or services in the designated area, but does not require certification that the person has met minimum requirements. An everyday example would be registering a handgun in a state that does not require passing a gun safety course.

Business Registration—required if a business intends to do business or offer specified products or services in a designated area, such as registering a liquor license. Some business license agencies require applicant testing or a background check. Others merely charge a fee after a cursory review of the application.

Special Permits—give the grantee specific permission to do something, whether it is to sell hot-dogs on the corner or to put up a three story sign. Permits are usually granted at the local rather than state government level.

Other Means of Licensing and Registration

Although much of the licensing and registration occurs at the state level, you should be aware of other places to search.

Local government agencies at both the county and municipal levels require a myriad of business registrations and permits in order to do business within their borders. Even where you think a business or person, such as a remodeling contractor, should have local registrations, it is still best to start your search at the state level.

County Recorder's Office and City Hall. If you decide to check on local registrations and permits, call the offices at both the county—try the county recorder—and municipal level—try city hall—to find out what type of registrations may be required for the person or business you are checking out.

Just as on the state level, you should expect that basic information will be just a phone call away and that you will not be charged for obtaining a status summary.

Professional Associations. As mentioned above, many professional licenses are based on completion of the requirements of professional associations. In addition, there are many professional designations from such associations that are not recognized as official licenses by government. Other designations are basic certifications in fields that are so specialized that they are not of interest to the states, but rather only to the professionals within an industry. For example, if your company needs to hire an investigator to check out a potential fraud against you, you might want to hire a CFE—Certified Fraud Examiner—who has met the minimum requirements for that title from the Association of Certified Fraud Examiners, see http://www.cfenet.com/.

Generally, a particular board handles one or several types of professional or business certifications. As such, certification information is relatively easy to verify.

Agencies and registries maintain a wealth of information about licensees or registrants in their files. As an employer you'll want to know if the applicant has a license or certification. They may deliberately omit the fact that it had been previously suspended.

What Information *May* Be Available

While some agencies consider this information private and confidential to one extent or another, most agencies will freely release at least some basic data over the phone or by mail. On the other hand, a recent study by BRB Publications, Inc. shows only 45% of the agencies indicate they will disclose adverse information about a registrant, and many of those will only disclose selected portions of that information.

In any event, the basic rule to follow when you contact a licensing agency is to find out **what specific kinds of information are available.**

An agency may be willing to release part or all of the following—

- Field of Certification
- Status of License/Certificate
- Date License/Certificate Issued
- Date License/Certificate Expires
- Current or Most Recent Employer
- Social Security Number
- Address of Subject
- Complaints, Violations or Disciplinary Actions

Even though license verification appears to be simple, an experienced vendor can usually do the task faster and they are articulate in obtaining the best information available. If a caller does not know what they can get and does not ask "all" questions, critical information can be missed. The fees for this type of service range from $10.00 to $14.00, not including any statutory fees.

> **Properly Licensed Or Not**
>
> XYZ Company believed that their screening policies were effective, but management decided to confirm this opinion by contracting a third party to investigate. Apparently, XYZ Company employed over a hundred employees who claimed to be certified emergency medical technicians (EMTs). When XYZ was questioned as to whether these certifications had ever been verified, the response was, "You can do that?" Thus, the verification process was initiated.
>
> After only a few phone calls to state agencies, it was uncovered that one of the licenses had never been issued and several had not been renewed. In the end, one liar was terminated and several employees were transferred pending renewal of their certifications. Best of all, the only cost involved was the phone calls.

Licensing Agency Search Fees

Several trends are common when verifying search fees of the various licensing agencies. They are as follows:

- There is no charge to verify if a particular person is licensed and this can usually be done over the phone.

- The fee for copies or faxes ranges from $0.25 to $2.00.
- A fee of $5 to $20 usually applies to written requests. This is due to the fact that the written certification releases more information than a verbal inquiry, i.e. disciplinary action or exam scores.
- A fee that is $25 or more is usually for a list of licensed professionals. For example, a hospital may request a roster of registered nurses in a certain geographic area.

How to Verify Military Service

	All Applicants	Management	When Claimed or Required
Military Service Records Check			•

Military records are accessible to the public under the Freedom of Information Act (FOIA) and are available for free by mail. In order to achieve maximum results, Standard Form 180 should be used. The form includes the specific locations to address inquiries, which are determined based on the branch in which the applicant served.

This form, known in all its various updates as Form 180, is produced by the Federal Government and can be obtained from the National Personnel Records Center in St. Louis, Missouri. The current version is online at www.nara.gov/regional/mprsf180.html. Also, the agency offers a fax-on-demand service.

Request For Military Records Form (Front)

A full size Request For Military Records form may be found in Appendix III.

Request for Military Records Form (Reverse)

STANDARD FORM 180 BACK (Rev. 4-96)

LOCATION OF MILITARY RECORDS

The various categories of military service records are described in the chart below. For each category there is a code number which indicates the address at the bottom of the page to which this request should be sent.

1. **Health and personnel records.** In most cases involving individuals no longer on active duty, the personnel record, the health record, or both can be obtained from the same location, as shown on the chart. However, some health records are available from the Department of Veterans Affairs (VA) Records Management Center (Code 11). A request for a copy of the health record should be sent to Code 11 if the person was discharged, retired, or released from active duty (separated) on or after the following dates: ARMY-- October 16, 1992; NAVY--January 31, 1994; AIR FORCE and MARINE CORPS--May 1, 1994. Health records of persons on active duty are generally kept at the local servicing clinic, and usually are available from Code 11 a week or two after the last day of active duty.

2. **Records at the National Personnel Records Center.** Note that it takes at least three months, and often six or seven, for the file to reach the National Personnel Records Center (Code 14) in St. Louis after the military obligation has ended (such as by discharge). If only a short time has passed, please send the inquiry to the address shown for active or current reserve members. Also, if the person has only been released from active duty but is still in a reserve status, the personnel record will stay at the location specified for reservists. A person can retain a reserve obligation for several years, even without attending meetings or receiving annual training.

3. **Definitions and abbreviations.** DISCHARGED--the individual has no current military status; HEALTH--Records of physical examinations, dental treatment, and outpatient medical treatment received while in a duty status (does not include records of treatment while hospitalized); TDRL--Temporary Disability Retired List

4. **Service completed before World War I (before 1929 for Coast Guard officers).** The oldest military service records are at the National Archives (Code 6). Send the request there if service was completed before the following dates: ARMY--enlisted, 11/1/1912, officer, 7/1/1917; NAVY--enlisted, 1/1/1886, officer, 1/1/1903; MARINE CORPS--enlisted, 1/1/1905; COAST GUARD--enlisted, 1/1/1915, officer, 1/1/1929.

BRANCH	CURRENT STATUS OF SERVICE MEMBER	WHERE TO WRITE ADDRESS CODE
AIR FORCE	Discharged, deceased, or retired with pay (See paragraph 1, above, if requesting health record.)	14
	Active (including National Guard on active duty in the Air Force), TDRL, or general officers retired with pay	1
	Reserve, retired reserve in nonpay status, current National Guard officers not on active duty in the Air Force, or National Guard released from active duty in the Air Force	2
	Current National Guard enlisted not on active duty in the Air Force	13
COAST GUARD	Discharged, deceased, or retired (See paragraph 1, above, if requesting health record.)	14
	Active, reserve, or TDRL	3
MARINE CORPS	Discharged, deceased, or retired (See paragraph 1, above, if requesting health record.)	14
	Individual Ready Reserve or Fleet Marine Corps Reserve	5
	Active, Selected Marine Corps Reserve, or TDRL	4
ARMY	Discharged, deceased, or retired (See paragraph 1, above, if requesting health record.)	14
	Reserve; or active duty records of current National Guard members who performed service in the U.S. Army before 7/1/72	7
	Active enlisted (including National Guard on active duty in the U.S. Army) or TDRL enlisted	9
	Active officers (including National Guard on active duty in the U.S. Army) or TDRL officers	8
	Current National Guard enlisted not on active duty in Army (including records of Army active duty performed after 6/30/72)	13
	Current National Guard officers not on active duty in Army (including records of Army active duty performed after 6/30/72)	12
NAVY	Discharged, deceased, or retired (See paragraph 1, above, if requesting health record.)	14
	Active, reserve, or TDRL	10

ADDRESS LIST OF CUSTODIANS (BY CODE NUMBERS SHOWN ABOVE) - where to write / send this form

#	Address	#	Address	#	Address	#	Address
1	Air Force Personnel Center HQ AFPC/DPSRP 550 C Street West, Suite 19 Randolph AFB, TX 78150-4721	5	Marine Corps Reserve Support Command (Code MMI) 15303 Andrews Road Kansas City, MO 64147-1207	8	U.S. Total Army Personnel Command 200 Stovall Street Alexandria, VA 22332-0400	12	Army National Guard Readiness Center NGB-ARP 111 S. George Mason Dr. Arlington, VA 22204-1382
2	Air Reserve Personnel Center/DSMR 6760 E. Irvington Pl. #4600 Denver, CO 80280-4600	6	Archives I Textual Reference Branch (NNR1), Room 13W National Archives and Records Administration	9	Commander USAEREC Attn: PCRE-F 8899 E. 56th St. Indianapolis, IN 46249-5301	13	The Adjutant General (of the appropriate state, DC, or Puerto Rico)
3	Commander CGPC-Adm-3 U.S. Coast Guard 2100 2nd Street, SW. Washington, DC 20593-0001	7	Commander U.S. Army Reserve Personnel Center ATTN: ARPC-VS 9700 Page Avenue St. Louis, MO 63132-5200	10	Bureau of Naval Personnel Pers-313D 2 Navy Annex Washington, DC 20370-3130	14	National Personnel Records Center (Military Personnel Records) 9700 Page Avenue St. Louis, MO 63132-5100
4	Headquarters U.S. Marine Corps Personnel Management Support Branch (MMSB-10) 2008 Elliot Road Quantico, VA 22134-5030			11	Department of Veterans Affairs Records Management Center P.O. Box 5020 St. Louis, MO 63115-5020		

Specific answers from the veteran greatly assist the processing of requests by the National Personnel Records Center. In addition, while some information can be obtained without the veteran's signature, it is most effective to include his or her signature. The results of the request will appear on a form that is known as "32 CFR 286, 32 CFR 310."

Confirmation of one's military background can be important, especially if the applicant has claimed to be the recipient of special training or experience as a result of service in the military. Such skills, should they prove to have been earned, might make a particular candidate a clear finalist for the position.

It is important to be aware that no matter who conducts the search for military records, experience has proven that one cannot expect to receive an answer in a timely fashion. The searches may have to be ordered more than one time. It often takes months to receive any kind of an answer.

How to Obtain Motor Vehicle Reports

	All Applicants	Management	When Claimed or Required
Motor Vehicle Reports	•	•	•

What are MVRs?

Reports on drivers are commonly known as driving records or MVRs (Motor Vehicle Reports). MVRs indicate the driving activities of the driver, such as moving violations, motor vehicle accidents, driving with a revoked license and driving while impaired. Obtaining and reviewing this information can enhance the assessment of an applicant. For instance, if Mr. Brady's MVR shows that he has been caught several times for driving while impaired, chances are he will not make an excellent bus driver or machine operator.

Some employers believe that MVR checks should only be required for employees whose positions require the operation of a motor vehicle. However, an applicant's driver report provides insight into his or her background and character regardless of the position for which he or she is applying. Also, the report can be used to verify the driver's license number, address, date of birth, and identity.

How to Obtain a Driving Record

Driving record information must be is retrieved from individual state motor vehicle departments. There is no national database, but the states communicate regarding out-of-state violations. With the advent of the Commercial Driver's License System (CDL) drivers may not carry valid licenses in more than one state. Thus, all commercial license history information is maintained by the home state of the licensed driver.

You Must Have a Signed Release or Affidavit to Obtain an MVR

The Federal Driver's Privacy Protection Act (DPPA) restricts the access of driving records to fourteen stated permissible users, unless a signed release is provided The permissible users list does NOT include employers unless they hire drivers with commercial drivers' licenses. Depending on the state, employers are entitled to the full information on an MVR only if:

- they provide either an affidavit attesting to the fact that the information is being used for employment purposes; or
- they provide a signed release from the applicant.

Some states require that the applicant's signature be notarized. Thus, providing a signed copy of the General Release Form may not prove sufficient when making a MVR request. All reputable screening companies will know if a specific state form is required. Nearly all states make their form available on the Internet.

The Driver's License Number

There is not a national numbering system. Each state determines its own system of assigned driver license numbers. All states use the Social Security Number (SSN) as an internal-identifier and many use the SSN as the actual driver's license number. Some states, such as New Jersey, New York and Washington, have concocted a code from the name and date of birth to form a unique license number.

Fees and Turnaround Times

The state fee varies anywhere from $1.00 to $16.00 (Rhode Island charges the most). The average fee is around $5.00. Usually, there is no additional fee for a CDL driver record.

If the local DMV is right around the corner and you can visit and pull a record, great! Otherwise, you will need to mail your request or use the services of a professional vendor to access a driving record. Typically, if you send a request by mail to the DMV, expect a one to four week wait. The hidden costs of doing the record search yourself include employee's time, postage and waiting for the results.

For a few dollars more, it may be worth hiring a vendor to access the record and deliver it to you. Vendors can usually process such requests within one to 48 hours, depending on the state. Also, the vendors are familiar with needed forms and will stop a useless search if an incorrect driver's license number is provided.

Sample Driving Record Abstract

The printed driving record is also known as an abstract. It contains a wealth of information about the licensee.

Lesson 7 - Background Checks

In the sample driving record abstract below, note that this license was suspended effective November 9, 1997, but the driver, one Kermit Dee Frogg, was allowed restricted driving privileges as of May 19, 1998. (We wonder if Miss Piggy knows how bad a driver "Kermie" is?)

ABC Driving Records Company, Inc.	PO Box 160147, Sacramento, CA 95816	
California Driver Record — B5036	Order Date: 11/6/1998	Seq #: 1

Name:	Frogg, Kermit Dee	As of:	11/11/98	
Address:	1234 Sesame St.	Misc.:	Ordered by your company	
City,St,Zip:	Sacramento, CA 95831	License #:	Q2398456	

Sex: Male	Weight: 35lbs	DOB:	11/11/1968	Age: 22
Eyes: Black	Height: 1' 08"	Issue Date:	11/11/1995	
Hair: Black		Exp. Date:	11/11/1999	

Year License First Issued: 1995   STATUS: VALID

Violations/Convictions — Failures To Appear — Accidents

Type	Viol.	Conv. ACD	V/C	Description	Location	Docket	License	PT
ABS 2541341	10/01/1996 123456	01/08/1997 1	S94	22350	prima facie spd viol–too fast cond		Encino	
FTA 04/14/1997 FTA	—	F04 2733D D45	4050A	Seat belt not used as req FTA for trial/court appearance	Encino	2540554		
ABS 2465154	06/01/1997 123445	04/30/1997 3	A11	23140a	DUI BAC at or over __ (DTL req.)		San Diego	
ABS 4561514	05/20/1998 1234567	08/19/1998 0	F04	2731D	Seat Belt not used as req.		Encino	

Suspensions — Revocations

Actions	Ord/Date	Eff/Date	End/Date	Code	Description
Suspended	10/10/1997	11/9/1997		16070	fail to maintain req. liability ins.
Priv Rein	05/19/1998			16072	restricted driving privilege

** Verbal Notice Document on File

Miscellaneous State Data

Restriction: Rest 01 – Must wear corrective lenses when driving
Restriction: Rest 52 – Restricted to driving to/from/during course of employment per CVC 16072

AKA   Kermie D Frogg
Driver Class: C Any housecare and 2 axle vehicles <26,001 GVWR
End of Report for Frogg, Kermit Dee

(Thank you to American Driving Records, Inc. for preparing this sample driving record abstract. For more information about American Driving Records, call 800-766-6877 or visit www.mvrs.com.)

What to Look for on Driving Record Abstracts

Does the name on the abstract match that on the job application?

Every state motor vehicle agency requires that the name on one's driver's license match that of one's birth certificate. However, if one has married or divorced, the name may differ. Also, keep in mind that the name written on the application is not necessarily a fake one, it may be a preferred name or nickname.

Is the driver's license number provided valid, and does it match the subject?

If the results read "Driver Not Found" or the results have a different individual's name or address on it, confirm that the number used to search is indeed the number supplied by the applicant. If the number was recorded correctly, ask the subject to present his or her license and verify the number.

Keep in mind that each state has its own format for driver's license numbers. In some states, a person's Social Security Number is also used as his or her driver's license number. In other states, the license number is coded to verify the driver.

For example, in New Jersey, the driver's license format is one alpha character followed by fourteen numeric characters. The initial letter is equivalent to the first initial of the driver's last name. The first nine numbers are coded to the driver's last name, first name and middle initial. The following four numbers are coded using the driver's month and year of birth. The last number is coded to the driver's eye color.

Does the address on the abstract match the address(es) provided?

Drivers' licenses are generally issued for a four to five-year period. Some people choose not to report address changes to the DMV until it is time to renew their licenses. Nonetheless, the presence of addresses on the driver's abstract that are *not* present on the application should be questioned further.

Does the date of birth match?

The date of birth on the I-9 Form or Release Form should match the one listed on the driver's license abstract.

A mother and daughter or father and son may have the same name or address. However, comparing the two dates of birth should confirm the subject's identity. MVRs provide yet another means by which to obtain a verifiable birth date.

What is the status of the license? Valid, expired, suspended or revoked?

If a license has been expired for a long period of time, the possibility exists that the subject may be holding a license in another state. If so, an additional abstract request should be made from that state, if it is identified.

Also, if the applicant's license has been suspended or revoked, the reasons should be noted as they may impact the hiring decision. Past suspensions, though no longer in effect, will usually appear on an MVR if they are less than 39 months old.

Examine violations, accidents and points

The presence or absence of violations, accidents and points can be useful in assessing the character of the applicant.

For those employers who wish to know more about driving records, we recommend two books by BRB Publications—*The MVR Book* and *The MVR Decoder Digest*. These annual references will tell you everything you need to know about driving records, including access procedures, privacy restrictions, and other regulations.

How to Search for Civil Records

	All Applicants	Management	When Claimed or Required
Civil Record Searches		•	

Civil records encompass a wide range of records from numerous types of government agencies. Civil records can be found at local courthouses, recorder's offices, Secretary of State offices, US District Courts and US Bankruptcy Courts. Most county courts are actually part of a state court system, which means you may have the luxury of earching the whole state system at once. Conversely, there may be multiple courts in the same county with different jurisdictions, either geographic or by type of case, all making the searching more complex.

Searching civil records can provide valuable insight into an applicant's character and financial background. These searches can uncover important and previously unknown information about the candidate, including additional names, addresses, former employer(s) and medical treatment/injuries as well as the existence of judgments, liens, bankruptcies, and pending litigation.

Because the cost for these searches is relatively low, many companies are including them as part of their standard screening procedures. But, as a norm, civil record searches are not performed for all applicants, but rather for promotional consideration as well as filling supervisory, management and other high-level positions.

Civil Court Searches

Civil court searches produce abstracts that identify the applicant as a plaintiff in civil cases and can identify the existence of open and closed litigation where the applicant is a defendant. The information obtained includes the following case information: type of action, location, docket number, date filed and identity of the defendants.

> **KEY POINT:** Court searches must often be conducted separately for plaintiffs and defendants. To maximize results, be sure to search for both.

Court searches should be conducted for each locality wherein the applicant has resided or worked. In those areas where entire regions or states are accessible, employers should start there to conduct the most extensive search possible.

Typical fees range from free to $5.00 per document plus copy and certification fees. Records at the US District courts are normally $15.00 each. You can generally search records with a full name and SSN; however, some court indices may only permit searching within a certain number of years without incurring additional fees. Again, court records indicate not only completed cases, but also when there is a pending or open case.

> **KEY POINT:** Many court will not permit their personnel to do record searches. If this is the case, employers must perform these searches themselves, in person, or arrange to have the search done by a third party, such as a public record retriever.

Many courts offer free public access terminals that permit requesters to view an index or list of cases within a general timeframe. If the requester wishes to view the document or order a copy, the terminal gives the index or docket number. It may take one to three weeks to receive a response by mail, so to save time it is recommended to go directly to the court or find someone to go for you.

Lien & Judgment Searches

Liens, judgments and real estate transactions are normally found at county recorder's offices. This type of search indicates fines, payments, restitution and other levies the applicant owes. Depending on the state, federal tax liens, state tax liens and Uniform Commercial Code filings may be recorded at county recorder offices, Secretary of State offices, or both.

The fees and response times for recorder office searching are very similar to those at the courts. Secretary of State offices are a different story. Many of these agencies offer free searching over the phone or on the Internet.

> **KEY POINT:** Check www.publicrecordsources.com for an updated list of state and county sites offering free access via the Internet.

Bankruptcy proceedings are a jurisdiction of the federal government and records are found at one of the 190 US Bankruptcy Courts. Each court has assigned counties of jurisdiction, and there is at least one US Bankruptcy Court in each state. Fees are generally $15.00 per record.

On many occasions, the results of lien and judgment searches have surprised employers. Candidates for executive positions have been discovered to have bankruptcies and excessive tax liens. These searches have also uncovered lawsuits filed by former employers. In one case, the applicant mentioned the lawsuit but neglected to include that is was filed because he or she apparently failed to return company property upon termination. Another suit involved the failure to return a company-leased vehicle. In fact, the applicant drove the car to the interview!

What to Look For in Civil Records

Variations of Names or Aliases

All names and variations of them, regardless of when they were discovered, should be searched for separately. Whether searches are conducted through a database or in person, the exact name provided is the name that the court searches, without variation. In other words, the court will not search using variations of the name unless the employer specifically provides a list of each name to be searched. Sometimes these names will not be uncovered until the results of the first search are received, in which case subsequent searches should be conducted.

Keep in mind, cases may be located under a shortened version of the proper name, under a maiden name, or a married name.

Additional Parties or Paper Trails

Reviewing litigation may reveal a connection between the applicant and a particular business. Whether it is a business he or she owns or used to work for, both options provide additional avenues for research.

Another example: suppose the driver's license abstract for an applicant is devoid of any problems. However, a court search reveals that the applicant was involved in an auto accident and related litigation. Some accidents are not reported to the police, and do not appear on MVRs.

Personal Identifiers

Personal identifiers are pieces of information that serve to identify a person. Typical identifiers are a Social Security Number, a date of birth, a driver's license number and even addresses.

Employers should compare the identifiers contained in the results of any search with those provided by the applicant. Doing so may reveal new information, confirm existing information, and verify that both sets of the documents refer to the same individual.

Identifiers are crucial in verifying that someone is truly involved in a court case, especially if he or she has a common name.

Dates of the Case

If a search uncovers a case involving a previous employer, the date of the case should be compared to the period of employment as it appears on the application/resume. Do the dates match? If not, the applicant may not have reported his or her employment history accurately.

Sometimes applicants will admit that they were involved in litigation with a previous employer, but they will "alter" the dates during which this occurred to make their position seem more justifiable.

The Statute of Limitations in most states is two years, and it is not uncommon to file a civil suit just before the statute runs out. Thus, the matter that provoked the lawsuit may have occurred up to two years prior to the actual filing of the suit.

Type of Case

Medical Malpractice/Tort/Auto

These are all personal injury cases. All suits and judgments in these categories should be thoroughly investigated. For protection, businesses should know about any prior injuries or medical treatments the applicant may have had.

Bankruptcy

If a bankruptcy is indicated, obtain a copy of the petition and list of creditors. These documents may provide information regarding employment, income, insurance, medical treatment, assets and business affiliations as well as other professional and character data.

Tax Lien/State Lien/Foreclosure

These cases can involve federal and/or state income taxes, property taxes, unemployment and disability, motor vehicle fines, alimony and child support. These kinds of cases also give insight into the applicant's character and financial situation.

Record Location

As with other types of public records, search all venues where the applicant may have had activity, i.e. lived, worked and/or visited for long periods of time. Know the location of the applicant's residence, past employers, etc. Does the applicant make frequent visits to another area for recreational purposes? Do they commute long distances or frequently visit family?

> **KEY POINT:** Do *not* assume that because an applicant lives in a particular area all cases involving him or her are filed in the same area. If an incident occurred somewhere else, it is possible that litigation arising from the incident was filed in that location instead. When in doubt, check it out!

Lesson 7 - Background Checks

Lesson Summary:

This lesson, while lengthy, is well organized with detailed explanations of each phase of performing a proper background check. Rather than regurgitate the entire lesson in outline format, let's have the following story speak for itself.

> **Which Company Policy Do You Follow?**
>
> A large company was impressed with an applicant's resume and education credentials. They were so impressed that they hired this individual to replace two vacant department head positions. Because of this supposed coup, they hired the individual without performing a pre-employment background investigation. Six months later, accounting irregularities surfaced, funds were missing! The individual was suspected and was terminated. The individual then sued for wrongful discharge and won, since proof was never established beyond a reasonable doubt that this individual was directly responsible for the irregularities.
>
> The individual applied for a new job in another city. The next company looking to hire this person was also impressed, but company policy dictated a background check. The results astounded them. The Social Security verification report and the credit report indicated that the individual had used more than one name and was in trouble with all of his credit accounts. The individual's motor vehicle report indicated that the license was revoked for various moving violations, including several DUIs. The most upsetting records came as a result of civil liens and judgment search. The court records indicated the subject was a plaintiff in several cases, including suing two prior employers for wrongful discharge.
>
> Because this particular company's policy outlined the requirement to have a clear Social Security Number verification, credit record, and motor vehicle report, the company was precluded from hiring this individual. While the civil litigation issue alone was not grounds for not hiring, certainly the issues of the credit report and motor vehicle record were.
>
> In the end, the company did not hire this individual and no doubt saved an enormous amount of time, money and possible negative publicity.

The bottom line is that no matter how good the candidate appears or how good the deal is, it is never wise to deviate from a company policy of performing a pre-employment background investigation.

Recommended Resources:

Web Sites

http://www.ssa.gov

> This is the web site for the Social Security Administration. Their fraud hotline number is 800-269-0271.

www.studentclearinghouse.com

> The National Student Clearinghouse will perform educational verifications for a moderate fee. This can be accomplished over the Internet.

http://www.publicrecordsources.com

> Lists vendors who specialize in educational verification (under the Search Firms button). There are also over 200 pre-employment screening firms profiled under the Screening Forms button. Also, this site presents links of state and county sites offering free access via the Internet.

http://www.nara.gov/regional

> NARA offers US government records access services to the public from facilities throughout the United States. Download Form 180 for searching military records from the web site of the National Personnel Records Center in St. Louis, Missouri. Also, the agency offers a fax-on-demand service.

Publications and CDs

The *Public Record Research System* by BRB Publications

> Many HR departments and screening vendors use this CD as a source of information for 26,000 government and private agencies dealing with public records. The system is also available as a web subscription at www.publicrecordsources.com. The book version, printed annually, is *The Sourcebook to Public Record Information*.

The MVR Book and *The MVR Decoder Digest*, by BRB Publications

> These annual references will tell you everything you need to know about driving records, including access procedures, privacy restrictions and regulation

The Criminal Records Book, by Derek Hinton, Facts on Demand Press

> The ultimate reference on criminal records, written for employers. Covers laws, regulations, access procedures, and privacy restrictions.

8

Pre-Employment Screening Firms
How to Select a Vendor or Pre-Employment Screening Company for Background Checks

There are many reasons to hire a professional firm to perform all or part of your pre-employment screening tasks. These firms are experts in public record information. They understand the legal issues and limits, and should be able to help you develop and improve your company screening policies. It stands to reason that a company that performs the same tasks for many clients often provides a better product at a lower cost and in a very professional manner. Another advantage to outsourcing is that you only need to use them on a demand basis.

The decision to outsource begins with knowing which functions you may want to undertake yourself, and which functions you wish to assign to a vendor. Remember the Screening Options Table in Lesson 6? A modified version of this table can be used to determine who will perform the function: one overall pre-employment screening vendor; a "specialty" vendor; or in-house.

For example, the table on the following page describes how the American Ultra-Tech Corporation handles their screening functions:

Lesson 8 - Pre-Employment Screening Firms

American Ultra-Tech Corporation **Screening Assignment Table**	ABC Screening	National Student Clearinghouse	Done In-house
Social Security Number Verification	•		
Credit History Checks	•		
Employment History Verification			•
Criminal History Checks	•		
Verification of Educational Background		•	
Confirmation of Professional Licenses & Registrations	•		
Military Service Records Checks	•		
Motor Vehicle Reports			•
Civil Record Searches	•		

American Ultra-Tech is located near the state DMV so they find it cost effective to send their own personnel to obtain driving records (Motor Vehicle Reports). Also, they have an account with the National Student Clearinghouse to verify attendance and degrees (www.studentclearinghouse.com). The remaining screening functions are performed by ABC Screening Company.

The question of whether to hire a specialty vendor and what to do in-house is inherent on a company's availability of personnel, knowledge of screening procedures, and the cost effectiveness.

 KEY POINT: Typically, the two aspects used most often to determine which vendor or screening company to choose are cost and response time. However, too many times a very important aspect is overlooked: the quality of the information.

Components of a Quality Screening Vendor

A screening firm does not necessarily need to be located in your city or state, as most professional pre-employment screening firms are national in scope and have the ability to provide quality background checks for all sizes of companies.

There are many ways to find screening vendors (see the end of this lesson). However, selecting the right vendor from several prospective companies is the real challenge. The things to look for in a screening company or specialty vendor are covered in the rest of this lesson. The more positive components a company has, the higher to score them. The more that is known about a potential vendor, the better. The ability to know what questions to ask and how to select the right vendor is extremely important. The potential vendor should be happy to answer any of the questions in the following areas.

Experience

It stands to reason that a company who has been in business for ten years or more and whose basic functions center on pre-employment screening is better than somebody brand new. That new company may be well meaning, but if they are without practical experience and totally relying upon someone else's expertise, they may not be able to fully fulfill your company's requirements. This does not mean that bigger is necessarily better. Often a small company who has focused on pre-employment issues for a good number of years may be more adept at providing total support to a business entity.

Expertise

A vendor who can demonstrate their expertise on employment issues can provide a great deal of guidance. The combination of experience and expertise can go a long way to keeping your company in line with Federal and State requirements. Their skills may result from the sheer number of backgrounds they have done over a good number of years. Their principles may have authored books, laws and testified in front of various government agencies regarding the legal issues impacting the hiring process. Is the vendor willing to help train your staff? Is the vendor willing to help with the company's policies and forms designed to comply with FCRA (see Appendix) and state laws? If they are in a different time zone, be sure to find out their hours of operation.

Do not be afraid to ask of their expertise, because if they have any, they would be more than happy to tell you.

Technology of Order and Delivery Features

Considering today's technology, the selected vendor should be able to provide the user with various modes of delivery. This is important to employers who wish to use the Internet to access both order and retrieval of screening documents. When considering use of an Internet delivery system, today's standard is "24 hours a day, 7 days a week" instant ordering and search retrieval. The ability to access your own account and see when orders were placed, when they were picked up through the system, which items are complete, what items are pending together with the ability to view and print even portions of completed orders should be standard. The better vendors have user-friendly systems that are safe, providing encrypted transmissions.

What might be acceptable today could be outdated tomorrow and it is a good thing to know if the potential provider is going down the same road.

Screening Services Offered

The nine screening services on the table at the beginning of this lesson were covered in detail in Lesson 7. To ensure that you can obtain any reports or services you may need in the future, it's important to know all the services that are offered by a vendor. Some agencies only provide the basics, which include a combination of SSN, credit, motor vehicle, criminal and prior employer checks. A vendor's ability to provide drug or psychological testing, military records, or foreign country records may not be required everyday, but could be essential in certain cases.

References

Find out if the vendor is a member of any national or state professional organizations. Also, check with the local Better Business Bureau. Some vendors will publish a selected list of their clients for their prospects to see, while others would rather not advertise their customer list but will supply references by appointment or request. It is always a good thing to ask for references and to follow up with those provided. Knowing that a vendor is not going to offer a disgruntled client as a reference, calls to those listed should include questions that are outlined herein relative to turnaround time, expertise and experience. The answers may differ from those provided to you by a vendor's sales person. If this happens, you may want to look elsewhere.

Compliance With Government Regulations

A potential vendor should be fully cognizant and able to engage in conversation about every level of compliance, from the Federal level to individual state requirements. Any bona-fide vendor should be able to supply copies or excerpts of any and all relevant laws to their potential client. The truth is, if a vendor doesn't require your company to sign a certification and have contracts that specifically include the legally-required notices, then there's sure to be trouble ahead.

Keep in mind that a vendor cannot legally ask questions or make inquires that would be illegal for you to do. For example, you—not the vendor—will be held liable by the EEOC (see Lesson 24) if illegal discrimination questions are asked of your applicant by the vendor.

An important feature concerns the length of time the results you ordered are retained. This is important for two reasons: first, to comply with FCRA retention regulations; and second, in case you misplace the documents. The ability to retrieve those files from the initial provider for at least up to three years should be a standard.

The FCRA and Database Searches

The Federal Trade Commission regulates the Fair Credit Reporting Act (FCRA) and legal requirements of the vendors (CRAs) who supply records to employers.

Employers must be cautionary about accessing records from certain databases compiled by private companies. For example, there are vendors who compile and store criminal records. These records are purchased in bulk format by the vendor from government agencies, and resold to clients such as private investigators. These records may be 30 to 90 days old, depending on the mode of purchase and frequency of updates.

In an opinion letter dated May 5, 1999, the FTC states that when a CRA uses reports from a stored data records company and the information is 30 to 90 days old, the CRA is not in compliance with the FTC. This in turn means the employer is not in compliance, and is open to a threat of litigation from the applicant or the FTC.

Section 613(2) of the FCRA states that "...when a CRA compiles and reports adverse public record information on consumers for employment purposes...have 'strict procedures' in place to ensure accuracy of the information...to insure whenever public record information which is likely to have an adverse effect on a consumer's ability to obtain employment is reported it is complete and up to date."

Pricing

The vendor should clearly explain what services and searches are being performed, and from what government agencies are accessed. Be sure to compare "apples to apples." A price quote that includes both a county and statewide criminal record search (which is advisable) will cost more than a mere county search.

The cheapest service isn't always best. Most professional vendors are within the same pricing range. There are some newer or smaller ones who charge a great deal more and get it (essentially whatever the market will bear). So, if one obtains three quotes from similar types of companies and they are all within the same range, it now is more important to look at the other components discussed—their features. It gets real simple if two companies appear to be standard and within the same realm, but one company is drastically higher. That can make a decision much simpler.

💡 **KEY POINT:** *DANGER* – Recently, there have been some companies who have made a big splash and indicated the lowest prices in the country *and* the fastest turn-around times. While everybody wants the quickest turnaround possible, it must be understood that every government agency is not on computer. This means very often one is not allowed to search the records without first going through court personnel and incurring court fees. Some vendors who offer cheap criminal backgrounds are quoting a price less than the actual court fee would be. Also, the courts that limit access and charge fees often lengthen the turnaround times. Simply put, you cannot legally obtain a search on a criminal history for less than the court fees or the time it takes court personnel to perform the search. Either it is being done illegally or there is no search being conducted at all. Be careful and ask probing questions. If it sounds to good to be true, then it probably is.

Insurance

If all the other components appear to be in place and are satisfactory, then it is time to inquire about the insurance coverage maintained by the potential provider. A Business Office Policy (BOP) or a basic workers compensation coverage is not the main issue here. Every business that operates as a business must have workers compensation insurance and the BOP only covers their general office liability. The issue to be concerned with is an Errors and Omission policy or professional liability policy. Remember, once a vendor is selected, they are responsible for the end results.

> **Be Leery of National Database Search Claims**
>
> There is a big distinction between doing a "national search" and "being able to search nationally." While many vendors claim that they are able to perform a criminal record or driving record search from any state, there is no such thing as a national database for either of these types of records. If you want a "national search" on a criminal record history, you will have to check every state and, in certain instances, every county in a state. Such an extensive search costs hundreds of dollars.

When a vendor relies upon another vendor to perform screening tasks for reasonable fees for the purpose of protecting the integrity of your company, that final protection should come from proof of insurance for any errors, omission or liability that could be the fault of the provider and not the company paying the fee.

Once you have the answers . . .

Does the vendor's performance match its claims? There is nothing wrong with asking a vendor to give you a free or low cost search, or to perform a test. Give several vendors the same applicant name and compare the results.

If your company does not have dedicated personnel or time to devote to searching, by all means consider hiring a professional to perform all or portions of the search. Regardless, by understanding all the components of the screening process, one can more easily decide which vendor is best for you.

Where to Find a Vendor or Screening Company

Now that you know how to screen for the right vendor, the question is *where to find one*! As mentioned previously, local is not always the answer, but you can always check out the yellow pages under *employment screening* or *credit reports*.

Another way to find a dependable vendor is to ask other businesses or business owners. Very often a local chamber of commerce can provide a list of screening vendors. Sometimes the local credit bureau will perform these services or know of someone who does. But merely because a service is recommended by a local entity, do not discard the elements of this lesson.

When you search for a vendor using a search engine on the Internet, you will find a myriad of screening companies. Some of the more professional web sites can indicate their high level of technical expertise and ability to meet fast turnaround times. That's all well and good, but be sure to look for their statements on compliance with FCRA.

Refer to Recommended Resources below for other ideas on where to find acceptable vendors.

Lesson Summary:

- Typically, the two aspects used most often to determine which vendor or screening company to choose are cost and response time. However, too many times, perhaps the most important aspect is overlooked: the quality of the information.
- The components of a quality screening vendor include; Experience, Expertise, Technology of Order and Delivery Features, Screening Services Offered, References, Compliance, Pricing, and Insurance.

- Be leery of vendors who offer "National Database Searches" for criminal records or driving records. There are no such national databases. To do a "national" search, each individual state or county must be accessed.

Recommended Resources:

Internet

http://www.publicrecordsources.com

Click on the section called *screening firms* and you will be able to search among 200+ of the nation's leading screening companies. Also, this site is an excellent source to find specialty vendors (click on *sources and search firms*).

Books

The *National Directory of Public Record Vendors* (BRB Publications, 800-929-3811) has an entire section dedicated to screening companies and also provides an excellent source for finding specialty vendors.

9 Pre-Employment Testing
How to Establish Testing Methods & Policies

This lesson will explore the following test method groups:
- Psychological and Aptitude
- Skills
- Drug and Medical

Pre-employment testing is not for everyone. Companies that typically use one or more of the basic test groups are generally large companies, or involved in sensitive areas such as government contracts or public safety. But that's not to say that any small firm shouldn't consider skills or aptitude testing as part of its company hiring policy.

Compliance with ADA

A significant factor to consider when establishing a company's pre-employment testing policy is to make sure your tests are in compliance with the Americans With Disabilities Act (ADA). To avoid claims of discrimination, make sure the testing procedures measure job skills and abilities, not test-taking abilities. Not accommodating an applicant who is disabled, but whose disability will not affect job performance, is opening the door to a potential lawsuit. For example, if a position does not require reading, make sure an applicant who is sight impaired or dyslexic is given a chance to take the test orally or with assistance.

The discussions on each of the testing groups will mention other tips for complying with ADA, when appropriate.

Psychological and Aptitude Testing

Aptitude and personality tests are meant to provide you with significant insight about the nature of and abilities of the applicant, but are also useful in screening.

Psychological testing as a screening method has been in use for a long time. Commonly known as "the pencil and paper test," the initial purpose was to identify applicants who are prone to theft. Over time, the creators of these tests developed surveys designed to provide employers with more tools. Now, tests can be used to determine characteristics such as loyalty, attendance, work ethic, drug avoidance and congeniality. There are now tests to help identify candidates who learn quickly, while others rate an applicant's verbal skills and specific job expertise. Often times, tests reveal that applicants are better suited for positions they haven't even thought about or applied for. On the other hand, a candidate may think they want a job not knowing that they would actually hate it and, therefore, their improper placement would make their performance less than stellar, which would make both the employee and the employer unhappy.

Today, psychological testing can be accomplished with the aid of computers or by telephone, depending on the provider used. These tests have become so sophisticated that their results appear to reveal qualities and traits that employers cannot detect during interviews. And, depending on the test and method selected, the cost may be lower than $2.00 per applicant.

Do be aware that the manner in which a psychological or aptitude test is given may screen out people who have physical or mental disabilities, and is therefore a violation of the Americans with Disabilities Act (ADA). As such, your company's best bet is to establish a logical need for such tests, to recognize when an applicant may give a false impression because of impairment, and to use an experienced and qualified vendor with proven testing techniques.

Using the Internet for Personality Testing

The Internet offers a wealth of useful and often fun sites that can allow an employer or an applicant to check out their own personality. There are also sites that are more serious and obviously want a company to use their services. One goes so far as to offer the viewer a free personality test that requires the answering of about 300 questions online. When the test is complete, the complete results are emailed. The type of tests range from general aptitude testing to programmers testing to communication skills and pretty much anything one could think about.

Three Recommended Web Sites

One site, www.employeeselect.com, allows you to take a really innovative but lengthy test. At www.saterfiel.com, if you add legality.htm the legal issues from case law are presented. Another good site one that offers an array of different types of tests is www.test.com.

If you want to look for more go into your search engine and look for "personality testing." You will get better results if you use "testing" versus just "test."

A Study by Reid Psychological Systems

Researchers at Reid London House (formerly Reid Psychological Systems), a national leader in the development of pre-employment screening programs for almost 50 years, found that over 95% of college students surveyed were willing to make at least one false statement to get a job, and 41% say they have already done so.

In conducting this survey, Reid researchers found ten areas in which participating students most frequently misrepresented themselves when competing for a job. The ten false statements include:

- Exaggerating involvement in school activities
- Exaggerating interpersonal skills
- Exaggerating the title of past business positions
- Exaggerating personal knowledge or impressions of prospective employer's corporate culture and history
- Exaggerating demeanor
- Exaggerating problem-solving skills
- Exaggerating computer experience
- Claiming untruthfully that one was well-respected by past employers
- Minimizing moodiness
- Exaggerating future goals

The results of the study revealed that participants were more likely to make false statements about qualities that employers could not readily prove. Qualities such as personality, hobbies and competence were the areas most often misrepresented. In general, people conceal or minimize undesirable acts and qualities while exaggerating desirable behaviors and traits.

Skills Tests

Skills test can come in many sizes and shapes. Some companies utilize written examinations that test an individual's knowledge of a subject or his or her intelligence level. If you hire someone to work at a hardware store, you want this person to know what PVC is, or how to use copper fittings, etc. Skills tests may involve clerical tasks such as writing a letter or using a word processor. Also, some tests may involve demonstrations of one's ability to handle physical labor, i.e. lifting objects that will be lifted often on the job. Certainly, if you were looking for someone with special skills, such as experience with a computer program, you would be remiss not to submit the prospect to some testing.

Your company's policy on skills testing should match the type of job or skill to the test used. Otherwise you open the door to ADA violations and possible lawsuits.

Drug and Medical Testing

In the public sector, pre-employment and random drug testing have been legal for many years. A number of employees in safety-sensitive positions have caused accidents and been found to be impaired by alcohol or drugs. Many railroad accidents, airline crashes, and the Exxon Valdez Oil Spill were drug or alcohol-related. The demand to protect the population and environment has compelled government agencies to develop policies and procedures designed to prevent such catastrophes. The policy of drug testing has expanded to include pre-employment, random, and post-accident. In fact, the first question after an accident is, "Were they tested?" It has become standard practice across North America to test any involved party for drugs or alcohol after an "accident." Operators involved in auto, construction or job-related accidents very often have blood samples taken at hospitals or doctors' offices, and are routinely tested for drugs or alcohol. In some cases, if an accident occurs in a public place, law enforcement personnel may make the request. If they don't, or if the accident occurs within your workplace, you may have to ask for the test, following the legal guidelines. If medical treatment is required, it may be necessary to perform a drug test to avoid adverse reactions.

In any event, the results can impact the involved parties. If an employee is found to have an illegal substance, a traffic or criminal charge may follow. If the employee is the only one injured, then an employer's insurance rates are sure to increase. On the other hand, when third parties are injured, the employer's liability increases automatically and litigation is sure to follow.

The following brief segments are provided as an overview for employers' examination.

Importance of Drug Testing to Business Today

The United States Department of Labor estimates that 75% of drug users are employed. Employment of drug abusers has been shown to increase health care costs as well as create a loss in productivity. The National Institute of Drug Abuse reports that nearly one in four employed Americans, between the ages of eighteen and thirty-four, used drugs in the past year, and that 3.1 million employed Americans, between the same ages, used cocaine in the past year.

According to the Psychemedics Corporation, government studies reveal that one out of six workers has a drug problem, and show that drug abusers, on average:

- Cost an employer $7,000 to $10,000 annually (National Institute of Health Statistics)
- Cost companies 300% more in medical costs and benefits
- Are absent up to 16 times more often
- Are 1/3 less productive

In surveys of drug abusers themselves:
- 44% admitted selling drugs to co-workers
- 18% admitted stealing from employers

While the statistics vary, it is a given by all companies comparing their operations before and after implementing drug testing, that the following occur:
- Substance abusers have many more on-the-job accidents than non-abusers.
- They use up to six times more sick leave.
- Have three times as many injuries and their utilization of workers' compensation claims can be as high as five times that of the non-abuser.

The issue of drug testing should become part of risk management. Drug use has notoriously resulted in problems that include higher insurance premiums, accidents, litigation costs, and other factors adversely affecting the bottom line of many companies. According to the American Management Association, 87% of major US firms now test employees, job applicants, or both for drug use. While many of the known statistics come from larger companies, it stands to reason that all companies, no matter what their size, should compare the additional costs of hiring a drug abuser versus the cost of drug testing.

How to Establish a Drug Testing Policy

Throughout this book we emphasize that all stages of pre-, ongoing, and post-employment procedures should be established in writing. Drug testing is no exception. No business should institute a drug testing program without first establishing a comprehensive policy and set of procedures.

Many vendors who provide drug-testing services can assist employers by furnishing basic policies, which can then be adjusted to an individual company's needs. They can offer answers to your questions about which tests to perform during the employment process, before an applicant performs a covered function, and when an employee is being transferred.

The following topics should be considered when a company establishes its drug testing policy:
- When drug testing may be administered for pre-employment.

- Types of drug tests to be used.
- Which substances are prohibited.
- What if a prospect, or employee, tests positive or refuses to submit to testing.

While there are various methods for drug testing, and the statistics in support of drug testing are noteworthy, the overriding consideration for having a solid drug policy may well be the financial impact of not having one.

How to Establish a Drug and Alcohol Abuse Policy

Not every company needs to test prospective employees for drug use. In fact, many companies feel this is an intrusive procedure when there is not a safety risk factor. However, it is still very important to establish a policy that drugs and alcohol abuse are not permitted in your workplace. The following text is suggested as a guide or basis for material that should be included in the orientation process.

> *The American Widget Company strictly prohibits the use of drugs or alcohol in the workplace. The company will take disciplinary action against any employee found using prohibited drugs or alcohol during working hours. Also, if an employee arrives at work under the influence of such drugs or alcohol, this person will be immediately sent home for the day, without pay. Repeated instances will result in a written warning, suspension or termination.*

Of course, how you word the statement depends on the nature of your business.

When Drug Testing May Be Administered for Pre-Employment

Pre-employment test drugs are permitted based upon federal and state laws as long as the testing is non-discriminatory. Companies having fifteen or more employees are regulated by the ADA and must follow their rules.

One primary reason to administer a drug test is to comply with federal regulations. Typical compliance regulations are propagated by a company's business with the Department of Transportation, the Department of Defense, the Nuclear Regulatory Commission, and the Department of Energy. Also, there are specific laws that affect railroad and public transportation companies. Any company who receives a federal grant or contract in the amount of $25,000.00 or more has specific rules to follow. Under these regulations, contractors, individuals, or sub-contractors are required to test for drugs and alcohol. A company that falls within any part of these guidelines should verify the laws that are applicable to their business. In certain industries, insurance carriers require these tests for specific types of employees, such as drivers or those employees handling dangerous machinery. The general rule of thumb is to offer employment after obtaining a negative drug test result.

In any event, when testing is considered, it is beneficial to notify all applicants that successful candidates will be asked to take the test prior to an offer of employment.

Administer Tests Uniformly

Employers will get into big trouble if a policy of testing only "certain people," such as people with long hair or just men or people with tattoos, is established. Do not approach drug testing with a border patrol mentality and open yourself to discrimination suits.

Other times Drug Tests are Administered:

Post-Accident:
- Chemical tests may be performed after an accident.

Random:
- Testing of employees by random selection and in a manner that provides that all employees have an equal chance of being selected.

Pre-Promotion Test:
- Testing candidates prior to promotion can decrease the opportunity of advancing someone who is currently abusing drugs.

Annual Physical Test:
- When companies routinely test employees on an annual basis this is also the time drug testing may be administered (so long as it is included in the policy).

For Reasonable Suspicion and For Cause:
- Testing of any employee who, because of their behavior or performance, can be reasonably suspected of having a drug or alcohol in their system.

Treatment Follow-Up Test.
- Testing employees periodically who have returned to work after participating in an alcohol or drug rehab program.

Drug Tests Used in Pre-Employment Screening

Urine testing is the most common way to test for most drugs, and this method appears to be the least expensive. In most cases, urine testing will only detect drug usage within the past two or three days. However, some drugs, including marijuana, are stored in fatty tissues and may register as positive for up to a month.

Blood testing is probably the second most popular method and is close to urine testing for accuracy and cost.

Saliva specimens are easy to collect and don't pose the troubles of privacy and intrusion that urine testing does. This type test is relatively new, and the full potential is not yet completely understood. Quantitative analysis shows this is not yet as accurate as urine or blood.

Adhesive **sweat patches** that can collect drugs and metabolites present in sweat. They can be worn for long periods before being removed.

Hair testing is not invasive and currently provides the longest window for the detection of drug abuse, estimated at 90 days. Psychemedics Corporation (www.psychemedics.com) had the first patent for hair testing. They recently were approved for a hair analysis to detect heroin use.

A recent US District Court decision, Western District of Missouri, declared that conducting pre-employment tests for **Carpal Tunnel Syndrome** does not violate ADA rules. This was based on the tests administered for specific job functions, as opposed to an overall group of physical demands or specific physical positions.

The Substances Tested for Usage

Below is a list of substances that are commonly tested for usage.

Alcohol: Liquor, Booze
Cannabis: Marijuana, Pot, Grass, Hash
Amphetamines: Speed
Ecstasy: XTC, Doves
Cocaine: Coke, Charlie, Snow, Crack
Opiates: Heroin, H, Smack, Stuff
Benzodiazepines & Barbiturates: Benzos, Downers, Valium
Hallucinogens: LSD, Magic, Tabs

If a Candidate or Employee Tests Positive or Refuses to Submit to Testing

If a test comes back positive, indicating the presence of a substance, a candidate may be rejected (without the employer's fear of a discrimination suit) IF a drug testing policy is in place and the candidate or employee has been notified in writing of this policy. The same holds true if the candidate or employee is asked to take a test and refuses.

If the issues are more complex, several good places to seek advice are listed at the end of this lesson.

The Other Side—Beating the Drug Tests

As employers have spent time and money to make the workplace a safer environment, the other guys have been busy too. It's just like "cops and robbers;" every time the cops come up with a way to catch the crooks, the crooks eventually figure out a way to counteract those methods. Once again, like the fake ID problem, books can be found that are written specifically on the subject of drug testing and how to beat it. Not only do they define ways, from the simple to the elaborate, to try to beat a drug test, these books also specify the detection times for each drug and how long it stays in one's system. Details of how to substitute another's urine for your own, where to get the containers, and what to put in them are spelled out. They even provide specific brand names, 900 telephone numbers and opinions on which products work the best. As with Fake IDs, one only needs to go to the Internet, type in "drug testing," and everything necessary can be obtained in minutes. The Internet even offers a product called *Clean'n Clear*. It comes with a double-your-money-back guarantee and guarantees passing of drug tests. The advertiser boasts that this product is undetectable, confidential, and has free same-day shipping — all for just $19.95.

Before we close this lesson, we should mention one testing mode that lately has been out of favor…

A Few Words About Lie Detector Tests

Most employers are prohibited from administering lie detector tests as a condition of employment under the federal Employee Polygraph Protection Act. The exceptions to this act include occupations that involve pharmaceuticals, national security, private security or defense.

The most common type of lie detector test measures the subject's level of stress when pertinent questions are intermixed with non-pertinent questions. However, it has been demonstrated that these tests can be manipulated or beaten with muscle control.

Lesson Summary:

- There are three prominent testing method groups used in pre-employment screening today:
    1. Psychological and Aptitude
    2. Skills
    3. Drug and Medical
- Companies that typically employ drug and medical tests or psychological and aptitude tests are generally large companies or involved in sensitive areas such as government contracts, or public safety. But that's not to say that a small firm

shouldn't consider skills or aptitude testing as part of its company hiring policy.
- Your company's policy on skills testing should match the type of job or skill to the test used; otherwise you open the door to ADA violations and possible lawsuits.
- The following topics should be considered when a company establishes its drug testing policy:
  - When drug testing may be administered for pre-employment.
  - Types of drug tests to be used.
  - Which substances are prohibited.
  - If a prospect or employee tests positive or refuses to submit to testing.
- If a drug test comes back positive, a subject can be rejected (without the employer's fear of a discrimination suit) IF a drug testing policy is in place and the candidate or employee has been notified in writing of this policy.

Recommended Resources:

The following sites provide excellent information related to drug testing and abuse:

www.drugfreeworkplace.org

    The Institute for a Drug-Free Workplace is an independent, self-sustaining coalition of businesses, organizations and individuals dedicated to preserving the rights of employers and employees in drug-abuse prevention programs.

www.health.org/wpkit

    Making Your Workplace Drug Free: A Kit for Employers. This site is geared toward helping employees establish a drug free work environment. Both employee and employer fact sheets are included.

The following sites provide computer-assisted employment products and services:

www.pstc.com

www.aspentree.com

www.telserve.com

www.wonderlic.com

The following sites provide psychological or aptitude testing direct on the Internet:

www.employeeselect.com

www.saterfiel.com

www.test.com

10 Conducting the Interview

The discussion of this topic can be quite lengthy. In fact, there are many excellent books devoted entirely to the interviewing process. Our purpose is to expose you to many good interviewing options, also, to make you aware of some legal issues.

"Before the Interview" Checklist

Involve Two+ People Reading the Resumes

As the saying goes, "Two heads are better than one." If possible, have more than one person read the collection of resumes and applications. Different perspectives will emerge. One reviewer might notice discrepancies in a particular resume that slipped by the other person who read it. Also, if two people each have a stack of resumes, and each removes from his or her stack all those lacking adequate experience, the selection process will move much faster.

Prepare a Uniform Question Format

Prior to the interview, prepare a set of questions that will be asked to each candidate. The questions should be concerned with job duties, skills, and experience. Remove those questions that can't or shouldn't be asked. By doing so, you lessen the risk that a rejected candidate will come back with a discrimination action.

We've observed that a lot of the same questions are used for interviews throughout the job market. Consider developing questions that aren't usually heard — ones that ask for unique answers that give you a chance to get to know even the most seasoned applicant. Develop specific scenarios that might arise were he or she to fill the position and ask for a sample response. This is not meant to try to catch someone off guard. Rather, consider it an opportunity for the applicant to demonstrate his or her capabilities.

If you are creating a question series or developing a new interviewing format for the first time, there are several things you can do to ensure a better interview. Using other trusted employees of good standing, do some rehearsing. This will help not only to lay out a consistent, fair format, but also will help the interviewer become more comfortable and "practiced" in conducting a smooth interview.

Assign the Applicant a Task Prior to the Interview

When you call an applicant to schedule an interview, give him or her an assignment as well. The task might be to visit your company's web site, retail location or that of a competitor. Ask him or her to make observations and develop suggestions.

During the course of the interview, ask the applicant about his or her experiences while performing the task. Some candidates, recognizing that the assignment is an opportunity to prove themselves, will go so far as to provide multi-page reports. Regardless, the assignment will illustrate how well an applicant can handle direction and execute a task. At a minimum, the assignment will make each interview worthwhile given that, at the very least, some feedback about the company will be received.

Interview Procedures

Working in Groups

Interviewing in teams can be beneficial, and here is why: When two people interview a candidate, the memory of the event is shared. In other words, the ability to recall the events of the interview no longer depends upon a single person from your company. Likewise, if the interview becomes significant to a legal proceeding later, the number of witnesses will be larger.

Assign roles: One interviewer might focus on phrasing questions properly, ensuring that all questions are asked and making sure that pertinent topics are covered whereas the other interviewer might be more of an observer, who studies the responses as well as attempts to record them clearly.

Make the Applicant Feel at Ease

While a face-to-face interview is a very good tool in the selection process, it has its limitations. There is an assumption by some that a candidate's little quirks exhibited during an interview will be magnified during employment. It is important to keep in mind, that though this may be true, these characteristics might remain little quirks. Nervous applicants might pull their ears, rub their foreheads, wring their hands or fidget in their seats. Other quirks include speaking rapidly or cracking of the voice.

Likewise, an interview that is flawless does not necessarily mean that the person's employment will be problem free as well.

A good approach to break the ice is to start with some personal dialogue designed to create an atmosphere of friendliness and trust. Comments on the weather or newsworthy event or what was on TV last night could be used as an opening. Then proceed by telling the candidate the importance of the position and how it relates to the company's operation. From there, mention such things of interest to the applicant such as job security, promotion opportunities, as well as the basics such as duties, hours, etc. For example: If a job requires weekend work, the hours need to be discussed as this may not be of interest to the applicant. By using this approach, you may avoid a "confrontational" or "adversarial" atmosphere and help the applicant feel more at ease during the interview process.

Give the Applicant Time to Ask Questions

Encourage all applicants to ask questions during the interview. An applicant that asks questions, as well as answers them, is typically well prepared.

Taking Notes

Inform the applicant you will be taking notes to jog your memory. Restrict the notes to comments that relate to the job. Do not record comments on the appearance or other superficial characteristics of the candidate. Such notes can be seen as discriminatory if used as evidence in a trial.

A Guide to Proper Questioning

What You Should Ask

The following questions are ones that are "safe." In other words, they will not be cause for discrimination claims and just about everyone should be able to answer them given the opportunity. In fact, starting with these types of questions can help the applicant relax. He or she will not feel as though you are simply getting down to business.

Where did you hear about the opening?

> Ask this question of *every* applicant, and keep track of the responses regardless of whether the applicant becomes a finalist. Why? It is important to track the source of your applicants. Don't assume that the ad in the local paper is the source. It might be word-of-mouth, the Internet or something else entirely. The tracking of this information need not be elaborate. It can be as simple as a tally sheet. Also, if you are not the person responsible for advertising your job openings, be sure to share your findings with that person.

What do you know about our company?

This question gives you the opportunity to find out how your company is perceived, as well as how prepared the applicant is. He or she may have taken the time to research the company, and this will give him or her the opportunity to showcase the ability to be prepared.

What motivates you?

Asking this question allows the interviewer to find out ways in which to motivate the person if he or she is hired. Perhaps the employee likes to hear words of encouragement. If this is the case, if hired, let the supervisor know what will motivate that new employee.

What are your interests?

This question should be easy to answer and may make the applicant more comfortable given that the applicant will be speaking about things about which he or she is passionate. In addition, if hired, the employer will know what kinds of rewards (other than raises) to implement. In other words, if the applicant responds to this question by saying, "I'm a big fan of the Phoenix Suns." Then the employer might reward good performance by purchasing tickets for him or her.

What interests you most and least about the position?

The answer to these questions can expedite the process of elimination. For instance, if the applicant says, "I don't like having to deal with customers," then the interviewer would realize that he or she is not the right person to answer the 800 line. Also, if there are multiple positions available, the answers to these questions can determine how to proceed, i.e. the position that best suits the applicant might become clear.

Can you give an example of a work experience of which you are proud?

Anyone can say, "I am a hard worker." Asking for examples of previous employment can enhance the assessment of the applicant. Perhaps the example provided is very similar to something that he or she would be doing for your company. And the example might indicate whether he or she would handle things to your satisfaction.

Have you signed a Non-Compete Agreement?

Now is the time to make sure an applicant will not be in violation a non-compete agreement he or she signed at other companies.

Also, if the applicant previously worked for a competitor, do not hire this person until the employment period for the other company has ended. Furthermore, once hired, do not allow the new employee who has worked for a competitor to solicit past clients from his or her previous job if this solicitation is forbidden by an agreement with the previous employer.

Avoid Improper Interview Questions

Many of the same concepts discussed in Lesson 5 are also applicable here. How many of the following questions do you consider proper interview questions?

- Do you own your own home?
- Have you ever had your wages garnished?
- Have you ever filed bankruptcy?
- Where were you born?
- What country are you from?
- What is your religion?

If you answered "none," you are, of course, correct.

There are so many restrictions as to what employers can ask applicants that the employer often feels handcuffed. There are some topics that should never be the source of questions in an interview. While some topics are open for discussion, some questions *definitely* cannot be asked without serious liability issues being raised

As mentioned in Lesson 5, it is considered discriminatory to ask for vital information such as an individual's date of birth, and this would not be the time to ask for the Social Security Number or driver's license number. However, in order to conduct an appropriate screening of an applicant, specific personal identifiers and prior names are required. Some of these questions are contained in the application and other portions are contained in the I-9 Form. The simplest way to avoid the appearance of discrimination while obtaining the necessary information is to include a line in the pre-employment inquiry release, which identifies the need for that information. The bottom line is that an employer can obtain the appropriate information using a proper form while not asking for this information in an interview, which could be considered discriminatory.

What follows are examples of topics that are commonly troublesome questioning areas. Examples of both acceptable- and unacceptable-phrased questions are.

AGE	
Possible Discrimination	How old are you? What is your date of birth?
Acceptable	Do you meet the state minimum age requirement for employment?

AVAILABILITY	
Possible Discrimination	Can you work Saturdays and Sundays?
Acceptable	Our hours of work are _____. At times, our work requires overtime — can you work such a schedule? Do you have any obligations that would prevent work-related travel?

CITIZENSHIP	
Possible Discrimination	Where were you born?
Acceptable	Are you legally authorized to work in the US?

CRIMINAL HISTORY	
Possible Discrimination	Have you ever been arrested?
Acceptable	Have you ever been convicted of a crime in the past seven years?

DISABILITIES	
Possible Discrimination	Do you have any disabilities? Do you have any health problems? Have you ever filed for workers' compensation?
Acceptable	Can you perform the essential functions of the job you are applying for with or without reasonable accommodations? **Note:** Once a conditional offer for a job has been made, it is legal to inquire past workers' compensation history.

	MEMBERSHIPS
Possible Discrimination	To what organizations do you belong?
Acceptable	Do you want to provide any additional information that relates to your ability to perform this job?

	MILITARY HISTORY
Possible Discrimination	Have you ever served in the armed forces of another country? What type of discharge did you receive?
Acceptable	Are you a US veteran?

	NAME
Possible Discrimination	Have you ever had your name changed?
Acceptable	Is there any additional information we need, about your name, to verify your employment and educational background?

	RELATIONSHIPS
Possible Discrimination	Who is the next of kin we should notify in the event of an emergency?
Acceptable	Is there someone we should notify in case of an emergency?

After the Interview

If you are the interviewer, give yourself at least five minutes between interviews during which you may compose yourself and mentally review the previous interview.

Ask yourself the following questions:

Did the applicant arrive on time?

If not, consider giving a second interview to see if he or she will arrive on time, especially if punctuality is very important to the position.

Did the person seem enthusiastic about the position?

Those who do the best work are those who love their jobs. Even though applicants aren't really qualified at this stage in the process to "love" their job, he or she may be passionate about the industry or eager to learn. Overall, an upbeat person might perform really well if the position is customer service oriented.

Did the applicant understand your questions?

If the position is technical in nature, the applicant should not ask for a definition of all the terms used during the interview. The applicant should already be familiar with the majority of them if he or she is truly qualified.

Also, did you have to explain most of your questions? If so the person may not be capable of handling the responsibilities of the position or your questions may need to be re-examined. As a test, try a few of them differently during the next interview, or ask fellow employees or laypersons to interpret the questions to determine if your meaning is clear.

Did the person respond promptly to most questions?

A great deal of hesitancy may indicate someone who is unprepared or who has overstated his or her qualifications. Likewise, someone who answers too quickly to every question may not be taking the time to listen, or is not thinking things through.

Applicant/Resume Evaluation Form

As mentioned in a previous lesson, the Applicant/Resume Evaluation Form is a handy tool for documenting your review of applicants.

This form complies with non-discrimination guidelines and ensures that the basis for hire or rejection are documented and job-related. An employer should not rely on memory to recall the specifics, which may be questioned later. Many of the suits filed against an employer are not filed by current employees, but by applicants who were rejected. These cases present a circumstance where there is very limited knowledge available about the plaintiff. It is not always easy to understand the motivations or background of an applicant given that the company's relationship with him or her is typically short-lived.

Note that this is an internal form used by the employer and does not require a signature from the applicant. A full-size version of the Applicant/Resume Evaluation Form is available in the Appendix.

> **APPLICANT/RESUME EVALUATION**
>
> *Completion of this form assists compliance with non-discrimination guidelines and ensures the basis for hire and reject decisions are documented and job related.*
>
> Name of Applicant: _____
>
> Date Application/Resume Received: _____
>
> Position Available: _____
>
> Will Applicant be Interviewed: ____ Yes Date of Interview: _____
>
> ____ No Reason for Rejection: _____
>   Code Number(s)
>
> Will Job be extended: ____ Yes Title: _____ Salary: _____
>
> ____ No
>
> Job-Related Reason Applicant is Best Qualified: _____
> _____
>
> If No, Reason for Rejection: _____
>   Code Number(s)
>
> _____
> Signature Interviewer/Evaluator   Position/Department   Date
>
> *You have the right to hire qualified individuals and to reject unqualified individuals. Selection and rejection decisions must be based on valid job-related criteria that are consistently applied to all applicants. The following are acceptable reasons for rejection provided the same statement could not be applied to the selected candidate. If numbers 1-8 do not apply, please complete 9 with a job-related reason.*
>
> 1. *Does not meet minimum job requirements*
> 2. *Meets minimum requirements but not best qualified*
> 3. *Cannot work required hours/schedule*
> 4. *Cannot perform physical requirements of job*
> 5. *Prior experience unrelated*
> 6. *Less related experience than person selected*
> 7. *Less related education/training than person selected*
> 8. *Lower skill level than person selected*
> 9. *Other (specify)* _____

These codes allow for very specific descriptions as to why an applicant was rejected. Combined with a copy of the submitted application and/or resume, this information can be crucial to winning a court case.

Computer-Assisted Interviewing

The use of computers is infiltrating almost every facet of life. Therefore, it is no surprise that computers have also become involved in the interviewing process.

Everything from interactive applications on screen to Interactive Voice Response (IVR) telephone interviews is now being used by major corporations. Of course, the expense of these technologies can make them cost-prohibitive. Nonetheless, these technologies have saved companies time and have helped to significantly reduce their turnover rates.

An article entitled "Computer-Assisted Interviewing Shortens Hiring Cycle" was published in a recent copy of *HR Magazine*. According to the article, Nike is one company using these technologies. In fact, the article also reports that when a new Nike store opened, "6,000 people responded to ads for workers needed to fill 250 positions. Nike used IVR technology to make the first cut. Applicants responded to eight questions over the telephone; 3,500 applicants were screened out because they weren't available when needed or didn't have retail experience. The rest had a computer-assisted interview at the store followed by a personal interview."

There are some who argue that using computers makes the interview process too impersonal and may result in the rejection of candidates who are truly worthy. But, computers cannot be accused of discrimination, unless they ask questions that have a disparate impact on a protected group.

Lesson Summary:

- Be sure to make the most of the interview process. This is an opportune time to learn about the applicant.
- Remember, in order for both sides to have the best experience, make the candidate feel comfortable.
- Formulate a standard of minimum questions to ask all candidates that will provide insightful answers.
- Keep a short list of the no-no's. Make sure you do not jeopardize your business by asking questions that can be viewed as discriminatory.
- Use an evaluation form; it not only helps keep you organized, but it is your documentation to show why an applicant is not chosen.

Recommended Resources:

http://www.pcmusa.com/CBI/index.htm

Competency-Based Interviewing®, part of SmartHire, is designed to enhance a company's interviewing skills and selection process. Check out the articles.

http://onlinestore.cch.com/default.asp?ProductID=1092

This site is from CCH and deals with shared learning, interviewing, and hiring practices. The online multi-media training program allows access to the course 24 hours a day, seven days a week.

http://www.HRTools.com

This site allows you to compare your organization's interviewing practice to other organizations. It offers a user poll and user input on the interviewing process.

11 Making the Job Offer
– The Proper Sequence

The applicants have been processed, screened and interviewed. It's time to make an offer of employment to the best qualified candidate.

💡 **KEY POINT:** If a group is used to accept (or reject) candidates, be sure that the body is composed of diverse individuals. If the group consists of people from only one gender or ethnic background, a rejected applicant may allege discrimination.

The act of procedure should be broken down into three distinct areas:
1. The Acknowledgement
2. Complete All Requisite Forms
3. Verify, Verify, Verify

1. The Acknowledgement

Make the moment a positive and memorable one by doing the following:

- Congratulate the applicant chosen.
- Acknowledge that the hiring process is a complicated one and that he or she "passed the test."
- Let them know that the company is proud to extend an offer of employment, and wants him or her to be a part of the team.

Above all, make a serious attempt to establish a friendly relationship from day one. Let the new hire feel excited, happy and ready to start work.

Welcome Package

Some companies prepare a welcome package for the new hire. This package includes the job description, a brief history of the company, appropriate policies, mission/vision statement, and an orientation schedule. Of course, these materials can also be given to the new hire during the orientation process.

Ask Again About Non-Compete Agreements

If this point was not covered in an interview, now is the time to make sure that the new hire will not be violation a non-compete agreements he or she signed at other companies. If the new hire previously worked for a competitor, do not hire this person until the paid employment period for the other company has ended.

2. Complete All Requisite Forms

Upon hiring, a new employee should be required to complete the following forms:

- W-4 Payroll Form
- State New Hire Form
- Employee Data Sheet
- New Employee Record Chart
- Induction Form

Also, depending on the new hire position, your company may find that use of Confidentiality or Non-Compete Agreement is essential.

The W-4 Payroll Form

Be sure to verify that the same Social Security Number is used on the W-4 as recorded on the I-9 Form and that the employee entered the number of dependents he/she wishes to claim.

State New Hire Form

A new-hire reporting requirement was hidden in the Personal Responsibility and Work Opportunity Action of 1996. This statute requires all employers to report specific information on all new hires to a state agency without exception. Each state then provides the information to the US Department of Health and Human Services (DHHS) for inclusion in a national database. The main purpose of these provisions is to aid in the collection of child support monies that are owed by deadbeat parents. The information can also be used to identify workers' compensation and employment insurance fraud.

Since each state is mandated to establish its own reporting system, as an employer you should contact your state government if you have not received a notice. The DHHS

Lesson 11 - Making the Job Offer

web site at www.acf.dhhs.gov/programs/cse provides state agency contact phone numbers, frequently asked questions and policy requirements.

Essentially, the same information about your company and the new-hire normally found on a W-4 Form is the same information that is required by this statute. The minimum time frame for reports is within 20 days of hire, but states can impose a shorter duration. As with other employer requirements, it is clear that employers are subject to fines for failure to comply.

KEY POINT: No one escapes this requirement. Do not let new-hire reports slip through the cracks.

The forms to use for new hire reporting vary by state. Also, there are provisions for multi-state employers. To determine the requirements for a particular state, contact that state's responsible agency directly (see below for a list of phone numbers) or through the Internet. Typically, the agency responsible is that state's department of wages or taxation, but other agencies may be involved.

If your company uses a payroll service, this service may be able to provide the necessary forms.

New Hire Reporting Offices

Alabama	334-353-8491	Kansas	888-219-7801
Alaska	907-269-6685	Kentucky	800-817-2262
Arizona	888-282-2064	Louisiana	888-223-1461
Arkansas	800-259-2095	Maine	207-287-2886
California	916-657-0529	Maryland	888-634-4737
Colorado	800-696-1468	Massachusetts	800-332-2733
Connecticut	860-424-5044	Michigan	800-524-9846
Delaware	302-577-4815	Minnesota	800-672-4473
D of Columbia	888-689-6088	Mississippi	800-241-1330
Florida	888-854-4791	Missouri	800-585-9234
Georgia	888-541-0469	Montana	888-866-0327
Guam	671-475-3360	Nebraska	888-256-0293
Hawaii	888-317-9081	Nevada	888-639-7241
Idaho	800-627-3880	New Hampshire	800-803-4485
Illinois	800-327-4473	New Jersey	888-624-6339
Indiana	800-437-9136	New Mexico	888-878-1607
Iowa	515-281-5331	New York	800-972-1233

North Carolina	888-514-4568	Tennessee	888-715-2280
North Dakota	701-328-3582	Texas	888-839-4473
Ohio	888-872-1490	Utah	801-526-4361
Oklahoma	800-317-3785	Vermont	800-786-3214
Oregon	503-378-2868	Virgin Islands	340-776-3700
Pennsylvania	888-724-4737	Virginia	800-979-9014
Puerto Rico	787-767-1500	Washington	800-562-0479
Rhode Island	888-870-6461	West Virginia	800-835-4683
South Carolina	888-454-5294	Wisconsin	888-300-4473
South Dakota	888-827-6078	Wyoming	800-970-9258

Employee Data Sheet

The Employee Data Sheet (see next page) should be completed as soon as possible after an applicant has accepted a position. The Sheet provides information which may not be asked at the time of application, but which is necessary for internal record keeping and administration. Personal information, such as date of birth and Social Security Number, is required for any death benefits and health insurance purposes. Additionally, the same information may be required on a spouse and children in order to declare them as beneficiaries.

Keep This Information Updated

The data on the Employee Data Sheet should be updated yearly. Keeping abreast of employee status in areas such as marriage, dependents, addresses and telephone numbers is important. Changes in marital status may affect a benefit program or provide insight into an employee's change in performance. If an employee's new address signifies that he or she has moved further away, an increase in travel time might explain a recent increase in tardiness. Overall, being aware of personal developments can help an employer understand and deal with changes in an employee's demeanor.

Lesson 11 - Making the Job Offer

Employee Data Sheet

A full size version of the Employee Data Sheet Form is available in the Appendix.

EMPLOYEE DATA SHEET

THE FOLLOWING INFORMATION IS NECESSARY TO MAINTAIN COMPANY RECORDS ON ALL OUR EMPLOYEES

EMPLOYEE #:_____ DEPARTMENT:_____ DATE OF HIRE: _____

NAME: _____

ADDRESS: _____

HOME TELEPHONE NUMBER: _____

SOCIAL SECURITY #: _____ DATE OF BIRTH: _____

RACE (PLEASE CIRCLE):

WHITE   BLACK   HISPANIC   ASIAN   AMERICAN INDIAN   OTHER _____

ARE YOU A CITIZEN OF THE UNITED STATES?   _____ YES   _____ NO

ALIEN REGISTRATION #: _____

MARITAL STATUS: ____ SINGLE   ____ MARRIED   ____ DIVORCED
                    ____ LEGALLY SEPARATED   ____ WIDOWED

DATE OF MARRIAGE: _____ SPOUSE'S NAME: _____

SPOUSE'S SS#: _____ SPOUSE'S DATE OF BIRTH: _____

CHILDREN:

NAME	DATE OF BIRTH	AGE	SEX
NAME	DATE OF BIRTH	AGE	SEX
NAME	DATE OF BIRTH	AGE	SEX
NAME	DATE OF BIRTH	AGE	SEX

WHO WOULD YOU LIKE US TO NOTIFY IN CASE OF EMERGENCY?

NAME: _____ RELATIONSHIP: _____

ADDRESS: _____

TELEPHONE NUMBER: _____

This information is necessary for benefits and deductions. It is best to update this information annually.

New Employee Record Chart

It is extremely important that a detailed report be kept of all employee data. The New Employee Records Chart lists the forms that must be filled out when hired and beyond. The form provides recruiters and personnel departments alike with the ability to ensure that the company's post-hiring paperwork requirements are met. A full size version of the New Employee Record Chart Form is available in the Appendix.

Note that this form does NOT require the signature of the new hire.

New Employee Record Chart

Employee _____ Position _____

Department _____ Date Employed _____

The above new employee must have checked item(s) in file.

Document	Required	Completed
Employment Application	_____	_____
Employee Data Sheet	_____	_____
W-4	_____	_____
I-9	_____	_____
Induction Form	_____	_____
Applicant Waiver Release	_____	_____
Substance Abuse Test Consent	_____	_____
Non-Compete Agreement	_____	_____
Confidentiality Agreement	_____	_____

You may want the employee to initial receipt and completion of all these documents.

Supervisor _____ Date _____

Induction Form

At the time of hire, it is a good practice to notify all employees the terms and conditions of their employment. Even though the company may include this

Lesson 11 - Making the Job Offer

information in an employee booklet or handbook, use of the Induction Form provides a concise and memorable synopsis of key rules and benefits.

There are several advantages to using the Induction Form. For instance, it eliminates confusion. When a supervisor "goes over" work hours, time keeping, holidays, vacations and other policies, the new employee often feels overwhelmed. Sometimes he or she is required to absorb so much information at once that not all of it is remembered correctly later. Misunderstandings develop, and then the employer must deal with a disgruntled employee. The Induction Form covers areas of great concern to employees and provides them with a clear, concise way to refer back to this information.

A copy of the completed Induction Form should be given to the employee and one should be retained in the employer's personnel file. Keeping a copy on file should provide the proof necessary to resolve any misunderstandings should they arise. A full size version of the Induction Form is available in the Appendix.

See Lesson 13 for more about bringing the new employee on board.

INDUCTION FORM

NAME: _____ SS#: _____

CLOCK #: _____ STARTING DATE: _____

JOB TITLE: _____

DEPT: _____ SUPERVISOR: _____

COMPANY BENEFITS AND RULES

1. HOURS: _____ AM/PM until _____ AM/PM a _____ lunch, and two _____ minute rest breaks, one at _____ and one at _____. The regular work week is _____ to _____.

2. TIME RECORDS: Punch only your own time card and in case of a mistake, take your card IMMEDIATELY to the office. After seven minutes, employees are docked 15 minutes for being late and repeated lateness is cause for discipline. If you are unable to come to work, call (___) ___-____ before the start of your shift.

3. HOLIDAYS: New Years Day, Good Friday, Memorial Day, 4th of July, Labor Day, Thanksgiving, Friday after Thanksgiving, and Christmas Day.

4. VACATIONS: You will earn _____ of vacation for each _____ of employment prior to _____ up to a maximum of _____ days. _____ weeks after _____ years of service and _____ weeks after _____ years.

5. INSURANCE: The company provides _____ insurance for all employees after _____ of service. If you wish coverage for your eligible dependents, this can be arranged through payroll deduction. After _____ months, the company provide $_____ of life insurance and a weekly sick and accident insurance program that pays a maximum of $_____ for 26 weeks after the first day of an accident and after the eighth day of illness.

If you have any questions at any time regarding your pay, benefits or job assignment, please discuss it with your supervisor.

I have read and understand the information above.

_____   _____
DATE   EMPLOYEE'S SIGNATURE

Witness:

_____   _____
Date   Signature

Using Confidentiality & Non-Compete Agreements

In every industry, employees have access to information that should be considered confidential. With regard to confidentiality, new employees are often overlooked. Entry-level recruits initially have minimal responsibilities, perhaps only handling mundane tasks, such as answering phones, typing and/or posting bills. They seem to present no threat to a business. Yet, while performing their duties, they may learn about customer lists, product costs, profit formulas, supply sources, trade secrets, business methods or confidential personnel information. The potential for disaster on a company-wide level grows unless adequate precautions are taken to ensure that confidentiality is maintained.

Yet, before a company can begin to monitor confidentiality, it must address exactly what is and needs to be confidential. When examining a particular subject, employers should ask:

- What if this information became public?
- What if this information was given to competitors?
- What effect would public/competitor knowledge have on the company?

The answers to these questions should provide a clear idea as to whether some form of confidentiality protection should be implemented. Typically, this is accomplished through the use of an agreement. Two such agreements have been provided within these pages.

The Confidentiality Agreement

A Confidentiality Agreement indicates that an employee has been notified has agreed to keep private the information that has been outlined in the pages that accompany the agreement.

The Non-Compete Agreement

A Non-Compete Agreement is used to prevent an employee from working for a company that is in the same business. The agreement can be written for a prescribed period of time. Typical time frames range from one to five years. Non-compete agreements often include restrictions regarding a specific area, region or number of miles from the employer.

Proper Use and Enforcement

Enforcing these agreements can be expensive and problematic depending upon the nature of the business and the terms of the agreement. Regardless, the use of such agreements represents a documented attempt to notify employees of company policy and to protect the integrity of the organization.

The typical practice is to assign a business attorney to tailor these agreements to meet your company's needs. Regulations governing the use and enforceability of such agreements vary, and are beyond the scope of this book. Nonetheless, signed copies of these agreements should be maintained for each employee. Likewise, the agreements should be updated yearly by having the employee initial and date the original.

Without the presence and proper use of these agreements, employees can justifiably claim that they did nothing wrong when they merely "passed on" information to someone else. They can also deny any verbal agreements of confidentiality. In other words, employers should not assume that every employee automatically agrees on what is confidential and what is not. Rather, the employer should make it exceedingly clear what is public and what is private. At the very least, these agreements are simple proof that such efforts have been taken.

Confidentiality Agreement

A full size version of the Confidentiality Agreement Form is available in the Appendix.

```
                    CONFIDENTIALITY AGREEMENT

    In consideration of being employed by _____ (Company), the
    undersigned hereby agrees and acknowledges:

    1.   That during the course of my employ there may be disclosed to me certain trade
         secrets of the Company; said trade secrets consisting of:

         a)   Technical information: Methods, processes, formulae, compositions, inventions,
              machines, computer programs, and research projects.

         b)   Business information: Customer lists, pricing data, sources of supply, and
              marketing, production, or merchandising systems or plans.

    2.   I shall not during, or at any time after the termination of my employment with the
         Company, use for myself or others, or disclose or divulge to others any trade secrets,
         confidential information, or any other data of the Company in violation of this agreement.

    3.   That upon the termination of my employ from the Company:

         a)   I shall return to the Company all documents relating to the Company, including but
              not necessarily limited to: drawings, blueprints, reports, manuals, correspondence,
              consumer lists, computer programs, and all other materials and all copies thereof
              relating in any way to the Company's business, or in any way obtained by me during
              the course of my employ. I further agree that I shall not retain any copies of the
              forgoing.

         b)   The Company may notify any future or prospective employer of the existence of
              this agreement.

         c)   This agreement shall be binding upon me and my personal representatives and
              successors in interest, and shall inure to the benefit of the Company, its successors,
              and assigns.

         d)   The enforceability of any provision to this agreement shall not impair or affect
              any other provision.

         e)   In the event of any breach of this agreement, the Company shall have full rights
              to injunctive relief, in addition to any other existing rights, without requirement of
              posting bond.


    _____          _____
    SIGNATURE                                                             DATE
```

Non-Compete Agreement

A full size version of the General Non-Compete Agreement Form is available in the Appendix.

General Non-Compete Agreement

For good consideration and as an inducement for _____ (Company), to employ _____ (Employee), the undersigned employee hereby agrees not to directly or indirectly compete with the business of the Company during the period of _____ years following termination of employment and notwithstanding the cause of reason for termination.

The term "not to compete" as used herein shall mean that the Employee shall not own, operate, consult to, or be employed by any firm in a business substantially similar to or competitive with the present business of the Company or such business activity in which the Company may engage during the term of employment.

The Employee acknowledges that the Company shall or may in reliance of this agreement provide Employee access to trade secrets, customers, and other confidential data and that the provisions of this agreement are reasonably necessary to protect the Company.

This agreement shall be binding upon and inure to the benefit of the parties, their successors, assigns, and personal representatives.

Signed under seal this _____ day of _____, 20___.

_____
Company

_____
Employee

3. Verify, Verify, Verify

This is also the time for your final check by verifying this information against the information provided in the application and found during the screening process.

KEY POINT: The various induction forms should be matched against the information given in the application and waiver forms. Do the Social Security Numbers match? How about the address and phone number? Taking this extra step can catch a liar before he or she enters your workplace!

For those employers who do not do a background search (shame on you), this is the last chance to defuse a possible unwanted situation should the new hire not be the same person as presented on the application.

Candidates may provide legitimate identifiers during the application process, especially when they know the employer will conduct a background investigation. Once they are to be hired, the money they will now earn may generate a different mindset. It is important to realize that applicants, especially those with something to hide, are schooled on how to avoid getting caught. They already know most employers do not compare their answers. They have been through the hiring process before, some of them many, many times. If they change one digit on transpose two digits on their Social Security Number, the W-4 or new hire report won't catch them. This is especially true if they owe money for child support or the Internal Revenue Service, or if they are a fugitive felon or in violation of parole or probation. Once hired, these people may not care what appears in their personnel file if they feel the employer will not check the information provided at this stage against the information on the application forms. Perhaps this sounds far-fetched, but the reality of this happening far exceeds your chances of winning the lottery. So, don't be duped, double check.

Lesson Summary:

- The act of procedure should be broken down into three distinct areas:
    - The Acknowledgement
    - Complete All Requisite Forms
    - Verify, Verify, Verify
- Upon hiring, a new employee should be required to complete the following forms:
    - W-4 Payroll Form
    - State New Hire Form
    - Employee Data Sheet
    - New Employee Record Chart

- - Induction Form
  - Also, depending on the new hire position, your company may find that use of Confidentiality or Non-Compete Agreements is essential.
- This is also the time for your final security checks by verifying any new information against the information provided to you in the application and used for the screening process. The various induction forms should be matched against the information given in the application and waiver forms.

Recommended Resources:

www.acf.dhhs.gov/programs/cse

    The Federal Office of Child Support Enforcement provides state agency contact phone numbers, frequently asked questions and policy requirements for the mandated New Hire Form.

www.hrtools.com/frames.asp

    Click on the "New Hires" button for articles and reference. This will also lead you to a map with state links to web pages where you may download the above-mentioned form.

12 How to Properly Reject Candidates

Generally, there are two groups of rejected candidates; those who were interviewed and those not. Some companies may even have second and third interviews before a final decision is made. Once the hiring decision is made, it is important to consider how to notify those candidates who were interviewed that they will not be hired. Although not as critical, some consideration should be given to notifying those rejected candidates who were not interviewed.

Options Not Recommended

The following options should not be followed:

- Do nothing to notify the rejected candidate.
- Notify the applicant *only* if he or she contacts you.

Why? First, these two options are simply rude. Consider the fact that if someone really wants to work for your company, the applicant may postpone any further job seeking until he or she hears from you. Thus, avoiding the inevitable will only delay the applicant's search for work, which may be financially damaging to him or her. In other words, follow *The Golden Rule* – "Do unto others as you would have them do to you."

Second, although the chances of a discrimination lawsuit are minimal, it is to your advantage to maintain copies of all reject letters that have been sent to non-hires.

Third, you do not want to "burn your bridges" in the event the new hire doesn't work out and you are forced to re-examine the next best candidates.

Options Recommended

- Notify the rejected applicant by phone.
- Notify the rejected candidate by mail.

The first option above is acceptable. However, it has its flaws. For instance, giving notice of rejection by phone does not create a "paper trail," i.e. it does not result in documentation that may be important in the future. Furthermore, rejection by phone can be awkward and uncomfortable for both parties.

The last option is the preferred method. Designing and implementing a form letter is the best way to handle a rejection. Rejection letters provide documentation and negate the need for an uncomfortable phone conversation.

It is a good idea to send rejection letters promptly to avoid awkward phone calls or visits from the rejected applicants. Also, for those applicants who were interviewed, maintain a copy of all rejection letters within a file devoted exclusively to each applicant.

What to Tell a Rejected Candidate

First and foremost, keep the conversation or letter simple and end with a thank you. Keep in mind that it is not necessary to give a rejected candidate a specific reason why he or she was not hired. If you speak to the rejected candidate on the phone, refrain from making any statements regarding the difference between the rejected candidate and the person hired. Simply state that the company has hired the person that was determined to be the most appropriate person for the position.

The next page contains a sample rejection letter. It is simple and to the point, thanking the candidate for the time and interest shown.

Rejection Letter Sample

A full size version of the Rejection Letter Sample is available in Appendix III.

(To be produced on your company letterhead)

(Insert date)

Dear *(insert name)*:

Thank you for your interest in working for our organization. Many talented and qualified people applied for this position, including you. After much consideration, we have hired another applicant.

Thank you for your time, and good luck in your job search.

Sincerely,

(Insert your name and signature here)

Lesson Summary:

- Once the hiring decision is made, it is important to consider how to notify those candidates who were interviewed that they will not be hired.
- The best notification method is by mail with a "rejection letter," but notification by phone is also acceptable.
- The rejection letter should be simple and end with a thank you. Do not give a specific reason for the rejection on the letter, other than that another candidate was selected.

Recommended Resources:

http://jobsearchtech.about.com/careers/jobsearchtech/mbody.htm

This site is an excellent resource for an array of sample rejection letters. Applicable letters are shown for various stages in the selection process.

Section One – Pop Quiz

Now that you've read and completely understand everything in Lessons 1 through 12, let's try a pop quiz! Below are five questions and two story problems.

The answers appear on pages 145-146.

Five Questions:

1. Can I ask for a date of birth on an application?
2. Can I obtain a driver's report (MVR) on applicants who will not drive a company vehicle?
3. How can I do pre-employment screening if I can't ask for a date of birth?
4. I only have a couple of employees; does the Fair Credit Reporting Act effect how I do screening?
5. My business is seasonal, do I have to use the I-9 forms?

Two Story Problems:

What Would You Do?

The following two scenarios are based upon real events. They may seem shocking, but they are all incidents that involve seemingly routine components of the hiring process.

Each story ends with several questions. The author's answers appear at the end of this section.

#1 - Verbal Innuendos:

The Story: During a phone conversation with a candidate's former employer, you were told that the employee had an excellent attendance record and job performance. In fact, the former employer answered all of the standard questions in a positive manner. However, several days later, the former employer called you and asked if he could mention a few items "off-the-record." He then proceeded to tell you that the candidate had been under some suspicion because of monies missing from cash drawers. Although the candidate's register always balanced, some of the employees next to him reported shortages several times a week, which could not be explained. Then the former employer went on to describe the candidate as having personality conflicts, stated that he didn't really get along well with other employees, and after several work place arguments, the candidate eventually resigned. The former employer went on to say that since the time that the candidate left, there wasn't a re-occurrence of missing money.

Question One: How would you treat and document this information?

Question Two: If this candidate had been promised the position before the second call, how would you now reject the applicant?

Question Three: What if he had already been hired?

#2 - Criminal Questions:

The Story: Suppose an applicant filled out the application in detail with large, legible handwriting, but a closer examination revealed that she left the question about criminal convictions blank. When asked about the blank, she mentioned that she had a DUI conviction and was not sure if it was considered a crime. Since the position in question did not require driving, and since she seemed to tell the truth, and since she had transportation to the office, you told her to check the box "no" and initial it.

Part of your hiring process involves a statewide criminal history search, a search that typically takes several weeks to receive the results. Since the applicant appeared to be the best candidate for the position and the need to fill the position was great, she was hired before the criminal report arrived. Eventually the state report did arrive, with two convictions—one for shoplifting and the other for writing bad checks. The arrest dates were within the last two years and the last conviction was only six months old.

Question One: What should you do?

Question Two: How do you protect yourself from a discrimination suit if you decide to fire her?

Answers to First Five Questions

1. No, you can't have questions that could indicate a person's age, like the year of high school graduation.
2. Yes. MVR's can be important in character assessment and verify addresses. Just be sure to obtain reports on the same class of employees.
3. The Applicant Waiver Form is your "permission slip" to conduct a background check. The Applicant Waiver Form should include the required identifiers to do so (date of birth, social security number, names).
4. Yes and no. The Fair Credit Reporting Act effects all employers if they use a "Consumer Reporting Agency" (CRA) to obtain items such as criminal record reports, driving records, credit report, verification of education or prior employment. If the employer does the verifications themselves, and do not obtain criminal, driving, credit reports, etc., then the employer is not bound by the FCRA rules.
5. Yes, every employer is required to utilize the I-9 forms for any employee.

The Solutions to Story Problems

There are no simple solutions here. Your liability as an employer, and your course of action, totally depend upon the manner in which the person was hired. Each solution depends upon the forms signed by the employee, the promises you've made in writing, and the overall process as outlined in your company's hiring policy.

#1 - Verbal Innuendos:

Answer One: Treat off-the-record information as such and do not make a written record. Because the former employer called a second time unsolicited, he may be sincere or he may be revengeful and wants to interfere with the former employee's advancement. Since there is no proof, the issue of missing money cannot be used. If it were used, there could be serious liability to both employers, the former for providing malicious or unsubstantiated information and the latter for using that same type of information to deny employment.

Answer Two: If the off-the-record information was timely, and you feel you want to hire another candidate, you can simply by saying the second candidate is the most qualified applicant. And, because you have all your documents in order, if some small omission or deception was uncovered during the screening process, such as an omitted address, that alone could be cause for rejection or termination. In short, anything covered by your employment policy, other than this newly disclosed information could now be brought into play. This is also a time where the "at will employment doctrine" could be of value.

Answer Three: This is tough because again judgment must be made on the information given and the motive behind it. Scenarios like this are where the employment policies can be of great value. You cannot terminate the employee for this reason. Remember though, if the employee is an at-will employee, you can terminate then for any reason.

Scenario 2: Criminal Questions

Answer One: If your policy is "no lies on an application" then you can terminate her without much cause for concern as long as you stick to your rules.

Answer Two: Your protection is her signed application, the signature on the waiver, and her initials to the question supported by the criminal history report itself. The issue here is not necessarily the presence of a criminal conviction, but rather the employee essentially lied on more than one occasion.

Section 2
Bringing the New Employee On Board

Once a hiring decision is made, you may heave a sign of relief, but don't go thinking you're home free. The next few steps are crucial. What you do – or don't do – will set a tone. This will affect the performance of the new employee and affect their attitude. To some degree it will affect your organization overall.

Remember that old line, "Our people are our most important asset?" This is far from mere rhetoric. Your people may very well make the difference between your business' success or failure. Have you considered what is and what isn't necessary to make a new employee feel welcome?

Properly introducing them to their new surroundings may be the easy part. There's other key things that must be taken care of behind the scenes. Proper documentation continues as an important protection device for both the employer and employee as was outlined in Lesson 11.

Pay special attention to these next four lessons. They focus on the correct procedures for bringing a new employee on board, how and when to conduct performance reviews, and how to retain good employees.

13 The New Employee Orientation Process

An effective orientation program should provide new employees with an understanding of the organization and how their performance contributes to the success of the organization as a whole. This is a must, regardless of the size of the company or the importance of the position. A successful program normally includes the following:

- The history of the company
- The company's structure and organization (e.g. names, titles and key staff)
- A copy of the company/department organizational chart
- A presentation on company benefits that includes supplemental literature
- A tour of the facility
- A copy of the employee handbook (see Lesson 14)

Keep in mind that for most new employees the first few days on the job are anxious and uncertain ones. Studies have shown that a lack of well-developed orientation programs can intensify this anxiety. The resulting stress can interfere with the progress of training and acclimation. Thus, many large companies designate one whole day for orientation and basic tasks. Smaller firms may need only a partial day, but the point is that a systematic orientation procedure is a must.

Creating an Orientation Program & Schedule

The size of the company and the type of position filled will dictate the orientation needs and schedule.

What follows is the orientation schedule for the American Ultra-Tech Corporation, which can be considered a medium to large-sized company. This list of procedures, where applicable, is a good starting point for any orientation program, regardless of the size of the company.

American Ultra-Tech New Employee Orientation Schedule

The first morning, the following should be accomplished:
- A welcome to the company with presentation of employee handbook
- Locations of locker and wash room facilities
- Locations of cafeteria and break facilities
- Review of security regulations
- Locations of work areas
- Review of safety rules and the required safety equipment
- Introduction to fellow workers
- Assign a "buddy"—someone to help show the new employee the ropes
- Reminder to ask questions and seek assistance

After lunch:
- Explain the department's work and how the employee's job ties into big picture
- Summary of work group's accomplishments and duties
- Practice on the job, including:
    - Preparation for work
    - Sample tasks
    - Follow-up

Near the end of the first day on the job, do the following:
- Review pay rate, hours, breaks and time keeping procedures
- Explain company benefit plans
- Discuss parking and car pooling
- Explain dispensary facilities
- Answer any questions

During the first two weeks on the job, the following should be accomplished:
- Review of benefit plans
- Check on safety habits
- Follow up on progress and performance
- Review any items about which the employee has questions

Lesson Summary:

- Employers should realize that making a new hire comfortable is an important step. Show that you value them by not merely putting them to work and walk away expecting perfection.
- A clearly conceived orientation process should be balanced with the work, training and acclimation of the new employee.

Recommended Resources:

These web sites have either software available or offer assistance to the orientation process:

www.deliverthepromise.com

www.intechnic.com

www.hrnext.com

14   The Employee Handbook

The employee handbook is one of the most useful and practical items given to a new hire. The handbook puts in writing what is expected on the new hire, thereby lessening the possibility of disputes and potential legal actions. The following areas are subjects that must be addressed for each position within a company. Obviously, the handbook for a small company will be less extensive, but whether the company is large or small, the handbook is an excellent means to implement personnel policies as the company grows. Therefore, it is imperative that the handbook be kept up-to-date. The handbook should have every page numbered and the date the policy was issued or modified. A corporate review of the book should be completed annually.

The topics below are suggestions of what could or should be included within a well-written handbook.

Hours of Employment

- What are the days of the work week?
- What are the hours of work?
- What are the start and stop times?

Salary Issues

- What is the pay period?
- What is the policy for breaks and lunches?
- What are overtime rules and compensatory time rules?

Benefits

- What benefits are provided?
- Who is eligible for benefits?
- What family members are covered, if any?
- What is the cost to employee?

Sick Leave

- What is the method of accrual?
- What are the limitations?
- What is the notification policy?

Holidays, Vacations and Job attendance

- Which holidays are paid holidays?
- What makes an employee eligible for holiday pay?
- How are vacation days determined?
- How long before the length of vacation time increases?
- What are the increments of use; by the hour, half-day, full-day?
- What types of absences are excused?

Conduct of the Employee

- What constitutes unexcused absences and excessive tardiness?
- Company policy on drug and alcohol abuse.
- Company policy of sexual harassment.
- Outline of a disciplinary policy including warning letters, suspension and termination.
- Company policy on violence in the workplace; zero tolerance.

A Few Words of Caution

The handbook is not a technical contract, but don't allow the handbook to serve as a limitation to disciplinary action or even termination. It is advisable to include a disclaimer that states the following:

The company reserves the right to discipline or terminate an employee for items and actions not stated in this manual.

Lesson Summary:

The Employee handbook goes beyond employee orientation and steps into employee management.

Whether the handbook is a short guide and directly to the point, or an extensive manual, this product is an enforcement tool and leaves less room for any errors or misunderstanding.

Recommended Sources:

www.canmummery.com

> This site provides a table of contents for constructing your own handbook and has other products.

www.employer-employee.com

> This site hosts many related products from handbooks to job descriptions.

www.knowledgepoint.com

> This site is another excellent source of products and self help tools.

15 About Probationary Employment, Temporary Help, & Subcontractors

Use of Probationary Employment

Who is a "probationary employee" and what is their purpose? This is a protective measure that allows employers a period of time to get to know the employee—can they perform, do they fit? Additionally, it allows your company more time to complete the verification process. A probationary employee may be terminated without explanation so long as that fact is made clear in the company policy at the time of hire. Probationary employment can be used in every state.

💡 **KEY POINT:** The establishment of a probationary employment policy must be in writing. A typical policy should include length of time of the probationary period.

The Probationary Employment Statement

The following statement should appear on the original application:

> "I understand that a 90 working day probationary period will be in effect in the event employment is offered. This is not a guaranteed employment time frame, it is a period during which I may be terminated at anytime with or without cause (except in Montana)."

If this statement is not on your application form, then either it should be placed on another form signed by the employee, or should be a separate form in and of itself.

Pay considerable attention to the wording of the details of the probationary period. Does your current form merely refer to a "60-day probation?" If so, employees might think that they are guaranteed the opportunity to work for the full sixty days, unless you make it clear in your policies. Also, consider using the term "working days" vs. "days" to extend the probationary period. A 90-working day period gives the employer four and a half months to observe the new hires behavior. This should be plenty of time to evaluate the new employee. Also, this is an important time to observe if "the three-month syndrome" takes place.

Protection From the Three-Month Syndrome

Under the three-month syndrome, a new employee is on their toes for about the first three months, minding their manners so to speak. By that time they've got the company's "program" figured out, they have seen how much (or little) policies are enforced and have learned what they can get away with. They think ownership/management won't notice a slip in productivity or bending of, if not ignoring, the rules. The three-month syndrome is not the norm, but it does happen. Even the best new hire can become a huge disappointment. Always keep the rules in favor of the employer, just in case.

Uniformity is Important

Be sure that your probationary policy is consistent throughout the company. Do not open the door to a discrimination suit, if you are forced to terminate an unwanted new hire for legitimate reason, by not showing these reasons in your company policy.

Probationary Employment in Action

The company below hired a new employee with a probationary period.

> **Problems with Harriett**
>
> A local company, ABC Trucking, was familiar with Harriet, who worked for one of ABC's vendors. ABC knew of Harriet's skill as a tape transcriber. It so happen that ABC had a job opening, and Harriet applied. The job description of the position that Harriet applied also called for other skills. Harriet claimed working knowledge of Microsoft Office Software and stated that she could perform all secretarial tasks, as well as answer the telephones. This was good enough for ABC, and they hired her. Even though she was a "known" quantity, ABC still enforced its hiring policy rules and had Harriett fill out and sign application and waiver forms, which included a 90-working day probationary period. The waiver form clearly stated that the employee could be terminated at anytime "during" a 90-day probation period.
>
> As it turned out Harriett was an excellent typist when using a tape and transcriber. However, she possessed little ability to use the ABC office software and spent an inordinate amount of time trying to figure it out, generally with unacceptable results. The worst came to light when the

> ABC realized that Harriett exhibited very poor phone skills, and that she could do little very little without specific directions. Thus, ABC's new "gal Friday" wasn't near or close to what she said she was, or what the company needed.
>
> During the second month of employment, ABC had several talks with Harriett about her shortcomings and attempted to provide training. Although she tried, she just wasn't capable and was given notice of termination at the end of the ninth week.
>
> The next week Harriett presented a demand letter to ABC. Essentially, the letter stated that she was not given a "fair trial" and that ABC employer had to either keep her as an employee or pay her for the remaining portion of the 90 days. She further stated that if her demands were not met she would seek legal advice at once (remember, she had previously worked for lawyers).
>
> ABC advised Harriett that the company was sorry she felt the way she did, but under the circumstances she would not be re-hired nor paid for the remainder of the 90 days. Harriett chose to pursue legal action
>
> After a short trial, ABC readily prevailed because the paperwork— the application and waiver forms—totally outlined the company policy and the job conditions and requirements. Without these forms, for evidence, ABC may have very easily lost.

If the ABC Company had asked Harriet to sign the application form without the probationary employment statement, then there could have been a sticky situation. Harriet would have had little trouble finding a lawyer to represent her. Even if ABC prevailed in a lawsuit, consider the negative impact of the time and money spent, as well as possible tarnish to ABC's reputation.

Using Temporary Help (Temps)

There are two big advantages to using temps: to increase help on demand without time and expense of the recruitment and selection process; and the ability to cancel services whenever the task is completed. A temp can be used on specific projects or for the seasonal rush. Another obvious advantage to the employer is that the temp agency pays the taxes, workers' compensation insurance, and any other benefits. An employer can even request a different or replacement temp employee from the agency if the original individual does not work out for any reason.

While there are many benefits associated with using these types of services, the serious question remains: what do you really know about these people?

How Well Are Temps Screened?

KEY POINT: The truth is while many providers maintain that they *screen their temps*, this usually refers to testing candidates ability to perform specific job functions.

The polling of a number of temporary help providers indicates that they may not conduct criminal history checks, pull motor vehicle records or verify Social Security Numbers. While they may check with prior employers, few are experienced in looking at the reasons for gaps in service. Most temp agencies indicate that they could not afford to do proper background checking because their clients wouldn't pay for it, even on a cost only basis.

> **Know Thy Temp**
>
> The XYZ Department Store hired temps on an ongoing basis to support increased workloads. As the work leveled off, XYZ offered full-time positions to those temps who seemed to be the most acceptable. No background checks were done: XYZ assumed that the temps had been screened by the agency. Six months later and after considerable expense with private investigators, XYZ solved a puzzling problem with employee theft. Two of the applicants had criminal records; one for shoplifting and the other for attempted murder. This shocked the XYZ management, since both temps turned employees had been exposed to the general employee population for over a year.

What is the moral to this story? Do not assume that others have done employee screening for you.

Questions to Ask a Temp Agency

Any business prepared to use temps should ask a number of questions, including:

- Does the temp agency screen its employees and, if so, to what extent?
- Will the temp agency perform deeper background check, if requested?
- Does the temp agency have liability insurance to protect you, the client? (Hint: If so, ask to see a copy of their certificate of insurance.)

Using Subcontractors

Generally, a company hires subcontractors (or independent contractors) to perform certain tasks on an ongoing basis. As with temps, there are many inherent advantages to hiring a sub. An employer using subs is not obligated to pay state or federal payroll taxes, or to pay workers' compensation, unemployment insurance, or pay for such benefits as health insurance or retirement funding. In addition, the company's liability for negligence of, or injury to, a subcontractor is minimal when compared to the same actions by the employer's true employees.

A downside to using subs is that big brother—the IRS—is watching you very closely. In 1998, the most recent year for which the IRS has statistics, it conducted just over 40,000 audits of independent contractor arrangements. The IRS defines the distinctions between a true employee and a subcontractor (see below). If an employer is treating an individual as a subcontractor, but the IRS determines this individual is a true employee, the employer is liable for the associated back taxes.

How Do You Determine if a Person is an Employee or an Independent Contractor?

> **KEY POINT:** The general rule is that an individual is classified as an independent contractor if the employer (payer) only controls or directs the results of the work and not the means and methods of accomplishing the result.

The IRS does provide some specific guidelines. The following text is taken from the IRS web site at http://www.irs.ustreas.gov:

> "The determination is complex, but is essentially made by examining the right to control how, when, and where you perform services. It is not based on how you are paid, how often you are paid, nor whether you work part-time or full-time. There is no statutory definition of what an employee is, but from common law three basic areas have been identified:
>
> - behavioral control,
> - financial control, and
> - type of relationship.
>
> "For more information on employer-employee relationships, refer to Chapter 2 of Publication 15-A, Employer's Supplemental Tax Guide. If you would like the IRS to issue a determination ruling, you may submit Form SS-8, Determination of Employee Work Status for Purposes of Federal Employment Taxes and Income Tax Withholding."

A PDF version of the IRS Publication 15-A is found at the IRS web site. Go to the "frequently asked questions" menu and type in the key words "independent contractor."

The IRS does not care how an employer may label or classify a worker. The IRS only looks at the substance of the relationship. And this is regardless if the worker is working full or part-time. The key is how the employer controls the subcontractor in question.

💡 **KEY POINT:** If you hire a subcontractor who does not "work" for other companies, and you require this person to perform certain tasks at a certain time of the day via a specific set of specifications, you have hired an employee.

The IRS Publication mentioned above has four excellent examples. These are route drivers, insurance sales, at-home workers, and traveling salespeople individuals hired as subcontractors, who in reality should be classified as employees.

The Benefits of Using a Subcontractor

The primary advantages of using subcontractors are similar to those described for temps. The employer does not have to pay for the following:

- Workers' Compensation
- State and Federal Unemployment Taxes
- FICA and Medicare
- Workspace
- Pension Plans, Health Care and Other Benefits

Also, there are the liability issues. While you can never fully limit all of your liability, you can at least minimize possible liability for injuries to, or injuries caused by, a subcontractor. As long as the subcontractor was not hurt on the company premises or through company negligence, there should be no liability issues. If a subcontractor causes damage to someone or something, the responsibility for negligence usually rests with the subcontractor. It is always a good idea to require and verify that a subcontractor has liability insurance in force.

Another benefit to using subcontractors rather than employees is that using subcontractors reduces or eliminates some federal or state requirements that are based upon the number of employees in a company. As an example, employers with less than twenty or more employees are not regulated by the age Discrimination Act of 1975. And, employers with less than fifteen employees are not bound by the American With Disabilities Act or the Civil Rights Act of 1964. In addition, fifteen states do not require an employer to provide workers' compensation insurance when their number of employees is less than three, four or five or if annual wages are less than a certain amount. (See Lesson 23.)

Put Subcontractor Agreements in Writing

When working with a subcontractor, it is a good idea to require a document, signed by both parties, that details the nature of the relationship. The contract should include the following:

- a statement that the purpose of the contract is to establish a subcontractor relationship

- a list of the duties to be performed by the subcontractor
- a statement that the subcontractor is to provide his or her own transportation and equipment
- instructions on the invoice cycle of when payment is made and avoiding hourly rate statements
- a statement that the subcontractor is free to provide similar services to other employers
- the subcontractor is to provide copies of their in-force insurance, driving record (if applicable), and Federal Tax ID Number or Social Security Number

Screening Subcontractors

As with temps, a subcontractor may represent the employer in some means or manner, including possible direct interaction, with accounts. Therefore, the employer has a right to know about a subcontractor's work experience, license (if required), criminal record, driving record, etc. If someone is hired as a subcontractor for an ongoing basis, we recommend using the same background checking policies appropriate for employees. Of course, be sure to have the subcontractor sign all relative waivers.

> **Know Thy Sub**
>
> A local grocery chain used subcontractors to perform cleaning services for all of their store locations. Since the work was performed after hours, the subcontractors' employees had keys to the stores.
>
> Early one morning upon arrival, a store manager was confronted by one of the cleaning persons armed with a gun. A demand for cash from the safe was made. The cleaning person didn't know the cash was put in a night deposit and the only cash in the store was starter sets for the registers. Angry because of the sparse proceeds, he stabbed the manger several times, stole his car and fled unknowing toward the county court house on a dead end road. The injured manager called 911 and several law enforcement agencies closed in on the fleeing cleaning person outside the courthouse where he then crashed the stolen vehicle.
>
> As it turned out, the cleaning person had a violent rap sheet, as did the owner of the cleaning service and most of their employees.

The lesson here is don't assume anything and don't be bashful. One way or another, it is wise to make sure your subcontractors have had background checks.

Leasing Employees or Using a PEO (Professional Employment Organization)

Essentially, employment-leasing companies, or PEOs, are brought in to manage specific tasks and thereby reduce some required staff effort and associated costs. Not to be confused with a temp, or independent contractor, this category is classified as true employees of a company. As such, regulations do not provide any provision for a company to escape tax payments, benefit packages, or lessen the number of employees for this category.

Benefits of Using Leased Employees

Ostensibly, leased employees remove headaches from the business owner and allow for savings based upon not having to budget salary for an administrator or by re-assigning duties to that person when lessening their workload. For example, some companies "lease" their human resource and benefit department. The outside company oversees insurance, tax filing, workers' compensation, unemployment compensation, etc. while the company controls the daily activity of "your" employees at the work place. Essentially the business writes one check to the lease organization who, in turn, handles all related issues.

The employees of the PEO perform the same tasks, work for the same people and earn the same wages as that job-holder did prior to this agreement. This allows the employer to focus on the core business and not to have to worry about the associated employee requirements. Some of these organizations only take over a company's employee population and have no provision for recruiting or screening, or only limited abilities.

Lesson Summary:

- The establishment of a probationary employment policy must be in writing with a specific time statement.
- While there are many benefits associated with using temps, a serious question remains: What do you really know about these people?
- An individual is classified as an independent contractor if the employer (payer) only controls or directs the results of the work, and not the means and methods of accomplishing the result. Check the IRS web site for specific definition.
- The primary advantages of using subcontractors or temps are that the employer does not have to pay for the following:
    - Workers' Compensation
    - State and Federal Unemployment Taxes

           - FICA and Medicare
           - Workspace
           - Pension Plans, Health Care and Other Benefits
- Before a person is brought in as a temporary or subcontractor, always inquire if the person is screened and by whom.

Recommended Resources:

http://www.irs.ustreas.gov

>The IRS web site has extensive information about the differences between employees and independent contractors (subcontractors). Look for IRS Publication 15-A.

http://www.fuba.org/fuba/letter/0009

>This site contains an article in a recent newsletter by the Florida United Businesses Association. The article discusses the differences in worker's compensation issues between subcontractors and employees.

HR Magazine, June 2001 Edition

>The Society for Human Resource Management has an excellent article in the June 2001 edition of HR Magazine. Titled *A Tough Target: Employee or Independent Contractor*, it reviews this classification dilemma. The article may also be read at their web site, www.shrm.org.

16 Retention Efforts — How to Keep Good Employees

Once you have a good employee, you want to make every effort to keep them. A good retention policy rests on these seven basic programs:

1. Recognition and Encouragement
2. Open Communication
3. Competitive Salary
4. Benefits Package
5. Ongoing Education
6. Out-of-the-Ordinary Perks
7. Making It Fun to Come to Work

These programs lead not only to personal loyalty, but also to the aura of an overall company pride, professionalism, and high company morale. All of these factors are key ingredients to the success of a business, and a means to avoid potential problems.

#1. - Recognition and Encouragement

The reality is that everybody wants to feel important and be recognized. Everyone likes to be treated nicely. Employers need to step back and take a hard look at the atmosphere of their workplace, regardless if there are two employees or two hundred. When someone puts in a forty-hour workweek and does an excellent job, but is rarely told so, they can develop resentment or uncertainty about their value and the value of their job. They might think, "No one around here cares how hard I work." This type of thinking chips away at an employee's morale, and the employee may not work as hard. They may feel like there is "no point; does anybody really care?"

Recognize a Job Well Done, Be it Large or Small

People remember when they are unexpectedly rewarded or given public recognition. Recognizing a job well done at a staff meeting, or at an impromptu company meeting, can be a great motivator and boosts morale. Perhaps a professional milestone has been reached, a goal met, a job completed or someone's efforts have made a difference, like fixing the copy machine at a critical time. There is no fixed time to show respect and gratitude to an employee. In earnest, let them know they are valued because of their efforts and contributions.

Make it a priority to find ways to let employees feel they are sharing responsibility for the company's performance. Not knowing that it's their own lack of appreciative gestures towards their employees, some companies take for granted that the turnover rate for entry level or low-pay positions is high. But it doesn't need to be that way. When all employees feel as if they are contributing, turnover decreases and the company wins.

#2 - Open Communication

When employees feel that they are part of the action, and not isolated in a dark corner somewhere, they are more productive. An open-door policy encourages employees to share ideas and responsibilities. Encourage new ideas. Hold company meetings when new projects are planned or underway.

Turn a Mistake Into a Learning Experience

Nobody wants to be corrected, especially in front of peers. If a problem occurs, turn the situation into a one-on-one constructive experience. It is important to cultivate a working environment where people are encouraged to take responsibility, stay focused, ask questions and look for better ways to produce results—and profits. A chew-out session takes away these initiatives. The old adage "praise in public, criticize in private" is always good advice, but is not always followed.

#3 - Competitive Salary

Make no mistake: admitted or not, salary is a key ingredient to keeping a happy employee. Large companies with human resources departments have access to review surveys and studies for determining fair salary levels. Smaller firms must do hands-on research, such as talking to other companies or reviewing the want ads, to determine an appropriate salary level for a position.

Salary Increases and Pay Raises

Salary increases are a very important aspect of keeping good employees. Employees are truly investments and their "rate of return" can and should increase over the years. Companies should be proactive about salary raises in their company policy. There should be a stated criteria when pay raises are earned, or when it is given to keep them in your employ.

If your company does not have a proactive plan, be prepared for a raise request from an employee. Before turning down a raise request, consider the cost of training a replacement employee and the probable loss of production their training period, which might extend for months.

#4 - Benefits Package

The benefits package can be vital for attracting or rewarding good employees. Typical benefits include healthcare insurance, and retirement or pension plans. There are plenty of good books, trained professionals, and advisory services that can and will explain the ins and outs of pensions, stock options and contributing investment plans such as 401Ks. A benefits package is not limited to insurance and retirement. Typically, applicants with strong management experience or with strong technical know-how may command premium dollars and a potent benefits packages before they undertake a career move. Some companies package additional benefits including transportation or parking, additional vacation or family days, gratis membership in trade associations, free conference attendance, and paid education.

Be Creative

New or smaller businesses don't usually offer extensive benefits packages, perhaps very little, but any business can offer profit sharing or bonuses when business is good. Some of the other topics that follow in this lesson can be implemented as part of a benefits package.

#5 - Ongoing Education

Employees need to know that the opportunity to advance and develop professionally exists within your organization. Holding classes and seminars is an excellent way to support ongoing education of employees. Let employees know they are encouraged to take class courses outside of working hours. If there is not a university in your area, consider community colleges or technical schools. If appropriate, encourage correspondent courses. More and more are now offered via the Internet, including online universities.

Depending on the value of the continuing education, offer to pay part or all of their tuition, or a tuition refund.

#6 - Out-of-the-Ordinary Perks

Consider offering flexible work schedules, work at home days, four-day work weeks, telecommuting, and other incentives.

If the success of your business depends on a solid stream of new clients, some employers offer employees a bonus for finding them. If a vacancy at your company needs to be filled, offer a bonus for referring qualified applicants. Employees know the company's structure and are in a good position to determine if someone they know is a good candidate.

Periodic goodwill gestures can be effective for increasing employee satisfaction. An extra day off, a free tank of gas or a gift certificate with a note for a "job well done" are inexpensive, personal means by which to express your satisfaction with an employee's efforts. Tickets to an amusement park, sporting event or a concert have become popular as well. Clothing such as caps, shirts and sweatshirts with the company logo on them last for a long time, generate good will and are effective advertising, too.

Some businesses buy their employees lunch every Friday. They have pizza, Chinese food, sub sandwiches or whatever the employees decide upon. The help is happy, and they let others know. Is this expensive? There is no way to measure how much good you get in return.

Be creative and do what works for the employees. Treat employees at least as good as you treat your clients.

#7 - Make It Fun to Come to Work

As an employer, do you dread walking through the door to work every morning, and dread it even more than that long rush hour drive to get there? Chances are, if you do, then so do your employees. Nobody wants to work where they don't receive some satisfaction and at least some warm fuzzies for their efforts. The attitude starts at the top. Remember the movie *Nine to Five*?

The Family Attitude

A good way to promote employee *and* company morale and loyalty is to develop a "happy family" attitude. This should not be seen as a company policy, but as something that comes genuinely from the heart. Bosses and supervisors should go out of their way to know something about each employee, making it a point to inquire about children, homes, recreational activities and so on. A simple, passing comment on a family picture an employee may have displayed makes a positive impression. This family attitude can be greatly enhanced by having as many company-sponsored events as practical, commensurate with company size and budget considerations. These could be casual events such as picnics, dinner parties and the like where the company bears

Lesson 16 - Retention Efforts

all expense. Inviting families to such an event allows friendships and personal ties to develop that will, in the long run, justify the cost.

Finally, beware of sustaining a "caste system" environment—divided sects, such as management vs. labor, old-timers vs. new hires, etc. This can lead to adversarial feelings and confrontations.

Lesson Summary:

- Employees need to feel important and be recognized.
- Find ways to make employees feel they are sharing responsibility for the company's performance.
- Employees are truly investments and their "rate of return" should increase over the years.
- The benefits package is a key enticement to attract and maintain top-notch personnel.
- Employees need to know that the opportunity to advance and develop professionally exists.
- Be creative and do what works for the employees, not just for the clients.

Recommended Resources:

http://www.meaningfulworkplace.com

> This web site is maintained by Tom Terez, the author of *22 Keys To Creating a Meaningful Workplace*. The book is filled with many ideas on how to strengthen your workplaces, and ways to motivate and treat employees. His web site summarizes much of the text of the book.

http://www.benefitslink.com

> BenefitsLink has provided free compliance information and tools for employee benefit plan sponsors, service-providers and participants.

http://humanresources.about.com/careers/humanresources

> Human Resources.com is a great source for articles on benefits, compensation, morale and motivations.

http://www.shrm.org/channels/

> The Society for Human Resource Management site has some excellent free access articles. Click on the Benefits and Compensation channels.

Lesson 16 - Retention Efforts

17 Using Performance Reviews

Performance reviews are an excellent way to maintain quality employment in your workplace. In fact, most companies consider performance reviews an absolute necessity and part of the corporate culture.

As mentioned in Lesson 3, the job description informs the employee of the company's expectations of him or her. Now, the performance review documents actual results against expectations.

The performance review allows the employer to give "official" feedback, both positive and negative, to the employee. Oftentimes, a performance evaluation is conducted in conjunction with a salary review, and therefore introduces performance as a factor in determining if a pay increase should be given, and if so, how much.

Caution Ahead

Employers must be cautious about conducting performance reviews in a manner that can be construed as degrading or distrustful. Because it focuses on them exclusively, some employees look upon the review process as demeaning and adversarial. The purposes of a review can vary, but a review should not be a conduit for sending a negative message to employees about their potential growth. The purpose is the reverse: a well-conducted review can be instrumental for better communication between the employer and employee.

When Should Reviews be Conducted?

Many companies have a policy of conducting an annual review for all employees. That's fine, but there are other times when a review may be conducted. Here are a few:
- The employee has reached the end of his or her probationary period.
- The employee is being considered for promotion.
- The employee has exhibited unsatisfactory performance.

- The employee has performed exceptionally well.

If the review was triggered by exceptional performance, this is the time to acknowledge a job well done. Also, consider the retention efforts presented in the previous lesson as a means to reward an employee, in addition to discussions of salary adjustment.

Documentation

By documenting performance reviews, two goals are accomplished:

- The employee has a written copy of areas that need improvement. This should include some written actions that the employee can implement to improve performance.
- The employer has a document that can be used to illustrate the history of the employee's work record. The document records progress or lack thereof.

Designing a Performance Review Form

Given that performance review descriptions vary widely, as do each company's needs, employers should develop their own form. Here some items that should be at the top.

- A place for the employee's name and job title.
- A place for the name of the supervisor conducting the review.
- A place for the date of the review.

The following areas should be given three or four blank lines each as well as a place for a letter grade or indication of "fair, poor, needs improvement, excellent, above average, decreased performance, satisfactory."

Time Management

- Has the employee been punctual, tardy or a combination thereof?
- What about breaks? Has the employee used break and lunch times properly?

Awareness of Job Requirements

- Does the employee seem to be aware of his or her responsibilities?
- Is he or she living up to the expectations of the job?
- Does the employee understand the relationship between his or her job and the company as a whole?
- Does the employee follow the company policy and accepted practices when seeking assistance or making grievances?

Behavior

- Is the employee polite?
- Is he or she well mannered, especially with customers?

Lesson 17 - Performance Reviews

- Does he or she use good judgment?
- Compliance with Policy
- Does the employee follow the rules?
- To what lengths does he or she go to adhere to policies and procedures?
- Has the employee neglected or ignored any of the rules?
- Does he or she follow safety rules?
- Dependability - can the employee be counted on to perform assigned tasks?
- Does he or she seem willing to help others?

Initiative
- Does the employee raise issues that need to be addressed?
- Does he or she develop solutions?
- Does the employee identify tasks that need to be accomplished and then perform them without being asked to do so?
- Does he or she provide ideas to better the company or its products?
- Is the employee self-motivated?

Interaction With Others
- Does the person get along well with other employees?
- Does he or she communicate and cooperate with them?
- What about with customers?
- How well does he or she manage suggestions and constructive criticism?

Independence
- Does the employee need constant supervision?
- Is the employee capable of tracking his or her assignments, or does he or she need to be reminded frequently?
- Does the employee arrive to work and begin accomplishing tasks, or does he or she always need direction?

Quality
- How accurate and professional are the results of the employee's work?
- What do customers and co-workers think of the employee's work?
- How frequently are errors made?
- Does the employee take action to correct errors?

Productivity
- Overall, what is the employee expected to contribute to the company?

- Does the employee end the work week with a significant number of tasks accomplished?
- Does the time the employee spends on tasks seem reasonable?

Summary of Performance And Call For Action

After dealing with the above specifics on the Performance Review Form, there should be space to write for overall evaluations. This is an important part of the review, as it is the documentation of progress, unusual events and changing expectations. The following should be included:

- New or noteworthy accomplishments since the last evaluation.
- Areas that are in need of improvement.
- Recommendations for improvement.
- An over-all letter grade or designation, such as "Excellent, Above Average, Average, Below Average, Unsatisfactory, Not Rated."

There should also be additional room for comments from the employee, a date for the next review, and a place for the signatures of both the reviewers and the employee.

Employee Copies

As with all employee documents, the employee should be given a copy of the performance review and the original copy should be maintained in his or her personnel file.

Keep in mind that documentation is imperative when the need to terminate an employee becomes apparent, as Lessons 18-21 will indicate.

On the next two pages is a sample Performance Review Form. A full size version is found in the Appendix.

Sample Performance Review Form

Performance Review

_____   _____
Employee Name   Reviewer Name

_____   _____
Job Title   Date of Review

	Circle One	*Reviewer Notes*
Availability Punctuality/Absence Time Awareness	Excellent Satisfactory Needs Improvement	_____ _____ _____
Job Awareness Accountabilities Sets Goals	Excellent Satisfactory Needs Improvement	_____ _____ _____
Behavior Interaction w/ Others Manners/Neatness	Excellent Satisfactory Needs Improvement	_____ _____ _____
Complies w/ Policies Follows Procedures Safety Rules	Excellent Satisfactory Needs Improvement	_____ _____ _____
Dependability Performs assignments	Excellent Satisfactory Needs Improvement	_____ _____ _____
Initiative Develops Solutions Provides Ideas	Excellent Satisfactory Needs Improvement	_____ _____ _____
Independence Tracks Assignments Needs Supervision	Excellent Satisfactory Needs Improvement	_____ _____ _____
Productivity Quality/Accuracy Corrects Errors	Excellent Satisfactory Needs Improvement	_____ _____ _____

Continued

Sample Performance Review Form (page 2)

Performance Review – Page 2

Employee Name

New and/or noteworthy accomplishments since last evaluation

_____
_____
_____
_____

Areas in need of improvement

_____
_____
_____
_____

Recommendations

_____
_____
_____
_____

Overall Performance Summary	**Excellent**
(Circle one)	Satisfactory
	Needs Improvement

Employee Comments

_____
_____
_____
_____

Employee Signature   Reviewer Signature

Date   Date of Next Review

The Non-Performance Review?

An interesting concept is presented in a book written by Tom Coens and Mary Jenkins. The authors believe that performance reviews are intrinsically flawed and do not work. In their book *Abolishing Performance Reviews,* they say, "It is time to start over and look for new ways to liberate the human spirit in organizational life."

Okay, a new twist couldn't hurt, so long as it doesn't backfire. While the book does not spell out a series of specific alternatives, it does stress that employers should first examine what they wish to accomplish, then create new tools based upon this criteria.

The ideas behind this book could help foster strong company morale. For instance, "the company trusts us to be professional, so we'll be professional." This may be all well and good, but these non-traditional concepts seem better oriented towards a non-corporate environment.

Lesson Summary:

- A properly administered performance evaluation system can increase employee efficiency. If correctly implemented, performance reviews may provide an important defense for wrongful termination lawsuits.
- A performance review should be instrumental for better communication between the employer and employee and not a conduit for sending a negative message to employees about their potential.
- A performance review must be documented and include areas for the employer's and employee's signatures.
- A performance review should include:
    - Availability
    - Awareness to Job Requirements
    - Behavior
    - Compliance With Policy
    - Initiative
    - Interaction With Others
    - Independence
    - Quality
    - Productivity
    - Overall Summary and Recommendations

Recommended Resources:

http://www.hrtools.com/frames.asp

This site has many performance tool and checklists under the "training and performance" button. You will have to register.

http://www.business-marketing.com/store/appraisals.html

Business Training media has a variety of tools and products devoted to employee appraisals and performance reviews. Check out the helpful articles available online.

http://www.office.com

At this site, do a search for their multi-paged article entitled "Conducting Performance Reviews."

Section 3
When Problems Arise

When problems arise – and they will – will you be prepared? Having performed proper checks, due diligence, and with all the documentation safely tucked away in your files, you should have a very good fighting chance of minimizing and surviving the challenge, and avoiding disaster.

However, the best screening, the best employee-appreciation programs, and the most well-meaning efforts on your part cannot protect you entirely. You cannot, for instance, control what an employee does in their off time. That may include drugs. Six months ago when you hired that person, they were THE perfect choice. Spotless record. Now, it's havoc.

Perhaps you, or someone you know, have your own war stories of complicated, costly employee-related problems, and much more than simple tales of employee misconduct. Workers' compensation rip-offs, fines and penalties for not obeying rules and regulations, lawsuits for wrongful termination, discrimination – it makes you wince. If and when it happens to you, you've got to handle it correctly.

How should you handle a "grievance" or a "complaint?" One thing is for sure: not handling it leads to something worse.

The lessons in this section help you solve those delicate problems facing employers today, and point you toward some right ways of handling them, including when to go beyond this book for expert advice.

18 How to Deal With Unsatisfactory Employees

At one time or another, most companies must deal with problems of *unsatisfactory employee performance* or *misconduct*. Since either of these problem types have severe negative effects upon the morale of the employees and safety in the workplace, employers must respond swiftly and decisively.

The first step in the solution is to determine whether to handle the problem as one of performance or misconduct. The way you handle employees who just won't do their jobs or are constantly tardy is much different than how to handle workplace violence or substance abuse problems. The "problem" is that many seemingly performance problems can ultimately be traced to some form of misconduct.

This lesson will provide you with important first steps in the prevention and initial solution of these problems. The topic of how to manage and disciple unsatisfactory employees is extensive goes well beyond the pages in this lesson. For more information about what to do when you encounter severe cases of anger, insubordination, alcohol and drug problems, we suggest reviewing the Recommended Resources section found at the end of this lesson.

Recognizing the Root of the Problem

When there is a problem with an employee, the real key to finding a solution is to first identify the real reason or reason why. The following are possible scenarios that may trigger unsatisfactory performance or misconduct. This list will help employers gain insight into the point-of-view of those whom they must discipline.

- Perhaps the employee was not informed of the company's policies or what constitutes *acceptable* behavior or job performance. If employees are ignorant of the rules, they cannot be expected to abide by them. Communication is key.

- The employee may not understand his or her importance to the company as a whole. Maybe the employee feels powerless or unimportant. All employees should feel empowered.
- The employee may have personal problems that are not left at the door when the person comes to work.
- Perhaps the employee lacks incentive. The rewards for good performance may have not been made clear.
- The employee's training may have been inadequate or incomplete. In this case, additional training is an option that should be explored.
- The wrong personality was hired for the job. Perhaps there was no consideration given to whether the employee was an introvert or an extrovert. For example, if an introvert is to perform the duties of a receptionist, they may have trouble with calls or not have the "voice of authority" needed.
- Poor job performance may be the result of the abdication of responsibility by former or current managers. Perhaps previous managers did not take the time to spell out, in measurable terms, the employee's job requirements.
- Perhaps a lack of workload gives the employee too much free time. The employee may not be challenged by their assignments.
- There may be a medical problem that the employee has not disclosed.

Recognizing the root of the problem may very well determine how to deal with a troubled employee. If items like "lack of training" or "the wrong person for the job" are issues, then the problem is yours. The solution calls for adjustments from both of you.

Disciplinary Measures vs. Corrective Actions

Disciplinary measures are called for when there is misconduct. Corrective actions are the norm for dealing with problems of unsatisfactory performance. Both can be handled with a corrective interview, although severe misconduct may require immediate action. The following conditions must be defined in your company's disciplinary policy:

- When prior warnings are necessary before action can be taken
- What and when supervisors may take disciplinary action
- What penalties are available

The action and penalty of a disciplinary measure may be spelled out in the company's employee handbook. If not, use the list above and the chart below to create your company disciplinary table.

Lesson 18 - Dealing with Unsatisfactory Employees

Prepare for the Common Problems

The better prepared for dealing with an employee problem, the better the possibility of creating a solution.

KEY POINT: An employer must always make time to listen to employees when problems develop.

Taking the time to listen gives the employer the opportunity to gather first hand information which, invariably, can be used to some degree in the process of solving the problem and prevent future problems. The problem may have resulted from a lack of communication, a loophole in a policy, not following proper procedures or something else entirely. Perhaps, a policy needs to be made clearer or a new one needs to be established.

As an exercise in preparation, take the list of common problems below and add your idea of the proper company policy or action. Under the warning column, jot down what you consider to be a "performance improvement period." For example, an initial warning for excessive tardiness could be monitoring arrival times for two months. Another occurrence of tardiness within the period could trigger a suspension.

	Warning	Action	Termination
Absenteeism			
Alcohol or drugs on the job			
Anger or threatening behavior			
Inability to get along with others			
Insubordination to a customer			
Insubordination to a supervisor			
Inadequate job performance			
Lack of productivity			
Tardiness			
Violence			

Of course, you may find there are problems not on this list that are inherent to your particular business. After you add those problems and corresponding answers, you have a good general outline of your company's policy of dealing with problem employees.

A Motivational Approach to Discipline

When disciplining an employee, be sure to make statements centered on the behavior rather than on the person. Also, make sure that the statements originate from you by including the phrase "I feel." For example, don't say, "You have a poor attitude when you answer the phone" or "You are not a very neat person." Instead, say, "*When you* answer the phone, *I feel* as though you have an attitude sometimes" or "*When you* write illegibly, *I feel* frustrated when trying to process your reports."

In other words, follow this basic model:

> "When you (fill-in-the-blank with a description of the unacceptable behavior), then I feel (mention your reaction and/or conflict here)."

Here are some more examples:

> "*When you* arrive late, *I feel* overwhelmed trying to handle the customers."

> "*When you* miss your deadline, *I feel* pressured to take up the slack."

By focusing on the behavior of the employee, you will not risk injuring his or her self-esteem, which can lower the employee's productivity and make him or her resent you. Also, by including "I feel" statements, you are expressing your opinion clearly, and acknowledging that it is only *your* opinion and not necessarily that of everyone else.

Oftentimes supervisors who use this approach will say, "When you (blank), I feel disappointed." Then, the supervisor will follow-up with some positive statements, indicating that he or she believes in the capabilities of the employee (e.g. "I know you can do better. I saw the excellent job you did on the [blank] project."). These types of statements usually result in the employee feeling that the supervisor cares about what he or she does. In fact, they will know that the supervisor is disappointed with poor performance and expects better from them. When such statements are used, employees may leave disciplinary meetings resolved to do better and feeling confident. Someone actually cares about their performance.

Give the employee an opportunity to provide a solution. Ask him or her, "What do you think you might do differently next time?" People are less resistant to their own suggestions. Plus, when a solution is provided directly from the person being disciplined, it feels less like a punishment.

How to Conduct Corrective Interviews

Many managers and supervisors shy away from conducting corrective interviews because they view them as distasteful. They feel that such interviews may create a caustic environment that will leave both sides unhappy. Realize that you cannot make progress with a difficult employee by shying away from the problem. The answer is to be direct and honest about the problem with the employee. The same Performance Review used in Lesson 17 is appropriate for a corrective interview.

The following guidelines will assist in conducting corrective interviews. While many of the points covered below assume that interview is corrective in nature, these points are valid when dealing with disciplinary actions.

Caution: Prepare for the interview beforehand.

Do the following:

- Get the facts.
- Identify the reason for the poor performance or conduct.
- Consider the employee's entire performance, not just the episodes of unsatisfactory behavior. Also, gather positive aspects of employee's performance.

Conduct all corrective interviews in private.

Many supervisors witness a violation of a work or safety rule and feel that they must act immediately to correct the employee. Consequently, the supervisor disciplines the employee in front of his or her peers. This negatively impacts the employee's self-esteem and it sends a mixed message to observers. It may even make you look rash or inconsiderate.

Set aside time.

Provide enough time so that the session will not be rushed and thus insignificant. Eliminate the possibility of interruptions. Also, do not schedule the meeting just before the employee's break or lunch period, or Friday afternoon or Monday morning.

Remain calm.

Avoid anger and irritation. It is not "get-even" time. Plan the interview so that you may open the dialogue in a relaxed manner. Remember to think objectively.

Stick to the topic.

Stay focused on the topic; do not get sidetracked. For example, do not discuss salary in relation to performance or misconduct.

Start slowly and positively.

Begin the interview with a "small talk." Expect a positive outcome no matter what the history. Don't talk about the employee's unsatisfactory performance right away. You should ease into it. However, there are situations where getting directly to the problem may be the most effective.

Be up front and firm.

Inform the employee of the purpose for the meeting. For example, "The reason for this meeting is to discuss your job and how I can help you overcome some of the difficulties you may be experiencing." They should feel that you are being objective, not intrusive.

Review the employee's job description.

Be prepared to discuss all of the employee's responsibilities, yet do not give the impression that the interview is strictly structured by having the job description or a hit list of the responsibilities in front of you.

Start with the good news.

Discuss the parts of the employee's job that he or she is doing best. Start by asking how the employee feels he or she is doing in the areas. The employee will probably respond that he or she feels "good" about them. Since it is true, respond that his or her performance in these areas is "better than good." Review of these positive aspects will make the employee realize that the meeting is not a "witch hunt" and should alleviate suspicions and defensiveness.

Progress from the good to the bad.

Continue the list of job responsibilities until reaching the area of poor performance. Ask him or her to rate performance in these areas as well. You might even have the employee choose from "excellent, good, fair or poor."

Be specific regarding the poor performance.

Point out an area in which the employee can improve. Give an example and add that you will do all that you can to help the employee better his or her performance. Be clear. Broad statements only result in confusion, resistance and defensiveness. Determine the examples *before* holding the meeting.

Refrain from explaining over and over.

Telling someone repeatedly what they did wrong will not motivate them to do something right. Ask questions instead of repeating faults.

Set them up for success.

To start, ask them to do something simple and easy. Give yourself a reason to give praise at a later meeting.

Give equal time to the employee.

He or she should be allowed to present his or her side of the story. Don't interrupt and never show displeasure or disagreement. You may find that you did not have all the facts.

End on a positive note.

Tell the employee that the interview was time well spent, and that you hope the employee also found it to be of value.

Follow-up.
>Schedule a specific time for a follow-up review. Saying you're going to check on the employee's progress and then fail to do so sends a bad message. However, do not crowd the employee by constantly looking over his or her shoulder. Continue to provide coaching as needed, and as performance improves, use your best judgment as to when to decrease your coaching on the issue.

Recognize Improvement

When an employee's performance improves, it is important to acknowledge it. Without recognition of a job well done, the employee may not realize that there are certain behaviors they should continue.

Lesson Summary:

- The first step in the solution process is to determine whether to handle the problem as one of performance or misconduct. The way you handle employees who just won't do their jobs or are constantly tardy is much different than how to handle workplace violence or drug problems.
- An employer must make time to listen to employees when problems develop. The problem may have resulted from a lack of communication, a loophole in a policy, not following proper procedures or something else entirely. Taking the time to listen will give the employer the opportunity to prevent future problems.
- When disciplining an employee, be sure to make statements centered on the behavior rather than on the person.
- The following are key points when conducting a corrective interview:
    - Prepare for the interview beforehand.
    - Conduct all corrective interviews in private.
    - Set aside time.
    - Remain calm.
    - Stick to the topic.
    - Start slowly and positively.
    - Be up front and firm.
    - Review the employee's job description.
    - Start with the good news.
    - Be specific regarding the poor performance.
    - Refrain from explaining over and over.

- Set them up for success.
- Give equal time to the employee.
- End on a positive note.
- Follow-up.
* Document the session. Indicate all employee concerns and reactions. Document the agreed upon actions to be completed by the employee and by the company. Schedule a tentative time for the next review.

Recommended Resources:

http://www.dol.gov/dol/asp/public/programs/drugs/employer.htm

Entitled *An Employer's Guide to Dealing With Substance Abuse*, this is an excellent site presented by the National Clearinghouse for Alcohol and Drug Information.

http://www.lectlaw.com/files/emp03.htm

From the 'Lectric Law Library, an excellent article entitled *An Employer's Guide To Dealing With Substance Abuse*.

http://humanresources.about.com/careers/humanresources

Click on the "Performance Management" heading; there's lots of good reading and ideas here.

19 How to Handle a Complaint, Grievance or Potential Litigation

Treatment of Complaints

If an employee thinks he or she has a complaint, whether real or imaginary, it is a complaint in any case and deserves fair, open-minded, patient and considerate treatment. A list of common items found as the basis of employee complaints include:

- threats or violence
- safety concerns
- harassment, sexual or otherwise
- unfair practices, or treatment by a supervisor
- discrimination in the workplace

Complaint Process

There should be a written company-wide complaint procedure policy. The policy should be accessible to all and be in the employee handbook. The policy should not be rigid, but instead it should encourage an employee to give notice of their compliant, be it perceived or real. The policy should include the following points:

- Certain company individuals are designated as those who have the authority to handle complaints. The reporting process for complaints should be accepted at multi-levels, especially in the event that the complaint concerns a supervisor.
- The employer will hold the information confidential to the extent possible.
- The employer will investigate all complaints in a timely manner, including interviewing all involved parties and witnesses.
- The employer will make a determination in a reasonable amount of time and take appropriate action.

This allows for an effective company complaint process. When an employer lays down these ground rules, employees know there is a process in place and that their complaint will be heard. Employees may feel better about fair treatment, which could result in fewer frivolous or redundant complaints. A simple compliant form can be the instrument of origin.

Treatment of Grievances

Do not make the mistake of believing that grievances only take place where there are unions or only in large companies. Every employee should know that he or she has the right to make a grievance, and that the organization and its procedures recognizes this right. Whether the grievance is justified or not, the employee should receive a timely decision and explanation for the basis of the company's answer.

The Grievance Process

Handling grievances is a tricky task. While larger companies usually have a grievance procedure in place, smaller firms usually manage grievance situations on a reactive basis. Regardless of which category you company falls into, the suggestions listed below will make your handling of the grievance process easier:

- The person who is the immediate supervisor of the employee should be the first person to whom the grievance is presented (unless that grievance is against that supervisor).

- Grievance procedures must allow for employees to appeal and take their grievances to a higher level, if the original complaint is ignored, neglected, unfairly handled or if the immediate supervisor refused to acknowledge the grievance.

- Every supervisor should be informed that it is an essential part of the job to properly handle the grievances from their employees, and that the organization holds its supervisor responsible for doing so.

- When dealing with an employee's complaint or grievance, the supervisor should discuss it in a friendly manner. The supervisor should not be argumentative, antagonistic, or defensive. He or she should avoid implying any threat of retaliation against the employee.

- When employees have complaints or grievances, the supervisor should listen fully to the employee's viewpoint, reserve judgment, discuss the grievance in private, and take prompt action on the problem, if possible.

- If the supervisor or organization is at fault, the mistake should be openly admitted and prompt action should be taken to correct it.

- As a supervisor, do not pass the buck in accepting a grievance, in acting on a grievance, in explaining the decision on the grievance, or rejecting a grievance. Only if the supervisor lacks the authority to handle the grievance, should they turn the matter over to a higher authority.

Treatment of Litigation

When litigation becomes a reality every employer gets that sick feeling. This feeling can't be helped. It goes without saying that you will need the services of a labor attorney.

Compile All Related Documents

The first thing to do is to compile and review all of the employee records of those involved. The review should include the application, screening results, performance evaluations and any complaints or disciplinary files. Realize that these documents may be part, if not the sole basis for, the defense. When the company's policies and procedures are compared to the records of the involved employee, often a clear picture emerges. Whether you are right or wrong, and to what degree, may be self-evident once this evaluation is completed.

However, if an employer does not have good hiring procedures, policies, posting and record keeping, it is time to start preparing to do some back peddling.

Look For Prior History

Employers who have been in business for several years, or have some history of dealing with such problems, should be able to rely upon past practices as a means to support their side in litigation disputes. For example, if a company has a history of terminating "other" employees who violated the same specific company rules, then the company has established "practice." As long as this termination practice is legal, per an attorney, it can be used as proof for a defense. This is especially important in cases when the litigant claims discrimination because of race or sex.

Involve Your Insurance Carrier

Finally, always examine your business insurance policy and call your insurance agent. You may have coverage, depending on the particulars. Coverage may even include an attorney.

Remember....

If you maintain good records you are already ahead of the game.

Consider Arbitration Agreements

Today, many employers are requiring workers to agree in advance to settle any employment-related disputes in arbitration. This avoids prolonged litigation and excessive costs. This trend was enhanced with a recent Supreme Court decision (Circuit City Stores vs. Adams, March 21, 2001). The US Supreme Court, in 5-4 decision, ruled that companies can insist that workplace disputes go to arbitration rather than to court. The ruling also stipulated that the Federal Arbitration Act covered employment contracts.

Lesson Summary:

- Whether the action is a complaint or a grievance, it most be taken seriously.
- Establish a company policy to handle complaints and grievances. Post the complaint policy and include it in the employee manual.
- The ongoing issue of having policies in place and documentation at hand is important to insure against the threat of litigation.
- Check with your insurance provider for coverage.

Recommended Resources:

http://www.healthwellexchange.com/nfm-online/nfm_backs/Jun_99/grievances.cfm

This is a well-written article entitled Working Through Employee Grievances, by Carolee Colter.

http://www.shrm.org/channels

The Society for Human Resource Management site has some excellent free access articles. Click on the Employee Relations Channel.

20 How to Handle Workers' Compensation Issues
Complying with Workers' Compensation Laws

Workers' Compensation is America's oldest social insurance program. For more than 80 years, most states have required all employers to maintain this insurance. The system is designed to cover the employer's medical expenses and lost wages for employees who are injured on the job.

KEY POINT: If you, as the business operator, fail to provide coverage, then you may be in violation of your state's laws, leaving you open to fines and penalties.

And, it gets a whole lot worse if an employee is injured and the employer is not covered. Who will pay the medical bills and lost wages? Even if the company can afford it, the chances of escaping serious problems are slim. In today's litigious society, even a minor injury may prompt a worker to contact an attorney. In fact, many employees deliberately look for an opportunity to file a compensation claim. Unfortunately, many workers view compensation as a benefit, i.e. time off with pay. Just as applicants are schooled in application tricks, some have a degree in abusing the workers' compensation system.

The consequences of noncompliance with workers' compensation laws vary in each state, but they are usually severe. It may become necessary for the state to assume financial responsible for medical, wage and disability payments. However, ultimately the company will assume responsibility for all the payments, plus horrendous fines, penalties and interest far beyond estimation. Some states suspend the employer's business license or revoke the corporate charter. If you cannot pay, the state can sue you, seize your assets and shut the company down. Essentially, you can lose everything. All of this is true, even if the compensation claim proves fraudulent. So, to protect your assets, check your state's requirements and adhere to the rules.

Set Company Safety Policies

Most medium- to larger-sized businesses have accident and injury reporting methods in place. For each injury, major or minor, documentation takes place. Progressive organizations have instituted safety committees who, monthly or quarterly, review all incidents and injuries in an effort to examine causes and to implement safety and prevention programs. Some firms even have their department heads generate reports that include comments, investigative narratives, and other statements on any incidents, all so that the employees may be educated and aware of safety issues and policies in their own work area.

As a result of having a correct safety and accident policy in place, when an accident or incident occurs, thorough information will be gathered, thus showing that strong efforts have been made to document the incident.

Your insurer is the best advisor as to what accident and safety policies are necessary for your business.

Cost Containment

This may not be enough. The cost of workers' compensation has soared by more than 40 billion dollars in the last decade. Part of this spiraling cost is a result of the methodology used by the insurance companies and current litigation practices.

> **KEY POINT:** But a large portion of the increased workers' comp expense can be directly traced to inability of today's management to recognize potential fraud.

The remainder of this lesson is devoted to how to spot signs of fraud and how to put an effective management system in place to control the abuse of workers' compensation and.

Guidelines to Reduce Fraud

Employers can reduce chances of workers' compensation fraud by implanting a series of company policies aimed specifically at the reporting of injuries. If you are an employer, consider the following proactive suggestions:

Use sound screening practices.

Under the American's With Disability Act, employers are not allowed to run a search for prior workers' compensation claims until they have made an offer of employment. Once a job offer is made, contact the state Workers' Compensation Bureau and request a prior claims search. Look for a repeating pattern, or a previous injury. Some fraudulent employees will claim the same injury over and over again.

Show your employees that you care about them.
>Train all employees on your company's method of reporting accidents and document the process.

Educate your employees on fraud.
>Educate employees as to what fraud is and what the rules are if they are found guilty. Notify employees that the company and the insurer will work together to investigate and prosecute those who file fraudulent claims. Establish a mechanism whereby employees can notify the company of fraudulent activities.

Educate Yourself.
>Have employees document the injury at first report; you may find that their explanations change over time. Get involved in the investigation and prosecution of fraudulent claims. Be aware of employees who are seasonal, facing a layoff, or have been problematic in the workplace. These are employees commonly associated with the filing of fraudulent claims.

How to Spot Signs of Potential Fraud

There are some proven indicators and telltale signs that signify a higher likelihood of the existence of fraud. The following are signs that an injury claim may be fraudulent:

- The employee was off for a period of time just prior to claiming the injury.
- The injury occurs late on the last day of the work week or immediately upon return to work.
- The injury was not witnessed.
- The injury was not properly reported or was reported late.
- The description of the injury is vague or changes.
- The recovery is taking longer than the injury warrants.
- Internal rumors suggest that the injury was faked.
- You hear that the employee is working elsewhere, is self-employed or is performing activities that he or she claims to be unable to do.
- After the incident, the employee is never at home, or a member of the household states that he or she "just stepped out" when a call is made.

Which Employees Commit Fraud the Most?

If the employee...

...has been problematic,

...is facing a layoff or termination and knows their employment will end,

...is new on the job,

or

....has a history of short-term employment, these employees may be more likely to commit workers' compensation fraud.

Suggested Remedies to Control Abuse

First, Some History

During the 1950s and 1960s, the typical on-the-job injury was handled much differently than it is today. Our parents and grandparents not only had a different work ethic and values, but were also subject to different rules concerning employee injury.

The Adjuster Relationship

In those days, an insurance company's adjuster controlled the medical treatment, records, and payment. The adjuster investigated the injury, its cause and circumstances, obtained reports, and conducted interviews in person. He or she would visit the scene, take photographs, and make diagrams where applicable. The adjuster determined if the injury was work-related and justified compensation. They were responsible for examining, adjusting and charting medical treatment, and paying the providers. The adjuster would often visit and make payment to the injured employee, again, in person. Many of the adjusters would see the claimant on a weekly or bi-weekly basis to update his or her paperwork, report on progress and issue payment.

The worker knew the adjuster was coming and had to be home or he or she wouldn't get paid. The company, through the adjuster's report, could monitor payments, progress, treatment, and prognosis. Adjusters also developed their own network of people, from all backgrounds, who would confide in them of suspected abuse and irregularities. Those adjusters could spot malingerers and would follow up on any information provided to them. After all, within their territory, adjusters were known in those communities and everyone knew they would be around. In actuality, as part of their jobs, they were the fraud unit.

The system wasn't perfect. Personal visits usually took place by schedule on a specific day of the week and at an approximate time of day. The employee had to be home or risk a delay in getting paid. If the employee wasn't home, he or she had to have an excuse and knew they would be questioned as to the reason for their absence.

Of course, there was a cost factor involved. The adjusters were paid their salary and they had the expense of an automobile. Some had company cars while others were reimbursed for their own. Regardless, the cost of the insurance, operation, and maintenance all added up. There was also the cost of cameras, film, developing, forms, photocopying, supervision, medical benefits, and pension.

Over time, the claims departments were viewed as expense factors. They were not income producers. Further reasoning indicated that the same results could be obtained by telephone contact and that the required reports could be obtained by mail. Eventually, these new practices were adopted, and through attrition and the reassigning of personnel, the street adjuster began to disappear.

Automation Takes Over

Soon only major cases received any personal attention. As time passed, new adjusters were trained to handle claims by phone and mail. The experienced adjusters who remained were assigned to investigate only major cases. The lack of hands-on management opened the door to the "get something for nothing" crowd who soon figured out how to beat the system. As a result, the cost of workers' compensation has soared, 40 billion dollars over the last decade alone. A hard look at the growing costs in workers' compensation claims indicates that the methods of the last twenty years or so are not and have not been working for a long time.

All of this means that now is the time to re-examine the elements of the claims process, from first report to medical treatment. So, what programs can help prevent abuse of workers' compensation by claimants and providers alike?

The following are examples of remedies that can be integrated with current policies and procedures. They are designed to aid in controlling the cost of claims and support you in the litigation process.

Proper Use of the First Report of Injury

The initial injury report is often the most critical document in a file. Yet, the initial report is often considered a nuisance to fill out, and therefore minimal information is recorded. This lack of detail allows an injured employee to exaggerate the claim as time goes by. Sometimes the claimants include, as part of their claims, pre-existing injuries, or injuries incurred subsequent to the initial event.

To curtail such faulty records, better reporting methods must be established. Standards should be set and forms completed fully. By providing precise forms, with instructions to those designated to take reports, a business will have established the primary requirement necessary to gain control over the claim. Regardless of severity, every injury should be documented as soon as possible — in detail.

Report Content

In addition to the basic "who, where and when," a descriptive narrative should be mandatory on the initial report. The narrative should include exactly how the injury occurred, what parts of the anatomy were affected, and what the employee was doing when it happened. All witnesses should be interviewed and their statements recorded.

If a finger is cut by a box cutter and requires two sutures, it may be a relatively simple matter. Painful, but should not result in much last time. However, if the injury resulted from a slip and fall, it is more complicated and an exact description should be recorded.

Here are some questions that are examples of getting specific:
"Which foot or leg went out from under you?"
"Did it go backward, to the front, or to a side?"
"What hit the ground—hand, elbow, arm, shoulder, head?"
"Was any other part of your body injured, cut, bruised, strained?"
"What caused you to fall—slippery surface, water, oil, object?"

If any witnesses were present, there should be documentation as to what they saw, heard, and the contents of any conversation they had with the injured worker, as well as their perceptions as to any cause of the injury. If other workers were present, but deny any knowledge, the employer should document that as well. If they didn't see it, ask, "What were you doing at the time, exactly?"

Taking the time to describe injuries in detail has several benefits. First, a well-documented injury report protects an honest worker from future misunderstandings that arise when details are unknown. It also assists the adjuster in total assessment. At the same time, it limits the malingerer's ability to include other injuries, which could not possibly have been physically related to the incident. Second, making an accurate initial report goes into the medical provider's file for comparison to future reports from the same individual.

Know the Medical Providers

It is no longer prudent to simply select a provider and contract out for treatment of on-the-job injuries. To adequately control total cost of workers' compensation these contracts must be very specific. The agreement should require that the injury and the treatment be causally related to the incident, as detailed by the worker and his or her supervisor.

If any other symptoms are present or claimed in the future, and they are not a result of the loss, then the claimant can be advised, "Yes, you have that condition, but it was not caused by this incident." Again, it is the details obtained at the first notice that can serve to limit the scope and duration of the claim.

Often times, an apparent minor injury becomes severe somewhere between the time of injury at the work place and the doctor's office. Usually, the physician only knows what he or she is told by the employee, and without supporting documentation has little choice but to accept the employee's word as the truth and that doctor's report may reflect this. However, if discrepancies are brought to the physician's attention early, they can be instrumental in spotting malingerers and curtailing fraud.

So, provide the treating physicians with the required forms to be completed at their office upon first treatment, or as soon as possible. The first portion of this form should be exactly the same as the initial report, except that now the injured worker answers the questions with a medical professional present.

The second half of the medical form should include a detailed, prior medical history. This process allows for a comparison with past and future reports, and any drastic differences would be obvious and questionable. Additionally, use of this form provides the employer, and hence the adjuster, with the identity of the family physician and potentially relevant access to the claimant's prior medical treatment history.

How to Control Lost Time Claims

Remember the adjuster who used to visit the injured worker? Some of that methodology needs to be put to work again. The values, ethics, and morals of old can't be forced on employees for the future, but the employer can attempt to change that employee's perception by being more pro-active. The criteria for implementing the following programs can vary depending on your organization's policies, structure, and claims experience.

Use of Home Visits and Interviews

During the recuperation period, the adjuster's personal visit to an injured worker's residence can provide valuable information that may affect the total claim evaluation. The first portion of the visit should be part of a wellness program; with questions designed to document medical treatment past and future, including current progress and projected recovery periods. Emphasis should be placed on caring about the worker's condition, ensuring satisfaction with medical treatment, and determining if any needs are not being addressed. Their good health is, of course, most important. The course of treatment and potential "return to work" date, as they understand it, can be correlated to the medical reports being received.

An honest employee will be happy that the adjuster, and therefore, the employer, cares enough to visit and ask of his or her needs and opinions. There is little doubt that morale plays a major role in both employee performance and recovery.

A review of medical treatment billings, including dates and scopes of services, should be conducted with the injured worker during the visit.

While the interviewer is present, he or she is in a position to observe the physical condition of the worker as well as other circumstances, which may be relevant. The interviewer should be trained to observe and detail anything that may indicate activity not consistent with the claimant's limitations. The range of details could include the presence of vehicles or equipment indicative of a side business, to the wearing

> It is not a coincidence that many workers' comp attorneys advertise on daytime television. An employee who feels that his employer does not care—who is not "in contact"—may begin listening to these ominous commercials!

of apparel that would be difficult to put on, considering the disability.

In some instances, due to the sheer volume of claims, coupled with staffing shortages, the ability to make this type of hands-on program work may be limited. Or, the success of the program can generate a desire to monitor even lesser claims. In any event, a patient interview and survey of medical treatment could also be undertaken by telephone. Although nothing can replace in-person contact, it is better to have a partial program than none at all. It also lets the providers know that their services are being monitored. A simple and well-orchestrated visit/interview can go a long way toward controlling many aspects of the claim cost.

Send a Message

Having such a program sends a message in your company policy to all claimants that someone will check up claims, and, that they can't just go home and do whatever they want. The implementation of this program should pay special attention to suspected malingerers with file histories containing obvious red flags or discrepancies. Identifying the fraudulent activity, prosecuting the subject and publicizing the results can achieve the short-term goal, which is to control workers' compensation claim costs. To avoid claims of fairness, always make sure you first check with your attorney when you do not "treat" all employees equally. Ultimately, employees who even consider stretching the truth will have second thoughts.

On the bright side, another benefit of this proactive, in-person approach is a strengthened bond between the employer and high-quality employees. Remember the earlier lesson on employee retention?

Anticipate the Results

Interview results may provide clues about questionable practices of providers. Further scrutinizing of these practices could demonstrate inappropriate treatment, billing overcharges or other actions. These issues should be dealt with as soon as they are discovered rather than allowing them to continue. Letting them continue says it's okay.

> **The Doctor said what?**
>
> Mrs. Cummings, an injured worker, tells the interviewer that she told her physician that she felt able to return to work, and yet the doctor told her to take a couple more weeks off "to be on the safe side." In scenarios like this, a closer look at that practitioner's files would be in order. The physician probably will have scheduled Mrs. Cummings for follow up with more visits. Hence, your company may be paying for unwarranted treatment and lost time.

Examine Previous Health Care Benefits

Some questionable claims can be refused based on an examination of the claimant's past health insurance utilization history. A number of "new" injuries have been documented as pre-existing or not work-related because of prior treatment by the employee's family physician, or at emergency care facilities. When these types of cases are identified, they can easily be supported by documents—not only by treatment records, but also by accident records that provide details of how, when and where an injury really occurred.

> **Loading Dock Scam**
>
> Mr. Leone worked on a loading dock it a trucking company. One day at a nearby lake, he suffered a fall on the deck of a boat, and fractured several of his ribs. In pain, he was taken to a nearby hospital for examination, and x-rays confirmed the injuries. The prescribed treatment was some pain medication, a chest wrap and plenty of rest. Lost time was projected to be six to eight weeks.
>
> Leone had exhausted most of his sick time and didn't want to lose out on his weekly paycheck. So, the morning after his fall, he went to the loading dock the morning and positioned himself on the ground. When another worker showed up, Leone alleged that he fell off the dock and hurt his ribs. He was taken to the local hospital for treatment, fully expecting workers' compensation. He thought he would be told to get some time to rest, recover *and* get paid. However, his act of fraud was discovered, by accident, when a change in health care providers produced a past treatment audit.

Another claimant alleged respiratory distress due to "workplace environmental conditions." The medical history taken by the workers' compensation providers denied any prior illness or treatment, and indicated the worker as a non-smoker. Yet, personal medical history obtained from the health insurance provider of a prior employer detailed a long history of respiratory ailments, including treatment, and that the worker had been a 2-1/2 pack-a-day smoker for many years.

Tie It All Together

Using the suggestions presented in this lesson will help any company properly manage their workers' compensation issues. But keep in mind—*prevention is the strongest cure*. Using sound pre-employment screening has proven to be the most effective measure when controlling abuse of workers' compensation.

Lesson Summary:

- If a business fails to provide workers' compensation coverage, it may be in violation of state laws, and subject to fines and penalties.

- Companies must have methods in place for employees to report accidents and injuries. Progressive organizations have safety committees that review all injuries and accidents to examine causes and to implement safety programs.
- Guidelines to Reduce or Prevent Workers' Compensation Fraud includes
    - Using sound pre-employment screening practices
    - Educating employees on what fraud is and what rules apply if they are caught.
    - Training employees on the correct method of reporting injuries or accidents.
    - There are nine telltale signs of potential fraud.
    - Understand how the medical providers' programs work.
    - Examine the previous healthcare benefits received by an injured employee, if fraud is suspected.

Recommended Resources:

http://www.dol.gov/dol/esa/public/regs/statutes/owcp/stwclaw/stwclaw.htm

This site, from the U.S. Dept. of Labor, contains overviews of individual state workers' compensation laws, including their benefit tables.

http://www.cwce.com

CWCE Magazine For The Workplace Community. This magazine is a great source of articles dealing with workers' compensation issues.

http://laborsafety.about.com/industry/laborsafety/mbody.htm

This site, part of the About The Human Internet, is another source of great reading material regarding workers' compensation issues.

http://www.workinjury.com

Although this site is heavily oriented towards California related workers' compensation laws and procedures, there is also plenty of useful information nationally.

21 Termination Procedures

The termination of an employee can be one of the hardest and most uncomfortable duties of a company supervisor, manager or owner. Any termination has the potential of creating an uncomfortable situations with the other employees and customers. If a termination is not handled correctly, litigation becomes much more probable.

There are five important steps in the termination process:
1. Determine if the reason is legitimate and unbiased
2. Do it swiftly
3. Do it legally
4. Determine if benefits are owed or if there is an exit package
5. Conduct an exit interview

Finally, there is one underlying task that ties into all of the steps above: to document, document, and document.

The first three steps in the termination process are covered in this lesson. The exit package and exit interview are covered in the Lesson 22.

Legitimate Reasons for Dismissal

The following are typical, acceptable reasons for termination:
- Dishonesty
- Failure to accomplish assigned duties, or poor performance
- Committing illegal acts while on the job or job site
- Endangering others
- Violation of company policies or non-compliance with them
- Wrongfully Disclosing confidential information
- Habitual tardiness

- Excessive absences
- Abusing employee benefits
- Insubordination
- Theft
- Fraud
- Misrepresentation

But, Are You Sure?

The reasons above are surely grounds for dismissal. But before you act, determine if you are reacting to a chain of events or an emotional circumstance. Ask yourself the following questions:

- Is this an "at-will" employee? (see below)
- If another employee did the same thing, would I still terminate?
- Could the cause of termination have been avoided with proper training or management?
- Did the employee clearly understand company policy?
- Is the employee involved in an action such as a workers' compensation claim, or scheduled to receive a benefit or bonus?

Nobody wants to be held hostage by an employee gone wrong. If you choose to terminate an employee, make sure that your decision is consistent with company policy, does not violate any contracts with the employee, and that there is documentation of your efforts to warn the employee. Imagine that you will have to explain your reasoning to a jury, complete with evidence. If you feel that your argument is weak, you may wish to reconsider the termination, for now.

Act Swiftly

The old adage about one rotten apple spoiling the barrel holds true here. A festering problem with an employee who should be terminated, but is not, may leave a negative impression among co-workers and customers. Once the decision is made to terminate, do it and don't procrastinate. Be sure that your decision is legal and strictly follows company policy.

Is the Termination is Legal?

Essentially, the manner in which an employee was hired determines that manner is which they can be terminated.

- If an employee was hired for a specific time period or has an employment contract, or has been given an express or implied provision that requires a reason for termination, then this employee can only be terminated for *just cause*.
- If an employee was hired under the Employment At-Will Doctrines, the employer has the right to end an employment relationship at anytime with or without cause.

How to Prove Just Cause

"Just cause" can be something as simple as contractual obligations that are not met. Common examples are if an employee simply fails to show up, cannot complete a shift, comes to work under the influence, removes company property, becomes violent, purposely damages goods or for any basic item contained in the "contract." Providing just cause for disagreements involving work product or time schedules requires additional effort or proof form management.

The best and perhaps only way to prove just cause is by documentation to show it. Any and all of the actions leading to termination must be documented. These actions include:

- performance reviews
- written warnings, and
- evidence of disciplinary meetings or sessions with the employee.

If a termination for just cause is necessary, then be sure to review all of the application and contract documents the employee has signed. If there are doubts or questions about a legal issue should contact an attorney who specializes in employment practices. Guesswork or depending on general theory obtained from some third party could result in embarrassment. Decisions made without expert advice can be very costly.

Employment At-Will

As discussed in earlier lessons, the common law doctrine of employment at-will is created when an employee agrees to work without a specification as to how long the parties expect the employment relationship to last. Under this century-old common law rule, employment relationships can, in general, be terminated at the discretion of either party.

This means that at any time, and without notice, at-will employees may quit work, or be dismissed by the employer "for good cause, for no cause, or even for cause morally wrong." However, though the employee may quit for any reason, there are many restrictions on an employer's right to terminate.

For the US worker, employment is considered to be of vital importance to the quality of life, although, statistically, the jobs of two out of every three workers depend almost entirely on the continued good will of their employers. The legal system, in general, presumes that the jobs of at-will employees may be terminated at the will of their employers. They also recognize that employees have a similar right to leave their jobs at any time.

Restrictions on the Right to Terminate At-Will

Congress and state legislatures have passed laws that restrict the authority of employers to exercise uncontrolled discretion in terminating employees. These laws have slowly eroded the right of employers to terminate employees for any reason or for no apparent reason. The prohibitions apply only to actions taken after the law's passage. Therefore, an employer can anticipate, catalog and implement the legislative exceptions with more certainty than is the case with exceptions created by the courts.

The following is a listing of the major federal statutes that place limits on the discretionary termination of at-will employees by employers:

- Prohibitions Against Dismissals in Retaliation for Behavior Worthy of Public Protection
    - Protected Labor Relations Activity
        - Railway Labor Act (1962)
        - National Labor Relations Act (1935)
    - Protected Activity in Support of Health and Safety Laws
        - Energy Reorganization Act of 1974
        - Federal Water Pollution Control Act (1948)
        - Air Pollution Prevention and Control Act (1977 amend.)
        - Occupational Safety and Health Act (1970)
        - Coal Mine Health and Safety Act (1969)
        - Railroad Safety Act (1975)
    - Miscellaneous Activities Worthy of Public Protection
        - Jury System Improvement Act of 1978
- Prohibitions Against Dismissals of Employees Who are Members of Protected Groups
    - Members of Groups that Have Been Victims of Past Discrimination
        - Title VII of the Civil Rights Act of 1964
        - Age Discrimination in Employment Act (1967)
        - Americans with Disabilities Act

- Members of Groups Requiring Protection Against Economic Disadvantage
  - Fair Labor Standards Act (1938)
  - Veteran's Employment Act (1976)
  - Employee Retirement Income Security Act (1974)
  - Consumer Credit Protection Act (1968)
- Members of Groups Requiring Protection Against Political Discrimination
  - Civil Service Act (1978)

These federal statutes prevent employers from taking action against an employee for exercising a right under these various laws. An employee that files a complaint, gives testimony or otherwise participates in a proceeding provided for by these laws, cannot be discharged for his or her actions. Many states also have statutes protecting employees from retaliation for filing claims or participating in proceedings under workers' compensation, disability laws, unemployment insurance laws, etc. Additionally, more and more judges are finding "whistleblower's" exceptions to employment at-will based upon employee conduct that is not the subject of a specific anti-retaliation statute.

Common Law Limitations—Important Exceptions

The legislative exceptions to the doctrine of employment at-will have created a lot of business for the court system. The courts in turn have performed their traditional role by enforcing these statutory rules in the cases brought before them.

Some judges have gone beyond the words of these statutes and have created an additional set of exceptions. Many of the exceptions are "judge-made" or common law exceptions based on public policies that the judge believes are embodied in a state statute.

There are also times when common law exceptions have nothing to do with statutes or public policy, but are based on traditional rules of contract law that the judge believes obligate an employer.

Common law exceptions can be categorized into two very traditional areas of the common law: contract law and tort law.

Contract law regulates the manner in which agreements between parties are interpreted and enforced.

Tort law regulates relationships between parties who may have no agreement or contract with respect to the matter at issue.

Lesson Summary:

- The five important steps in the termination process are:
    - Determine if the reason is legitimate and unbiased
    - Do it swiftly
    - Do it legally
    - Determine if benefits are owed is there an exit package
    - Conduct an exit interview
- Before you act, determine if you are reacting to a chain of events or an emotional circumstance. Ask yourself the following questions:
    - Is this an "at-will" employee?
    - If another employee did the same thing, would I still terminate?
    - Could the cause of termination been avoided with proper training or management?
    - Did the employee clearly understand company policy?
    - Is the employee involved in an action such as a workers' comp claim, or scheduled to receive a benefit or bonus?
- The rule of the common law doctrine of employment at-will is created when an employee agrees to work without a specification as to how long the parties expect the employment relationship to last. Under this century-old common law rule, employment relationships can, in general, be terminated at the discretion of either party.
- Congress and state legislatures have passed laws that restrict the authority of employers to exercise uncontrolled discretion in terminating employees

Recommended Resources:

http://www.businesstown.com/people/firing.asp

This is a great resource for articles on managing employees and how to terminate. Full of professional information; many articles are available.

http://www.irem.org/nyholm.htm

This is an article titled *Firing without Getting Burned* and is written by Sandy Gail Nyholm. This is well written article is highly informative.

22 Exit Interviews, Packages, & Termination Meetings

While the previous lesson deals only with employees who are terminated, this lesson covers the exit procedures for all employees, whether they resign, are laid off, or are terminated.

An exit interview should be held with an employee who has resigned or has been laid off. A termination meeting should be held with an employee who has been fired or terminated. At either meeting, the *exit package*, meaning the severance pay, explanation of benefits, and status of insurance, needs to be covered with the former employee. Also, these meetings must be documented.

Exit Interviews

The two-page **Exit Interview Report Form** found in Appendix III is an excellent starting point to create your own customized exit report.

The Exit Interview Report should include the following:

- The reason why the employee is leaving the company.
- Checklist of items required to be returned, such as keys and company property.
- Checklist of restrictions placed on the exiting employee, such as a non-compete agreement.
- A series of questions that give insight to the exiting employee's feeling about the company's operations, working conditions, strengths, weaknesses, and policies.

Exit interviews can indicate trouble spots or point out areas where company improvements can or should be made. Any allegations made by an employee during the exit interview must be kept confidential if he or she so desires. If there are lingering questions as to why an employee has resigned, these answers can surface in an exit interview.

The Exit Interview Report Form should be kept in the now former employee's personnel file.

Exit Packages

The amount of severance pay to give to an employee who is leaving is very subjective. The amount may depend upon the reasons for the exit, the years of service, the position, and the atmosphere surrounding the exit. Some companies have policies in place that determine the amount of severance pay and other benefits. Certainly, a generous severance check will create goodwill and help defuse any adversarial situations that could lead to litigation. A typical severance package for a non-administrative employee that has been terminated is two-three weeks of pay.

In certain situations, federal law designates that retirement funds and health insurance are among benefits that must be part of an exit package. Withholding these benefits can trigger litigation against the employer.

Retirement Funds

If a company has a retirement plan in place and the employee has met the minimum length of service for vestment, federal law stipulates he or she is entitled to these funds. Holding these funds is grounds for civil litigation against the employer.

Health Insurance

The federal government requires that all companies with 20 or more employees that provide a health insurance benefit must offer COBRA insurance to an employee who resigns, is laid off, or is fired. Note that COBRA is not paid by the employer; it is paid by the employee. COBRA permits the employee to keep the same level of insurance previously paid by the employer in force. One notable exception is if an employee is fired due to "gross misconduct." Of course, COBRA is not applicable if the company did not pay for health insurance in the first place.

Termination Meetings

Many times, the termination meeting is the time an employee is told that his or her services are no longer needed. The meeting should be direct, to the point, and short in length. The meeting should be documented, using the same Exit Interview Report mentioned previously.

The following is a list of suggestions that will make the termination meeting less stressful for both the employer and employee.

First, review any signed contracts between the employer and employee

> It is also a good idea to determine if this employee was hired as an "at-will" employee or if contracts and written promises were made at the time of hire.

Lesson 22 - The Exit Interview

You open the door to litigation if you do not follow the terms of such agreements.

Meet at the beginning of the day

The employee may feel that something is "going to happen." The morning hours or the beginning of the employee's work shift is the proper time to terminate. Also, if the termination decision has been made, whenever possible do not wait until the end of the week.

The meeting should be held private and face-to-face.

This is a common sense rule. Nobody wants to be terminated in public, nor over the telephone. It is a good idea to limit the number of company personnel to one or two people, and include the immediate supervisor if possible.

Provide the reason(s) for the termination

The employee should be told why he or she is being let go. If appropriate, show the employee copies of warnings or adverse reports from their personnel file. Providing documentation of a pattern of poor performance or a repeated series of misconduct is better than basing a termination on one incident.

Review the checklists on the Exit Interview Report

Make sure that all company property is recovered and that the former employee is reminded of restrictions such as company trade secrets, a signed non-compete agreement, etc.

Listen to what the employee has to say

Give the employee a chance to speak, keeping in mind he or she may be upset (another reason to keep the meeting private). If the employee is allowed to vent in person, it may reduce the chances of the employee filing a lawsuit. Also, a candid conversation with the employee may reveal unknown problems to the employer. The following story is an excellent example:

> **Tip of the Iceberg:**
> An employee of a security patrol company was repeatedly caught violating company rules. The verbal and written warnings did not seem to help, and ultimately the company had no choice but to terminate the employee. When told of the termination the employee did not deny the charges against him, but he became very upset. He refused to leave the premises and demanded to see the company's owner to no avail. The company's policy for release of the final paycheck dictated that all company-provided uniforms, badges, ID's and equipment had to be turned in. The next day the employee showed up at the main office with his company equipment, and again demanded to see the company's owner. This time the company consented and the owner sat down with the former employee. And the stories started. The upset former

employee claimed he had gotten fired for playing the radio loud and driving the car too fast on the premises. But, he said that he was turned in by people who didn't like him and who were abusing company rules and policies. He proceeded to tell stories of who was punching other employees' timecards in and out, of an ongoing scheme of stealing fuel from the company, and of female employees who were leaving their posts to spend time in the back of the compound with local police officers.

While the story seemed outrageous, the owner was impressed by the fact that the former employee was naming names and dates. He asked the former employee to settle down and repeat each of the accusations in detail while he took notes. The owner felt he had to verify the allegations, so an internal investigation began. Much to the owner's shock, everything the former employee said was confirmed. The owner immediately instituted a policy of requiring an exit interview with anyone leaving his company.

Be specific about severance benefits

Do not mention benefits or bonuses that *may* be given to the employee. Mention only those benefits that will be delivered and stick to that list. Otherwise you open the door to litigation and you may very well not have the court's sympathy.

Termination meetings are not fun for either side. Being fair and courteous will be much easier for both parties and something good can come of it. However, to borrow some thunder from the Boy Scouts, always **be prepared**!

Lesson Summary:

- Whether the reason for leaving is a resignation, a termination for cause, or a lay off, a documented Exit Interview Report should be completed.
- The Exit Interview Report should include the following:
    - The reason that the employee is leaving the company.
    - Checklist of items required to be returned, such as keys and other company property.
    - Checklist of restrictions placed on the exiting employee, such as a non-compete agreement.
    - A series of questions that give insight to the exiting employee's feeling about the company's operations, working conditions, strengths, weaknesses, and policies.
- In certain situations, federal law requires that retirement funds and health insurance benefits be part of an exit package. Withholding these benefits can trigger litigation against the employer.

Recommend Sources:

http://sanantonio.bcentral.com/sanantonio/stories/1998/05/04/smallb4.html

> This is an excellent article on exit interviews that appeared in an edition of the San Antonio Business Journal.

http://www.ewin.com/articles/exit.htm

> This article, *How and Why to Conduct Exit Interviews,* is posted by Winning Associates. It is well written and ends with a useful checklist.

Section 4
Abiding By The Law

Are you in compliance with state and federal laws?

You may know your state laws well enough, but what if your screening firm pulls a report from another state? Are you in compliance with that state's laws?

Good question. And, it's not the screener's fault if you aren't in compliance.

In Section Four's lessons you will learn quite a bit about state and federal laws that apply to employers. It's a safe bet that more than half will apply to you.

Lesson 23 features state employment discrimination laws. Lesson 24 will help you understand and comply with federal employment discrimination laws. Lesson 25 covers how to comply with other legal issues including sexual harassment, hiring the handicapped, AIDS, and other sensitive issues that now have the support of legislation.

Information in this section is for your general information and is not intended as legal advice and should be construed as such. For advice on your specific legal issues, please use an attorney. Laws and rules reproduced here are taken from official sources, but not all are presented verbatim.

23 How to Comply with State Discrimination Laws

All states have employment laws. These laws can have three nuances of note. They may only apply according to the number of people employed by an employer. They may prohibit specific types of discrimination. They may mandate that rules must be "posted" for employees' examination. Many of the state discrimination laws are patterned after the federal laws.

Laws Defined by Number or Type of Employees

In most cases, the number of employees is the benchmark for determining when employers are subject to specific law provisions. While some state law provisions start at three or less employees, most seem to follow the Americans With Disabilities Act— ADA— (which is a minimum of fifteen). Some state laws detail the number of employees that work a minimum number of days, essentially covering part-timers or for a seasonal business. Some states exclude "domestic help" from the employee classification, and a few more have done the same for "farm workers."

State Specific Discriminatory Laws

The federal laws reviewed in the next lesson also affect employers. These laws can, by large, cover some of the same state's own specific regulations. These state standards make it illegal to discriminate against employees or applicants on the basis of race, creed, color, natural origin, age (over forty), sexual orientation, religious accommodations, political affiliation, AIDs or genetic traits, lawful use of tobacco products, or unequal pay based on sex. While this seems redundant where a federal law exists, an employer should be aware of distinctions between home rule and the federal regulations. It is important to note that none of these state laws remove liability from the federal requirements.

Posting

Most states require employers to "post" notices of state laws that relate to the employee. The notices must be prominently displayed in a location where employees normally have access, and not in some closet or dark corner.

Very often, the topics and language in state posting requirements duplicate federal posting requirements. This is to the employer's advantage. For example, should an employee complaint be filed "late" and become a litigation matter, these "postings" could help defend against a charge of alleged inaction by an employer. This "documentation" could be vital, especially if the charges are failing to properly respond. After all, most "notices" offer multiple means of complaining.

An Overview of Certain State Law Topics

The remaining portion of this lesson examines these six specific categories of state employment discrimination laws:

1. Reasons for Terminating Employees
2. Obtaining Criminal Record Checks for Employment Purposes
3. Alcohol and Drug Testing
4. Former Employer Immunity for Reference Checks
5. Workers' Compensation

Within each category, the general standard or norm and the states that have adopted that norm are reported. Also indicated are those states that have strong variances from the norm, or no law at all. These laws may become the basis for litigation involving negligent firing and economic interference.

If you have any questions about your state's specific rules, we recommend visiting your local law library or calling your state attorney general's office.

#1 - Reasons for Terminating Employees

The Standard

Forty-five states and the District of Columbia have passed legislation restricting the firing of employees for most or all of these exact circumstances—

- serves on jury duty
- files a workers compensation claim
- takes time to vote
- files safety complaints

- union activity
- usees family leave
- has a child support wage garnishment
- tells others of wage earnings
- is a protected reservist or veteran
- refuses to work on Sunday or their Sabbath
- is a member of a fire service

The laws do not say you have to pay them for this time, but you cannot fire them.

Non-Standard States

These six states do not have employment laws that restrict termination for the reasons given above:

>Colorado   Idaho
>Louisiana   Montana
>Wisconsin

#2 - Obtaining Criminal Record Checks for Employment Purposes

The Standard

Among other things, the Fair Credit Reporting Act regulates the use of criminal record checks. In addition, *every* state has some specific laws regarding the use of criminal record for employment purposes.

Some have **limitations** on the time frames allowed for consideration—how far back you may look. Many forbid the use of, or even asking about an arrest that did not result in a conviction, or a record that was sealed or expunged. If this disqualified information is used in the decision making process for employment, then there are grounds for discrimination. Most states allow the use of arrest, indictment or pending trial information.

Many of states **require criminal record checks for specific positions,** including; healthcare workers, day care (child or adult), school bus drivers and school employees, law enforcement, security personnel and private detectives, youth sports (paid and volunteer). Other areas where criminal record checks are required are **occupations that involve state licensing or registration**. Typical industries and professions include insurance agents, racing, gambling, and liquor sales.

Some states require **sex-abuse or child-abuse registry** checks.

Interestingly, some states have an overall policy that does not permit employers or the general public to gain access to their statewide criminal records database. These same

Lesson 23 - State Discrimination Laws   222

states have laws on the books requiring criminal background checks for certain occupations. As a result, these states must then specify, by statute, which occupations require a criminal record check. This can become quite confusing when legislators make changes to one statute but not to another, thus not giving the means to access, when access is required.

So, once again it is important to know your own state's requirements limitations.

#3 - Alcohol and Drug Testing

The Standard

States with alcohol and drug testing statutes generally mirror the federal policies and standards. Some states require additional reporting, others impose limitations. A few have job specific testing requirements.

Many of the state laws "allow" employers to use state "drug free workplace programs" that outline testing procedure guidelines that must be followed. Seven states offer workers' compensation premium discounts to companies who follow the program. Two states have provisions where employees forfeit workers compensation benefits for refusing to test or testing positive.

The issue again is to know the home rule and make work it for you.

States with Rules or Limitations

Alabama	Alaska	Arizona
Connecticut	Florida	Georgia
Idaho	Illinois	Indiana
Louisiana	Maine	Minnesota
Mississippi	Montana	Nebraska
North Carolina	North Dakota	Ohio
Oklahoma	Oregon	Rhode Island
South Carolina	Tennessee	Utah
Vermont	Washington	

#4 - Former Employer Immunity for Reference Checks

As a rule, employers are reluctant, if not afraid, to provide derogatory or negative information on a past employee's performance or conduct. The stories of costly litigation and enormous jury awards have virtually shut down one of the most important channels of information a new or prospective employer could rely on. Some employers refuse to respond to a reference check. Others only provide name, rank and dates of employment. This is the only way to protect a company. Or is it?

Forty-one states have enacted litigation providing immunity to employers who provide truthful references concerning an employee's qualifications, job performance and reason for termination. As long as the information is truthful and without malice, the employer is free from civil liability. Many employers may not be aware that they reside in a protected state. Therefore, when checking the reference from a protected state, it is a good idea to remind that employer of his immunity.

In fact, there has been a backlash of litigation against companies and their insurers for withholding damaging information about a former employee. Cases where one employer knew of dangerous or costly actions by their former employee and knowingly withheld that information from an inquiring prospective employer have resulted in disaster. For example:

> **Oh, He's OK**
>
> ABC Company caught an employee, Mr. Jones, embezzling a large amount their money. Eventually the employee, although fired, made restitution and charges were withdrawn. Several years later, Mr. Jones applied for a job with XYZ Enterprises. XYZ contacted Company ABC for a reference and was provided with a glowing picture of Mr. Jones. Within a year after hiring Jones, he was caught embezzling nearly $100,000. The insurance company for WYZ performed an investigation and discovered the knowledge withheld by Company ABC then sued them. In the end the insurance company won the case against ABC and was awarded double the value of the embezzlement.

The moral of this story is to know your state laws, the state laws of the company you contact for references, and be careful.

States with Laws for Immunity for References from Former Employers

Arizona	Arkansas	California
Colorado	Connecticut	Delaware
Florida	Georgia	Hawaii
Idaho	Illinois	Indiana
Iowa	Kansas	Louisiana
Maine	Maryland	Michigan
Minnesota	Missouri	Montana
Nebraska	Nevada	New Mexico
New York	North Carolina	North Dakota
Ohio	Oklahoma	Oregon

Rhode Island	South Carolina	South Dakota
Tennessee	Texas	Utah
Virginia	Washington	West Virginia
Wisconsin	Wyoming	

States NOT Having Laws for References From Former Employers

These states have no provisions regarding blacklisting or references or immunity to employers.

Alabama	Alaska	District of Columbia
Kentucky	Massachusetts	Mississippi
New Hampshire	New Jersey*	Pennsylvania
Vermont		

*New Jersey has introduced legislation in the Senate and Assembly.

#5 - Workers' Compensation

Small Employer Exceptions

Standard

Every state has workers' compensation laws. Except in two states, coverage is mandatory. However, some states require a minimum number of employees. Again check your state's laws or with an attorney to make sure your company is complying with all of the applicable laws.

Non Standard States

Non-Mandatory:	New Jersey and Texas permit the employer to choose whether to offer workers' compensation.
Three or More Employees:	Arkansas, Georgia, Michigan, New Mexico, North Carolina, Virginia, and Wisconsin.
Four or More Employees:	Florida, Rhode Island, and South Carolina
Five or More Employees:	Mississippi, Missouri, and Tennessee

Further Exceptions

If you are in the construction business in Florida, Missouri, or New Mexico, you can forget the rules above. Insurance is required with one or more employees. Wisconsin reverts to one employee in more than $500 in wages were paid the previous year. There are other exceptions in Arkansas, Kansas, South Carolina, and Tennessee. Again, check your state's laws, or do so through your attorney.

Discounts for Drug Testing

The seven states listed below offer as much as a 5% reduction in workers' compensation premiums under a "drug free workplace" initiative. There are also specific testing requirements and policies that employers must follow. These seven states are:

Georgia	Idaho	Mississippi
North Dakota	Tennessee	Virginia
Washington		

Other Notes about Worker's Compensation

Arkansas — An injured employee who refuses to test forfeits workers compensation medical payments and indemnity.

Florida — An employee who tests positive forfeits workers compensation benefits.

Recommended Resources:

http://www.employmentlawcentral.com

This site does an excellent job of disseminating employment law. There are pages and links to recent laws, opinions, and court cases. A great site!

http://www.icle.org

The Institute of Continuing Legal Education offers impressive educational and legal resource materials, including an Employment Law Central link.

http://www.hrtools.com

Do a search under "workers comp" and this site will provide a wealth of information about state worker's compensation laws.

http://guide.lp.findlaw.com/11stategov

Findlaw.com is a great resource of legal information. The URL listed above provides a gateway to every state's "cases, codes and regulations."

http://www.references-ect.com/main.html

This company has an terrific page of state employment laws. Find your way to www.references-ect.com/state_employment_statues.html.

24 How to Comply with Federal Discrimination Laws

Employers must abide by a myriad of federal laws and statutes. In the US, it is illegal to discriminate on the basis of race, color, religion, sex, age or national origin in all employment practices, which include hiring, discharging, promotion, compensation, and all other terms, privileges, and conditions of employment. But, some laws only pertain to certain employers, some are based on the number of employees working for an employer, and some federal laws can by superseded by state laws.

In an effort to present an effective overall analysis, Lesson 24 profiles seventeen significant laws and statutes. Each profile includes the type of employer affected, an explanation of the act, the government agency administering the act, and where to view a copy of the act on the Internet, if available.

The second portion of this lesson gives brief descriptions to fourteen specific areas of concern to employers, such as wages, medical leave, etc.

Finally, at the end of this lesson is a one-page chart that shows how federal laws or statutes affect employers with varying number of employees.

Important Federal Discrimination Laws

Age Discrimination in Employment Act of 1967/1975

Who it Affects: Employers of 20 or more persons.

Details: Prohibits discriminating against persons who are 40 years of age or older. Certain apprenticeship programs, retirement or benefit systems are exempted from these prohibitions. Forty-four states also have age laws, some of which have no age 40 to 70 limitation; therefore, all ages are protected. The act was amended in 1975.

For More Info: US Equal Employment Opportunity Commission
202-663-4900
www.eeoc.gov

Act found at www.eeoc.gov/laws/adea.html

Americans with Disabilities Act (ADA)

Who it Affects: Employers with 15 or more employees.

Details: Prohibits using job applications that include questions about an applicant's health, or about the nature or severity of a disability. This Act also limits an employer's use of physical examinations, and there are different sets of requirements depending on whether the examination involves an applicant or an employee. Pre-employment physical examinations may not be given under this Act before a job offer has been made. However, once an offer has been made, the rules change. After an offer has been made and before an applicant begins work, an employer may require a medical exam, and condition the job offer on the exam results, providing the following conditions are met:

- The medical exam must be given to all new employees in the same job category, regardless of any disabilities.
- Information gathered during the exam must be maintained on separate forms and in separate files for each employee.

The information must be kept confidential, except for the fact that when appropriate, supervisors and managers may receive information about necessary work restrictions and accommodations.

For More Info: US Equal Employment Opportunity Commission
202-663-4900
www.eeoc.gov
Act found at www.eeoc.gov/laws/ada.html

Civil Rights Act of 1866, 1871 & the Equal Protection Clause of the 14th Amendment

Who it Affects: All persons within the United States.

Details: The Civil Rights Act of 1866 prohibits discrimination on the basis of race in contract and property rights. The Civil Rights Act of 1871 prohibits public officials from violating any constitutional rights of persons, including discrimination against race, sex, etc. The Equal Protection Clause of the 14th Amendment provides equal protection under the law for all persons within the United States.

For More Info: US Equal Employment Opportunity Commission
202-663-4900
www.eeoc.gov

Civil Rights Act of 1964 (Title VII), as amended by Equal Employment Opportunity Act of 1972

Who it Affects:
- All private employers of 15 or more persons.
- All educational institutions, both public and private.
- State and local governments.
- Public and private employment agencies.
- Labor unions with 15 or more members.
- Joint labor-management committees for apprenticeship and training.

Details: Prohibits discrimination on the basis of race, color, religion, sex, or national origin. It also prohibits practices caused by statistically determined adverse impact, as well as intentional, unequal treatment.

For More Info: US Equal Employment Opportunity Commission
202-663-4900
www.eeoc.gov

Act found at www.eeoc.gov/laws/vii.html

Executive Orders 11246, 11375 & Revised Orders 4 & 14

Who it Affects: All organizations that hold government contracts. The orders apply specifically to contractors and subcontractors who have government contracts in excess of $50,000 or who employ 50 or more people.

Details: These are Presidential orders rather than laws. These orders prohibit discrimination in employment and require Affirmative Action Plans by all federal contractors and subcontractors. Revised Order 4 covers under-utilization of females and minorities. Rule 401:2741 covers payment of dues in private clubs that discriminate on the basis of race, sex, etc.

For More Info: Office of Federal Contract Compliance
Department of Labor

Act Found at www.dol.gov/dol/esa/public/ofcp_org.htm

Equal Pay Act of 1963

Who it Affects: All employers in the US. Subject to the Fair Labor Standards Act.

Details: Requires equal pay for men and women performing work substantially similar in skill, effort, responsibility, and working conditions unless wage differentials are due to bona fide systems of seniority, merit, output or some business factor other than sex.

For More Info: US Equal Employment Opportunity Commission
202-663-4900
www.eeoc.gov

Act found at www.eeoc.gov/laws/epa.html

Title IX, Education Amendments Act of 1972

Who it Affects: Employees or students of any educational institution receiving federal financial aid.

Details: Extends coverage of the Equal Pay Act and prohibits discrimination on the basis of sex against employers of students.

For More Info: US Equal Employment Opportunity Commission
202-663-4900
www.eeoc.gov

Credit Reporting Act (FCRA)

Who it Affects: All employers, screening firms, credit card companies and any entity involved in providing or using "consumer reports."

Details: The purpose of the Act is to benefit consumers by strengthening privacy provisions and defining more clearly (maybe) the responsibilities and liabilities of businesses that provide information and use and consumer information reporting agencies.

This Act is one of the most influential laws to impact not only employers and employees, but also all Americans. Refer to page 177 for a more detailed explanation.

For More Info: The Consumer Response Center
Federal Trade Commission
Washington, DC 20580
(202) 326-2222
www.ftc.gov

Act found at www.ftc.gov/os/statutes/fcrajump.htm

Consumer Reporting Employment Clarification Act of 1998 (Amendment to FCRA)

Who it Affects: All employers, screening firms, credit card companies and any entity involved in providing or using "consumer reports."

Details: This Act, which is retroactive to October 1, 1997, clarifies criminal record convictions and driving records on commercial drivers.

The Act removes the time limitation on the use of criminal records of older than 7 years within consumer reports. Previously, the FCRA stated that unless an applicant was applying for a position that paid a certain salary or more per year, criminal record information older than 7 years could not be reported by a consumer reporting agency. However, criminal *arrest* information, without conviction, still has a limitation of 7 years.

For More Info: The Consumer Response Center.
Federal Trade Commission
Washington, DC 20580
(202) 326-2222
www.ftc.gov

Freedom of Information Act (FOIA) & Privacy Act Of 1974 (PA)

Who it Affects: All employees. Also, all US citizens with regard to access to information on public officials and information compiled by the CIA and FBI.

Details: The FOIA is an information access law, whereas the PA is an information protection law with limited access provisions. Anyone may submit a FOIA request for any type of record, but a PA request may only be made by the individual (or their legally authorized representative) covered by the requested records. The Privacy Act provides employees access to all information maintained and used in the hiring process, as well as to grant salary increases and promotions (e.g. performance appraisals), and allows for such information to be contested or rebutted in a written document; that must be maintained in the same file.

For More Info: www.usdoj.gov/foia

Immigration Reform & Control Act Of 1986 (IRCA)

Who it Affects: All employers and employees.

Details: Prohibits employers from hiring illegal aliens. This means that employers are required to verify that employees hired after November 6, 1986 are legally entitled to work in this country. Employees must provide employers with documents that show eligibility to work, and identity. Employers must complete an Employment Eligibility Verification Form, known as Form I-9 and provided in this book, attesting under penalty of perjury that they are either US nationals or aliens authorized to work in the United States.

For More Info: Department of Justice
US Immigration & Naturalization Service
202-514-2000
www.ins.usdoj.gov/graphics/index.htm

National Labor Relations Act & Related Laws

Who it Affects: Employers involved in unions and interstate commerce.

Details: The National Labor Relations Act is the primary law governing relations between unions and employers in the private sector. The statute guarantees the right of employees to organize and to bargain collectively with their employers or to refrain from all such activity. Generally applying to all employers involved in interstate commerce--other than airlines, railroads, agriculture, and government--the Act implements the national labor policy of assuring free choice and encouraging collective bargaining as a means of maintaining industrial peace. Through the years, Congress has amended the Act and the Board and courts have developed a body of law drawn from the statute.

For More Info: National Labor Relations Board
1099 14th Street
Washington, D.C. 20570-0001
www.nlrb.gov

Pregnancy Discrimination Act of 1978

Who it Affects: All employers and female employees.

Details: Prohibits discrimination in employment practices on the basis of pregnancy, and requires that medical coverage and leave policies for pregnancy be the same as other medical coverage and/or disability policies.

For More Info: US Equal Employment Opportunity Commission
202-663-4900
www.eeoc.gov

Personal Responsibility & Work Opportunity Reconciliation Act of 1996 (PRWORA)

Who it Affects: All employers and employees.

Details: Also known as the *New Hire Reporting Program.* New Hire reporting is a process by which an employer must report information on newly hired employees to a designated State agency shortly after the date of hire. States will match New Hire reports against child support records to locate parents, establish an order or enforce an existing order for child support. Once these matches are done, the State New Hire agency transmits new hire reports to the National Directory of New Hires (NDNH).

For More Info: Federal Office of Child Support Enforcement
(210) 401-9267
Department of Health and Human Services
www.acf.dhhs.gov

Rehabilitation Act of 1973

Who it Affects: Companies, holding government contracts of $10,000.

Details: The Act requires these employers to take affirmative action to employ and advance qualified, handicapped individuals who meet reasonable standards for employment, that are job related and consistent with business necessity and safe performance of the job. As part of a company's affirmative action plan, reasonable accommodations must be made to the physical and mental limitations of an employee or applicant, unless it can be demonstrated that such an accommodation would impose an undue hardship on the conduct of the company's business.

For More Info: US Equal Employment Opportunity Commission
202-663-4900
www.eeoc.gov
Act found at www.eeoc.gov/laws/rehab.html

Vietnam Era Veteran's Readjustment Assistance Act

Who it Affects: All organization holding a government contract in excess of $25,000.

Details: This prohibits discrimination and requires affirmative action in all personnel practices for special disabled veterans, Vietnam Era veterans, and veterans who served on active duty during a war or in a campaign or expedition for which a campaign badge has been authorized. It applies to all firms that have a nonexempt Government contract or subcontract of $25,000 or more. An affirmative action program is required.

For More Info: The Office of Veterans' Reemployment Rights
Department of Labor
www.dol.gov/dol/esa/public/ofcp_org.htm

Other Topics of Employer Concern Administered by the US Department of Labor

The US Department of Labor is responsible for the administration and enforcement of over 180 federal statutes. These legislative mandates and the regulations produced to implement them cover a wide variety of workplace activities for nearly 10 million employers and well over 125 million workers, including protecting workers' wages, health and safety, employment and pension rights; promoting equal employment opportunity; administering job training, unemployment insurance and workers' compensation programs; strengthening free collective bargaining and collecting; analyzing and publishing labor and economic statistics.

What follows is a brief description of the principal statutes most commonly applicable to businesses. The intent is to acquaint you with the major labor laws and not to offer a detailed exposition of laws and regulations enforced by the Divisions within the Department of Labor. Some of the text below is taken from the US Department of Labor's web site. For detailed information on all of the 180 federal statutes, visit the US Department of Labor's web site at: http://www.dol.gov/dol/public/regs/main.htm.

Agriculture & Migrant Workers

The Migrant and Seasonal Agricultural Worker Protection Act regulates the hiring and employment activities of agricultural employers, contractors and associations using migrant and seasonal workers. The Fair Labor Standards Act has special child-labor regulations that apply to agricultural employment, except for family farms that do not hire outside workers. Administration is by ESA's Wage and Hour Division.

The Immigration and Nationality Act requires employers who want to use foreign temporary workers to get a certificate from the Employment and Training Administration certifying that there are insufficient available and qualified Americans to do the work. The Immigration Reform and Control Act requires all employers of such workers to furnish reports on them to the government.

Construction

Several agencies administer programs related solely to the construction industry. OSHA has special occupational safety and health standards for construction; ESA's Wage and Hour Division, under Davis-Bacon and related acts, requires payment of prevailing wages and benefits; ESA's Office of Federal Contract Compliance Programs has special regulations on non-discrimination and affirmative action hiring; the antikickback section of the Copeland Act precludes a federal contractor from inducing any employee to sacrifice any part of the compensation required.

Employee Protection

Most labor and public-safety laws and many environmental laws mandate whistleblower protections for employees who complain about employers. Remedies can include job reinstatement and payment of back wages. Enforcement is usually by the agency most concerned; e.g., OSHA enforces protections afforded by the Occupational Safety and Health Act.

Family & Medical Leave

Administered by the Wage and Hour Division of ESA, the Family and Medical Leave Act requires employers of 50 or more employees to give up to 12 weeks of unpaid, job-related leave to eligible employees for the birth or adoption of a child or for the serious illness of the employee or a family member.

Garnishment of Wages

Garnishment of employee wages by employers is regulated under the Consumer Credit and Protection Act and administered by the Wage and Hour Division of ESA.

Government Contracts, Grants or Financial Aid

Recipients of government contracts, grants or financial aid are subject to wage, hour, benefits and safety and health standards under:

- The Davis-Bacon Act, which mandates payment of prevailing wages and benefits to employees of contractors engaged in US government construction projects;
- The McNamara-O'Hara Service Contract Act, which set wage rates and other labor standards for employees of contractors furnishing services to the US government;
- The Walsh-Healey Public Contracts Act, which requires the Department of Labor to settle disputes of awards to manufacturers supplying products to the US government.

Administration and enforcement is by ESA's Wage and Hour Division. Non-discrimination and affirmative action requirements related to this subject, found in other statutes, are regulated by ESA's Office of Federal Contract Compliance Programs.

Layoffs and Plant Closings

Such occurrences may be subject to the Worker Adjustment and Retraining Notifications Act (WARN). WARN offers employees early warning of impending layoffs or plant closings. It is administered by the Employment and Training Administration.

Mining Safety & Health

The Federal Mine Safety and Health Act of 1977 covers all people who work on mine property. Administration is by the Mine Safety and Health Administration (MSHA).

The Act ensures employer responsibility for the health and safety of miners; mandates regular inspections of underground and surface mines; establishes miners' training requirements; enables dangerous mines to be closed and prescribes penalties for health and safety violations. MSHA enforces safety and health regulations at more than 4,600 underground and surface coal mines and 11,000 non-coal mines. Health and safety regulations cover numerous hazards, including respirable dust, airborne contaminants and noise; design and maintenance requirements for equipment; roof falls; flammable and explosive gases, dust and smoke; electrical equipment; fires; storage, transport and use of explosives and access to mine entrances and exits.

Pensions & Welfare Benefits

The Employee Retirement Income Security Act (ERISA) regulates employers who offer pension or welfare benefit plans for their employees. It preempts many similar state laws and is administered by the Pension and Welfare Benefits Administration (PWBA). Under the statute, employers must fund an insurance system to protect certain kinds of retirement benefits, with premium payments to the federal government's Pension Benefit Guaranty Corp. Pension plans must meet a wide range of fiduciary, disclosure and reporting requirements. Employee welfare plans must meet similar requirements. PWBA also administers reporting requirements for continuation of health-care provisions, required under the Comprehensive Omnibus Budget Reconciliation Act of 1985 (COBRA).

Transportation

Most laws with labor provisions regulating the transportation industry are administered by agencies outside the Department of Labor. However, longshoring and maritime industry safety and health standards are issued and enforced by OSHA. The Longshoring and Harbor Workers' Compensation Act, administered by ESA, requires employers to assure that workers' compensation is funded and available to eligible employees.

Unions & Their Members

The Labor-Management Reporting and Disclosure Act (also known as the Landrum-Griffin Act) deals with the relationship between a union and its members. It safeguards union funds, requires reports on certain financial transactions and administrative practices of union officials, labor consultants, etc. The act is administered by the Office of Labor-Management Standards, which is part of the Employment Standards Administration.

Veteran's Reemployment Rights

Certain persons who serve in our armed forces have a right to reemployment with the employer they were with when they entered service. This includes those called up from the reserves or National Guard. These rights are administered by the Office of the Assistant Secretary for Veterans' Employment and Training.

Wages & Hours

The Fair Labor Standards Act prescribes standards for wages and overtime pay, which affect most private and public employment. The Wage and Hour Division of the Employment Standards Administration administers the act. It requires employers to pay covered employees the federal minimum wage and overtime of one-and-one-half-times the regular wage. It prohibits certain types of work in an employee's home. It restricts the hours that children under 16 can work and forbids their employment in certain jobs deemed too dangerous. Wage and Hour Division also enforces the workplace provisions of the Immigration and Nationality Act that apply to aliens authorized to work in the US.

Workplace Safety & Health

The Occupational Safety And Health Act (OSHA) is administered by the Occupational Safety and Health Administration (OSHA). Safety and health conditions in most private industries are regulated by OSHA or OSHA-approved state systems. Employers must identify and eliminate unhealthful or hazardous conditions; employees must comply with all rules and regulations that apply to their own workplace conduct. Covered employers are required to maintain safe and healthful work environments in keeping with requirements of the law. Effective OSHA safety and health regulations supersede others originally issued under these other laws: the Walsh-Healey Act, the Services Contract Act, the Contract Work Hours and Safety Standards Act, the Arts and Humanities Act and the Longshore and Harbor Workers' Compensation Act.

Quick Guide Federal Law Chart

Name of Law:	Affects . . .
ALL EMPLOYERS	
Civil Rights Act of 1866, 1871 & the Equal Protection Clause of the 14th Amendment	Discrimination based on race & sex
Equal Pay Act of 1963	Discrimination based on sex
Immigration Reform & Control Act of 1986	Discrimination based on citizenship
National Labor Relations Act & Related Laws	Interstate commerce, discrimination based on race, national origin, religion, sex, religion & union activity/affiliation
Title IX, Education Amendments Act of 1972	Employers of students, discrimination based on sex
Personal Responsibility & Work Opportunity Reconciliation Act of 1996	New hire procedures
EMPLOYERS WITH 15 OR MORE EMPLOYEES	
Title VII, Civil Rights Act of 1964 as amended by the Equal Employment Opportunity Act of 1972	Discrimination based on race, color, religion, sex & national origin
Americans with Disabilities Act	Discrimination against the disabled
EMPLOYERS WITH 20 OR MORE EMPLOYEES	
Age Discrimination in Employment Act of 1967	Discrimination against age
Age Discrimination in Employment Act of 1975	Discrimination against age
EMPLOYERS WITH 50 OR MORE EMPLOYEES	
Executive Orders 11246, 11375 & Revised Orders 4 & 14	Discrimination against race & sex
Rehabilitation Act of 1973	Discrimination against disabled
Pregnancy Discrimination Act of 1978	Discrimination against pregnant women

Recommend Sources:

Private Web Sites:

http://www.employmentlawcentral.com

>This site does an excellent job of disseminating employment law. There are many pages and links to recent laws, opinions, and court cases.

http://www.icle.org

>The Institute of Continuing Legal Education offers an impressive Internet site of educational and legal resource materials, including an Employment Law Central link.

http://guide.lp.findlaw.com/11stategov

>Findlaw.com is a great resource of legal information, including the federal government.

http://www.nolo.com

>Nolo Press is a leading publisher of legal "self-help" books. Their site is filled with great information regarding employment law and compliance.

Government Web Sites:

http://www.eeoc.gov

>US Equal Employment Opportunity Commission oversees a number of the laws mentioned in this lesson.

http://www.ftc.gov

>The Federal Trade Commission oversees the Fair Credit Reporting Act. Go to www.ftc.gov/os/statutes/fcrajump.htm to view the act and notices.

http://www.nlrb.gov

>The National Labor Relations Board oversees employers involved in unions and interstate commerce.

http://www.dol.gov

>The US Department of Labor is responsible for the administration and enforcement of over 180 federal statues dealing with workplace activities.

25 Answers on How to Comply with Other Legal Issues

Sexual Harassment

Sexual harassment is a form of sex discrimination that violates Title VII of the Civil Rights Act of 1964. Portions of the text below have been taken from the web site of the US Equal Employment Opportunity Commission (EEOC) at www.eeoc.gov.

Facts About Sexual Harassment

Unwelcome sexual advances, requests for sexual favors, and other verbal or physical conduct of a sexual nature constitutes sexual harassment when submission to or rejection of this conduct explicitly or implicitly affects an individual's employment, unreasonably interferes with an individual's work performance, or creates an intimidating, hostile or offensive work environment.

Sexual harassment can occur in a variety of circumstances, including but not limited to the following:

- The victim as well as the harasser may be a woman or a man. The victim does not have to be of the opposite sex.
- The harasser can be the victim's supervisor, an agent of the employer, a supervisor in another area, a co-worker, or a non-employee.
- The victim does not have to be the person harassed but could be anyone affected by the offensive conduct.
- Unlawful sexual harassment may occur without economic injury to or discharge of the victim.
- The harasser's conduct must be unwelcome.

It is helpful for the victim to directly inform the harasser that the conduct is unwelcome and must stop. The victim should use any employer complaint mechanism or grievance system available.

When investigating allegations of sexual harassment, EEOC looks at the whole record: the circumstances, such as the nature of the sexual advances, and the context in which the alleged incidents occurred. A determination on the allegations is made from the facts on a case-by-case basis.

Develop a Company Policy on Sexual Harassement

Prevention is the best tool to eliminate sexual harassment in the workplace. Employers should take steps necessary to prevent sexual harassment from occurring and clearly communicate to employees that sexual harassment will not be tolerated.

Employers should establish a complaint or grievance process and take immediate and appropriate action when an employee complains. The *Grievance Process*, discussed on page 192 in Lesson 19, lays out the components for an effective program. This policy should be posted for all to see and printed in the employee handbook. Without a policy in place, an employer's exposure to liability and possible litigation increases dramatically.

Hiring the Handicapped

Title I of the Americans with Disabilities Act prohibits private employers, state and local governments, employment agencies and labor unions from discriminating against qualified individuals with disabilities in job application procedures, hiring, firing, advancement, compensation, job training, and other terms, conditions and privileges of employment.

Enforcement of this act, by the EEOC, pertains to employers with 15 or more employees. As such, these employers must make accomadations for an individual who:

- Has a physical or mental impairment that substantially limits one or more major life activities;
- Has a record of such an impairment; or
- Is regarded as having such an impairment.

A qualified employee or applicant with a disability is an individual who, with or without reasonable accommodation, can perform the essential functions of the job in question. Reasonable accommodation may include, but is not limited to:

- Making existing facilities used by employees readily accessible to and usable by persons with disabilities.
- Job restructuring, modifying work schedules, reassignment to a vacant position;

- Acquiring or modifying equipment or devices, adjusting modifying examinations, training materials, or policies, and providing qualified readers or interpreters.

An employer is required to make an accommodation to the known disability of a qualified applicant or employee if it would not impose an "undue hardship" on the operation of the employer's business. Undue hardship is defined as an action requiring significant difficulty or expense when considered in light of factors such as an employer's size, financial resources and the nature and structure of its operation.

An employer is not required to lower quality or production standards to make an accommodation, nor is an employer obligated to provide personal use items such as glasses or hearing aids.

Age, Race, Ethnic Background, Religion, Pregnancy

US Equal Employment Opportunity Commission (EEOC) regulates job discrimiation for these areas. We suggest visting the EEOC web site at www.eeoc.gov for detailed information regarding these topics.

Retention of Employee Records

Under the Civil Rights and Age Discrimination Acts, all applications must be retained for specific periods, but not less than three years. However, most companies keep the personnel records of former employees much longer to answer reference checks and other inquiries involving insurance.

At a minimum, all personnel records should be retained for a period of three years. Other employee support information, such as time cards or time sheets and work tickets, needs to be kept only for two years.

Employers Monitoring Employees

According to a 2001 Survey performed by the American Management Association, more than three-quarters (77.7%) of major US firms record and review employee communications and activities.

Inspections

Typically, inspections are not for all businesses but should be considered if there is a potential or real problem. Keep in mind, this type of policy can be bad for company morale.

If an attempt to discourage theft, consider a policy that requires employees, upon request, to open briefcases, lunch boxes, desks, lockers, toolboxes, packages and personal automobiles on company property for inspection. If an employer plans to implement such a spot-check program, the following should be considered:

- Provide ample advance notice your rights as an employer and intention to implement the inspection program. Have new-hires sign an acknowledgement that permits a search of personal property at the employer's discretion.

- Insure that the inspections or searches are not discriminatory, nor aimed at a protected class of employees.

- Be sure to have reasonable cause for conducting the search. The US Supreme Court has ruled that, in the public sector, employers may search employer property such as employee offices, desks, and files, without a warrant or probable cause, as long as the search is "reasonable." Apply the inspection uniformly; avoid the appearance of being "out to get" an individual or group of individuals.

Employee Searches

Employee theft is a major problem that involves an individual's privacy rights in the workplace. Again, if appropriate, an employer can begin to control employee theft by implementing a consistent policy that makes the following clear to all employees:

- Company supplies, products or manufactured items of any type may not be removed from their normal locations, (e.g., concealed on an employee's person, or in their toolbox or locker) nor removed from company property.

- Company supplies, products, or manufactured items shall not be given to an employee as a gift, reward or token, except by personnel specifically authorized to do so. Such authorization must be in writing and a removal pass must accompany the item.

- No employee may remove discarded, rejected, or scrap items; specific authorization must be obtained in advance.

Surveillance of Employees

There are no specific federal requirements that restrict the private-sector employer's right to monitor employee activities at work. However, some states restrict electronic monitoring of the employee work, rest, and recreation areas. A few state legislators are proposing legislation that would limit computer monitoring of employees' work habits.

There are numerous bills pending on state and federal levels on this issue, and they periodically receive media attention. Be sure to check the appropriate jurisdiction's status so as not to end up on the wrong side of the law.

Hours of Employment

The Fair Labor Standards Act, which is commonly referred to as the Wages and Hour Act, contains provisions and standards concerning minimum wages, equal pay, maximum hours and overtime pay, record keeping, and child labor. The requirements apply to employees in certain enterprises. However, the law provides exemptions from its standards for employees in certain types of employment.

The amount of money an employee should receive under the minimum wage and overtime provisions cannot be determined without knowing the number of hours he or she has worked. The FLSA does not specifically define "hours of work." The Wage and Hour Division of the US Department of Labor has issued regulations on the subject (29 Code of Federal Regulations, Sec. 785.1-785.50), which are summarized below.

"Suffered Or Permitted" To Work

An employee is working if all of the time an employee is required to be on duty: on the employer's premises; at a prescribed workplace; and all time during which he is "suffered or permitted" to work for the employer. Even if the employer has not requested the employee to perform the work, the employee may only desire to finish a task, correct errors, prepare time or production reports, the reason is immaterial and the time must be counted as hours worked if the employer "knows or has reason to believe" that the employee is continuing to work. This basic rule also applies to work performed away from the employer's premises, job site or even at home. It is the duty of management to exercise its control and to see that work is not performed if it does not want it to be performed.

Preparatory and Concluding Activities

Hours worked include all the time the employee spends engaged in the principal activities that he or she has been employed to perform. Work time does not include activities that are "preliminary or postliminary" to work unless there is a contract or custom providing for payment of wages for this time. For example, normal commuting from home is not ordinarily considered work time. However; time spent walking from the time clock to the workstation is a matter of custom and generally counted as work time. Time spent changing clothes on the employer's premises is usually not considered work time unless the employee is required to wear certain clothes to perform the job.

Dealing With AIDS

Individuals who have been exposed to the AIDS virus pose another major privacy issue. AIDS, like any other workplace privacy issue, requires discretion, education and confidentiality.

A recent US Supreme Court decision (Bragdon v. Abbott 1998) ruled that a person's HIV infection is a disability under the ADA (Americans with Disabilities Act). The ADA prohibits disability discrimination in employment and requires that employers offer accommodations for the disabled.

See below for a first class web site for employers dealing with AIDs.

Recommended Resources:

http://www.eeoc.gov

> The US Equal Employment Opportunity Commission oversees violations of multiple laws including the Civil Rights Act and Americans With Disabilities Act. Their Publications Center can be reached at 1-800-669-3362.

http://www.shrm.org/channels

> The Society for Human Resource Management site has some excellent articles for free. Click on the Employee Relations Channel.

http://www.aidsfund.org/bossguide.htm

> The National Aids Funds provides a great deal of information for employers and managers on how to deal with aids in the workplace. Highly recommended.

http:// www.amanet.org

> The American Management Association is a worldwide leader in management development. With over 7,000 corporate and 225,000 individual members, their web page is an excellent resource for learning programs including e-learning and self-study courses.

Appendix I
The Fair Credit Reporting Act (FCRA) Explained

The Fair Credit Reporting Act (FCRA), first enacted in 1970, was designed to manage the relationship between information users, subjects and providers. The law set standards for providers, rules for users and protections for subjects. It was also meant to eliminate abuses such as using credit information against the best interests of the individual, defining what content consumer credit reports could include, and identifying the permissible purposes for which the information could be used.

Intended to guarantee that the information supplied by Consumer Reporting Agencies (CRAs) is as accurate as possible, the original 1970 FCRA was, by the late 1990's, in need of an update. Foremost among complaints were consumers' frustrations about information providers' (known in the law as "Consumer Reporting Agencies" or "CRAs") unwillingness to quickly correct erroneous information. The FCRA was amended effective September 1997, and again November 1999, to correct some problems. It remains the law of the land.

There are three sections in Appendix I:
1. An Employer's Obligations
2. The Summary of Consumer Rights
3. Quiz

Much of the text was taken from the Federal Trade Commission (FTC) web site. We feel it is an excellent explanation of the FCRA and how the act relates to employers. To view the full text of the FCRA and notices of rights, visit http://www.ftc.gov/ftc/formal.htm and click on the Fair Credit Reporting Act heading on bottom left of the screen.

1. An Employer's Obligations

As an employer, you may use consumer reports when you hire new employees and when you evaluate employees for promotion, reassignment, and retention — as long as you comply with the Fair Credit Reporting Act (FCRA). Sections 604, 606, and 615 of the FCRA spell out your responsibilities when using consumer reports for employment purposes.

The FCRA is designed to protect the privacy of consumer report information and to guarantee that the information supplied by consumer reporting agencies is as accurate as possible. Amendments to the FCRA — which went into effect September 30, 1997 — significantly increase the legal obligations of employers who use consumer reports. Congress expanded employer responsibilities due to concerns that inaccurate or incomplete consumer reports could cause applicants to be denied jobs or cause employees to be denied promotions unjustly. The amendments ensure (1) that individuals are aware that consumer reports may be used for employment purposes and agree to such use, and (2) that individuals are notified promptly if information in a consumer report may result in a negative employment decision.

What is a Consumer Report?

A consumer report contains information about your personal and credit characteristics, character, general reputation, and lifestyle. To be covered by the FCRA, a report must be prepared by a consumer-reporting agency (CRA) — a business that assembles such reports for other businesses.

A fundamental principle of the FCRA is that only entities with a permissible purpose may obtain consumer reports. In other words, the use of personal credit and related information about an individual for purposes other than those enumerated in the Act is not allowed, not for politics, not for newspaper reports, not for fun. This provides everyone with a degree of personal financial privacy.

Employers often do background checks on applicants and get consumer reports during their employment. Some employers only want an applicant or employee's credit payment records; others want driving records and criminal histories. For sensitive positions, it's not unusual for employers to order investigative consumer reports — reports that include interviews with an applicant or employee's friends, neighbors, and associates. All of these types of reports are consumer reports if they are obtained from a CRA.

Applicants are often asked to give references. Whether verifying such references is covered by the FCRA depends on who does the verification. A reference verified by the employer *is not* covered by the Act; a reference verified by an employment or reference-checking agency (or other CRA) *is* covered. Section 603(o) provides special procedures for reference checking; otherwise, checking references may constitute an investigative consumer report subject to additional FCRA requirements.

Key Provisions of the FCRA Amendments

The applicability of the FCRA is much more pervasive than most people realize. For example, every employer using a consumer report to determine the worthiness of employees and potential employees must be especially diligent to obey the guidelines and rules of the FCRA. Doing so will avoid serious legal problems.

Written Notice and Authorization

The amended FCRA states that an employer who wishes to utilize a consumer report must make the individual — whether they are a job applicant or a current employee — aware that a consumer report may be obtained, and the individual must agree to such use. Additionally, the individual must be notified promptly if information in a consumer report *may* result in a negative employment decision. Before you can get a consumer report for employment purposes, you must notify the individual in writing — in a document consisting solely of this notice — that a report may be used. You also must get the person's written authorization before you ask a CRA for the report. Certain exceptions apply to the trucking industry—see next page.

How Long Can a CRA Report Negative Information?

Seven years. But, there are certain exceptions:

- Information about criminal convictions may be reported without any time limitation.
- Bankruptcy information may be reported for ten years.
- Information reported in response to an application for a job with a salary of more than $75,000 has no time limit.
- Information reported because of an application for more than $150,000 worth of credit or life insurance has no time limit.
- Information about a lawsuit or an unpaid judgment against you can be reported for seven years or until the statute of limitations runs out, whichever is longer.

Adverse Action Procedures

If you rely on any part of a consumer report—even in part—for an "adverse action"—denying a job application, reassigning or terminating an employee, or denying a promotion—be aware that:

> **Step 1**: Before you take the adverse action, you must give the individual a pre-adverse action disclosure that includes a copy of the individual's consumer report and a copy of "A Summary of Your Rights Under the Fair Credit Reporting Act" — a document prescribed by the Federal Trade Commission. The CRA that

furnishes the individual's report will give you the summary of consumer rights. (A copy of the FCRA-prescribed text is included at the end of this appendix.)

Step 2: After you've taken an adverse action, you must give the individual notice — orally, in writing, or electronically — that the action has been taken. This is called an adverse action notice. It must include:

- the name, address, and phone number of the CRA that supplied the report;
- a statement that the CRA that supplied the report did not make the decision to take the adverse action and cannot give specific reasons for it; and
- a notice of the individual's right to dispute the accuracy or completeness of any information the agency furnished, and his or her right to an additional free consumer report from the agency upon request within 60 days.

Certifications to Consumer Reporting Agencies

Before giving you an individual's consumer report, the CRA will require you to certify that you are in compliance with the FCRA and that you will not misuse any information in the report in violation of federal or state equal employment opportunity laws or regulations.

In 1998, Congress amended the FCRA to provide special procedures for mail, telephone, or electronic employment applications in the trucking industry. The federal FCRA, in some circumstances, does not required these employers to make written disclosures and obtain written permission in the case of applicants who will be subject to state or federal regulation as truckers. (State FCRAs or Department of Motor Vehicles may still require written permission.) Finally, no pre-adverse action disclosure or Section 615(a) disclosure is required in the circumstances in which a written release exception is utilized. Instead, the employer must, within three days of the decision, provide an oral, written, or electronic adverse action disclosure consisting of: (1) a statement that an adverse action has been taken based on a consumer report; (2) the name, address, and telephone number of the CRA; (3) a statement that the CRA did not make the decision; and (4) a statement that the consumer may obtain a copy of the actual report from the employer if he or she provides identification.

Consequences of Non-Compliance

There are legal consequences for employers who fail to get an applicant's permission before requesting a consumer report or who fail to provide pre-adverse action disclosures and adverse action notices to unsuccessful job applicants. The FCRA allows individuals to sue employers for damages in federal court. A person who successfully sues is entitled to recover court costs and reasonable legal fees. The law also allows individuals to seek punitive damages for deliberate violations. In addition, the Federal Trade Commission, other federal agencies, and the states may sue employers for non-compliance and obtain civil penalties.

Editor's Note: The following text is taken directly from the FTC web site. This is required language of the summary that must be issued to applicants who are not hired because of an "adverse action," as explained earlier.

2. Prescribed Summary of Consumer Rights

The prescribed form for this summary is as a separate document, on paper no smaller than 8x11 inches in size, with text no less than 12-point type (8-point for the chart of federal agencies), in bold or capital letters as indicated. The form in this appendix prescribes both the content and the sequence of items in the required summary. A summary may accurately reflect changes in numerical items that change over time (e.g., dollar mounts, or phone numbers and addresses of federal agencies), and remain in compliance.

A Summary of Your Rights Under the Fair Credit Reporting Act

The federal Fair Credit Reporting Act (FCRA) is designed to promote accuracy, fairness, and privacy of information in the files of every "consumer reporting agency" (CRA). Most CRAs are credit bureaus that gather and sell information about you -- such as if you pay your bills on time or have filed bankruptcy -- to creditors, employers, landlords, and other businesses. You can find the complete text of the FCRA, 15 U.S.C. 1681-1681u, at the Federal Trade Commission's web site (*http://www.ftc.gov*). The FCRA gives you specific rights, as outlined below. You may have additional rights under state law. You may contact a state or local consumer protection agency or a state attorney general to learn those rights.

- **You must be told if information in your file has been used against you.** Anyone who uses information from a CRA to take action against you -- such as denying an application for credit, insurance, or employment -- must tell you, and give you the name, address, and phone number of the CRA that provided the consumer report.
- **You can find out what is in your file.** At your request, a CRA must give you the information in your file, and a list of everyone who has requested it recently.

There is no charge for the report if a person has taken action against you because of information supplied by the CRA, if you request the report within 60 days of receiving notice of the action. You also are entitled to one free report every twelve months upon request if you certify that (1) you are unemployed and plan to seek employment within 60 days, (2) you are on welfare, or (3) your report is inaccurate due to fraud. Otherwise, a CRA may charge you up to eight dollars.

- **You can dispute inaccurate information with the CRA.** If you tell a CRA that your file contains inaccurate information, the CRA must investigate the items (usually within 30 days) by presenting to its information source all relevant evidence you submit, unless your dispute is frivolous. The source must review your evidence and report its findings to the CRA. (The source also must advise national CRAs -- to which it has provided the data -- of any error.) The CRA must give you a written report of the investigation, and a copy of your report if the investigation results in any change. If the CRA's investigation does not resolve the dispute, you may add a brief statement to your file. The CRA must normally include a summary of your statement in future reports. If an item is deleted or a dispute statement is filed, you may ask that anyone who has recently received your report be notified of the change.

- **Inaccurate information must be corrected or deleted.** A CRA must remove or correct inaccurate or unverified information from its files, usually within 30 days after you dispute it. **However, the CRA is not required to remove accurate data from your file unless it is outdated (as described below) or cannot be verified.** If your dispute results in any change to your report, the CRA cannot reinsert into your file a disputed item unless the information source verifies its accuracy and completeness. In addition, the CRA must give you a written notice telling you it has reinserted the item. The notice must include the name, address and phone number of the information source.

- **You can dispute inaccurate items with the source of the information.** If you tell anyone -- such as a creditor who reports to a CRA -- that you dispute an item, they may not then report the information to a CRA without including a notice of your dispute. In addition, once you've notified the source of the error in writing, it may not continue to report the information if it is, in fact, an error.

- **Outdated information may not be reported.** In most cases, a CRA may not report negative information that is more than seven years old; ten years for bankruptcies.

- **Access to your file is limited.** A CRA may provide information about you only to people with a need recognized by the FCRA -- usually to consider an application with a creditor, insurer, employer, landlord, or other business.

- **Your consent is required for reports that are provided to employers, or reports that contain medical information.** A CRA may not give out information about you to your employer, or prospective employer, without your

written consent. A CRA may not report medical information about you to creditors, insurers, or employers without your permission.
- **You may choose to exclude your name from CRA lists for unsolicited credit and insurance offers.** Creditors and insurers may use file information as the basis for sending you unsolicited offers of credit or insurance. Such offers must include a toll-free phone number for you to call if you want your name and address removed from future lists. If you call, you must be kept off the lists for two years. If you request, complete, and return the CRA form provided for this purpose, you must be taken off the lists indefinitely.
- **You may seek damages from violators.** If a CRA, a user or (in some cases) a provider of CRA data, violates the FCRA, you may sue them in state or federal court.

3. Quiz—Let's Look at the Following Four Scenarios:

Question One: You advertise vacancies for cashiers and receive 100 applications. You want to order credit reports on each applicant because you plan to eliminate those with poor credit histories. What are your obligations?

Answer One: You can get credit reports — one type of consumer report — if you notify each applicant in writing that a credit report may be requested *and if* you receive the applicant's written consent. Before you reject an applicant based on credit report information, you must make a pre-adverse action disclosure that includes a copy of the credit report and the summary of consumer rights under the FCRA. Once you've rejected an applicant, you must provide an adverse action notice if credit report information affected your decision.

Question Two: You are considering a number of your long-term employees for a major promotion. You want to check their consumer reports to ensure that only responsible individuals are considered for the position. What are your obligations?

Answer Two: You cannot get consumer reports unless the employees have been notified that reports may be obtained and have given their written permission. If the employees gave you written permission in the past, you need only make sure that the employees receive or have received a "separate document" notice that reports may be obtained during the course of their employment — no more notice or permission is required. If your employees have not received notice and given you permission, you must notify the employees and get their written permission before you get their reports.

In each case where information in the report influences your decision to deny promotion, you must provide the employee with a pre-adverse action disclosure. The employee also must receive an adverse action notice once you have selected another individual for the job.

Question Three: A job applicant gives you the okay to get a consumer report. Although the credit history is poor and that's a negative factor, the applicant's lack of relevant experience carries more weight in your decision not to hire. What's your responsibility?

Answer Three: In any case where information in a consumer report is a factor in your decision — even if the report information is not a major consideration — you must follow the procedures mandated by the FCRA. In this case, you would be required to provide the applicant a pre-adverse action disclosure before you reject his or her application. When you formally reject the applicant, you would be required to provide an adverse action notice.

Question Four: The applicants for a sensitive financial position have authorized you to obtain credit reports. You reject one applicant whose credit report shows a debt load that may be too high for the proposed salary, even though the report shows a good repayment history. You turn down another, whose credit report shows only one credit account, because you want someone who has shown more financial responsibility. Are you obliged to provide any notices to these applicants?

Answer Four: Both applicants are entitled to a pre-adverse action disclosure and an adverse action notice. If any information in the credit report influences an adverse decision, the applicant is entitled to the notices — even when the information isn't negative.

Appendix II
The Social Security Number Check

Social Security Number Allocations

The Social Security Administration holds information about an individual as confidential, and, by law, cannot disclose it except in very restricted cases where regulations allow release of personal information. However, for verifying the authenticity of a card, Social Security Numbers are very revealing, especially when the numeric codes used for the assignment of the nine digit numbers are known. Those codes are given here.

Using Social Security Number Chart 1

A Social Security Number's first three digits, known as the area number, are determined by (but do not necessarily match) the Zip Code of the mailing address shown on the application for a Social Security Number. In using Social Security Number Chart 1, keep in mind these rules about the Numbers :

- Any Social Security Number beginning with 000 is not valid.
- An asterisk (*) indicates new areas where Social Security Numbers will be allocated, but are **not yet issued**. If a job applicant would present a card that begins with one of these numbers, it would not be a valid card.
- 700-728 - Once issued to railroad employees, the practice was discontinued as of July 1, 1963. This sequence does not appear on the chart.

While at first it would seem that if a person's Social Security Number did not match their primary state of residence or birth state, then the card would be suspect. That is not always the case as there are certain three digit numbers that have been transferred from one state to another. Or, in some cases, an area has been divided for use among certain geographic locations. These exceptions are given in the following chart. Numbers designed as "not yet issued" are intended for use later for the state indicated.

Social Security Number Chart 1

This is a numerical listing of Social Security Number "area" codes. Includes US Territories and locations where United States Social Security Numbers have been issued. Italicized items (each accompanied by an asterisk) are card numbers not yet issued as of May 1, 2001.

Numbers Inclusive	Location	Numbers Inclusive	Location	Numbers Inclusive	Location
001 – 003	New Hampshire	429 – 432	Arkansas	585	New Mexico
004 – 007	Maine	433 – 439	Louisiana	586	Guam
008 – 009	Vermont	440 – 448	Oklahoma	586	American Samoa
010 – 034	Massachusetts	449 – 467	Texas	586	Philippine Islands
035 – 039	Rhode Island	468 – 477	Minnesota	587	Mississippi
040 – 049	Connecticut	478 – 485	Iowa	*588**	*(MS - not yet issued)*
050 – 134	New York	486 – 500	Missouri	589 – 595	Florida
135 – 158	New Jersey	501 – 502	North Dakota	596 – 599	Puerto Rico
159 – 211	Pennsylvania	503 – 504	South Dakota	600 – 601	Arizona
212 – 220	Maryland	505 – 508	Nebraska	602 – 626	California
221 – 222	Delaware	509 – 515	Kansas	627 – 645	Texas
223 – 231	Virginia	516 – 517	Montana	646 – 647	Utah
232 – 236	West Virginia	518 – 519	Idaho	648 – 649	New Mexico
232	North Carolina	520	Wyoming	650 – 653	Colorado
237 – 246	North Carolina	521 – 524	Colorado	654 – 658	South Carolina
247 – 251	South Carolina	525	New Mexico	659 – 665	Louisiana
252 – 260	Georgia	526 – 527	Arizona	667 – 675	Georgia
261 – 267	Florida	528 – 529	Utah	*676 – 679**	*(AR - not yet issued)*
268 – 302	Ohio	530	Nevada	680	Nevada
303 – 317	Indiana	531 – 539	Washington	*681 – 690**	*(NC - not yet issued)*
318 – 361	Illinois	540 – 544	Oregon	*691 – 699**	*(VA - not yet issued)*
362 – 386	Michigan	545 – 573	California	750 – 751	Hawaii
387 – 399	Wisconsin	574	Alaska	*752 – 755**	*(MS - not yet issued)*
400 – 407	Kentucky	575 – 576	Hawaii	*756 – 763**	*(TN - not yet issued)*
408 – 415	Tennessee	577 – 579	Dist of Columbia	764 – 765	Arizona
416 – 424	Alabama	580	Virgin Islands	766 – 768	Florida
425 – 428	Mississippi	580 – 584	Puerto Rico	*769 – 772**	*(FL - not yet issued)*

Social Security Number Chart 2

This is an alphabetical listing by state or territory name, including all locations where United States Social Security Numbers have been issued.

Location	Numbers Inclusive	Location	Numbers Inclusive	Location	Numbers Inclusive
Alabama	416 – 424	Iowa	478 – 485	North Dakota	501 – 502
Alaska	574	Kansas	509 – 519	Ohio	268 – 302
American Samoa	586	Kentucky	400 – 407	Oklahoma	440 – 448
Arizona	526 – 527, 600 – 601, 764 – 765	Louisiana	433 – 439, 659 – 665	Oregon	540 – 544
				Pennsylvania	159 – 211
Arkansas	429 – 432,	Maine	004 – 007	Philippine Islands	586
(not yet issued)	676 – 679*	Maryland	212 – 220	Puerto Rico	580 – 584, 596 – 599
California	545 – 573, 602 – 626	Massachusetts	010 – 034		
		Michigan	362 – 386	Rhode Island	035 – 039
Colorado	521 – 524, 650 – 653	Minnesota	468 – 477	South Carolina	247 – 251, 654 – 658
		Mississippi	425 – 428, 587	South Dakota	503 – 504
Connecticut	040 – 049	(not yet issued)	588*	Tennessee	408 – 415,
Delaware	221 – 222	(not yet issued)	752 – 755*	(not yet issued)	756 – 763*
Dist of Columbia	577 – 579	Missouri	486 – 500	Texas	449 – 467, 627 – 645
Florida	261 – 267, 589 – 595, 766 – 768,	Montana	516 – 517		
		Nebraska	505 – 508	Utah	528 – 529, 646 – 647
(not yet issued)	769 – 772*	Nevada	530 & 680		
Georgia	252 – 260, 667 – 675	New Hampshire	001 – 003	Vermont	008 – 009
		New Jersey	135 – 158	Virgin Islands	580
Guam	586	New Mexico	525 & 585, 648 – 649	Virginia	223 – 231,
Hawaii	575 – 576, 750 – 751			(not yet issued)	691 – 699*
		New York	050 – 134	Washington	531 – 539
Idaho	518 – 519	North Carolina	232, 237 – 246,	West Virginia	232 – 236
Illinois	318 – 361			Wisconsin	387 – 399
Indiana	303 – 317	(not yet issued)	681 – 690*	Wyoming	520

Appendix II - The Social Security Number Check   260

Social Security Number Chart 3

While the first three digits of every nine digit Social Security Number denote the *area* or state where the application for an original Social Security Number was submitted, the middle two digits (digit four and five, which are known as the *group numbers*) are also numerically coded. Lastly, within each nine digit Social Security Number, are the *serial numbers*, which comprise the last four digits. These four serial numbers run consecutively from 0001 through 9999. Once serial number 9999 is assigned, the next *group number* (the two middle digits) is assigned, and serial number 0001 would be the first assigned with it.

These fourth and fifth digits range from 01 to 99 but they are not assigned in consecutive order. For administrative purposes, the first two-digit group numbers consist of the ODD numbers from 01 through 09. Later, the EVEN numbers from 10 through 98 are issued.

After all the numbers in group 98 of a particular area are issued, then the EVEN groups 02 through 08 (02, 04, 06, 08) are used, followed by the ODD groups, 11 through 99.

Thus, the order of issuance of the two middle digit numbers are:

1st: ODD - 01, 03, 05, 07, 09 2nd: EVEN – 10 to 98

3rd: EVEN – 02, 04, 06, 08 4th *and finally:* ODD – 11 to 99

By examining the latest monthly Highest Group Issued Table for the *latest* SSN area ranges to date, an invalid number can spotted when it greater than the number the Social Administration has issued.

For example, if presented with an Social Security Card with the number 606-39-0001, check the latest Highest Group Issued Table (Social Security Chart 3 below is effective as of May, 2001). Finding that the latest 606 number issue was 606 25, number 606 39 could *not* have been issued, therefore it is not legitimate. However, a card with 606 03 would be a number that had been issued.

Consider this: if the card read 606-23-0001, it could be a valid card, although it would probably have to belong to someone quite young, as 606 23 is quite close to the latest number issued, 606 25.

Social Security Chart 3 – Highest Group Issued Table shows the Social Security Number area (first three) numbers and group (middle two) numbers that are in the process of being issued as of May 1, 2001.

Appendix II - The Social Security Number Check

Social Security Chart 3 – Highest Group Issued Table as of May 1, 2001

Area #s	Group #s	Area #s	Group #s	Area #s	Group #s	Area #s	Group #s	Area #s	Group #s	Area #s	Group #s
001	96	002	94	003	94	004	02	005	02	006	02
007	98	008	84	009	84	010	84	011	84	012	84
013	84	014	84	015	84	016	84	017	84	018	84
019	84	020	84	021	84	022	84	023	84	024	84
025	84*	026	82	027	82	028	82	029	82	030	82
031	82	032	82	033	82	034	82	035	68	036	68
037	66	038	66	039	66	040	02	041	02	042	02
043	02	044	02	045	02	046	02	047	02	048	02
049	02*	050	90	051	90	052	90	053	90	054	90
055	90	056	90	057	90	058	90	059	90	060	90
061	90	062	90	063	90	064	90	065	90	066	90
067	90	068	90	069	90	070	90	071	90	072	90
073	90	074	90	075	90	076	90	077	90	078	90
079	90	080	90	081	90	082	90	083	90	084	90
085	90	086	90	087	90	088	90	089	90	090	90
091	90	092	90	093	90	094	90	095	90	096	90*
097	90*	098	90*	099	88	100	88	101	88	102	88
103	88	104	88	105	88	106	88	107	88	108	88
109	88	110	88	111	88	112	88	113	88	114	88
115	88	116	88	117	88	118	88	119	88	120	88
121	88	122	88	123	88	124	88	125	88	126	88
127	88	128	88	129	88	130	88	131	88	132	88
133	88	134	88	135	08	136	08	137	08	138	08
139	08	140	08	141	08	142	08	143	08	144	08
145	08	146	08	147	08*	148	06	149	06	150	06
151	06	152	06	153	06	154	06	155	06	156	06
157	06	158	06	159	80	160	80	161	80	162	80
163	80	164	80	165	80	166	80	167	80	168	80

An Asterisk (*) indicates a change that became effective 4/2001

Continued Next Page

Appendix II - The Social Security Number Check 262

Social Security Chart 3 *Continued* – Highest Group Issued Table as of May 1, 2001

Area #s	Group #s	Area #s	Group #s	Area #s	Group #s	Area #s	Group #s	Area #s	Group #s	Area #s	Group #s
169	80	170	80*	171	78	172	78	173	78	174	78
175	78	176	78	177	78	178	78	179	78	180	78
181	78	182	78	183	78	184	78	185	78	186	78
187	78	188	78	189	78	190	78	191	78	192	78
193	78	194	78	195	78	196	78	197	78	198	78
199	78	200	78	201	78	202	78	203	78	204	78
205	78	206	78	207	78	208	78	209	78	210	78
211	78	212	61*	213	59	214	59	215	59	216	59
217	59	218	59	219	59	220	59*	221	94	222	92
223	89	224	89	225	89	226	89	227	89	228	89
229	89*	230	87	231	87	232	47	233	47	234	47
235	47	236	47	237	95	238	95	239	95	240	95
241	95	242	95	243	95	244	95*	245	93	246	93
247	99	248	99	249	99	250	99	251	99	252	99
253	99	254	99	255	99	256	99	257	99	258	99
259	99	260	99	261	99	262	99	263	99	264	99
265	99	266	99	267	99	268	06	269	06	270	06
271	06	272	06	273	06	274	06	275	06	276	06
277	06	278	06	279	06*	280	04	281	04	282	04
283	04	284	04	285	04	286	04	287	04	288	04
289	04	290	04	291	04	292	04	293	04	294	04
295	04	296	04	297	04	298	04	299	04	300	04
301	04	302	04	303	23	304	23	305	23	306	23
307	23	308	23	309	23	310	23	311	23	312	23
313	23	314	23	315	23*	316	21	317	21	318	98
319	98	320	98	321	98	322	98	323	98	324	98
325	98	326	98	327	98	328	98	329	98	330	98
331	98	332	98	333	98*	334	96	335	96	336	96

An Asterisk (*) indicates a change that became effective 4/2001

Continued Next Page

Social Security Chart 3 *Continued* – Highest Group Issued Table as of May 1, 2001

Area #s	Group #s	Area #s	Group #s	Area #s	Group #s	Area #s	Group #s	Area #s	Group #s	Area #s	Group #s
337	96	338	96	339	96	340	96	341	96	342	96
343	96	344	96	345	96	346	96	347	96	348	96
349	96	350	96	351	96	352	96	353	96	354	96
355	96	356	96	357	96	358	96	359	96	360	96
361	96	362	27	363	27	364	27*	365	25	366	25
367	25	368	25	369	25	370	25	371	25	372	25
373	25	374	25	375	25	376	25	377	25	378	25
379	25	380	25	381	25	382	25	383	25	384	25
385	25	386	25	387	21	388	21	389	21	390	21
391	21	392	21	393	19	394	19	395	19	396	19
397	19	398	19	399	19	400	57	401	57	402	57
403	57	404	57	405	55	406	55	407	55	408	91
409	91	410	89	411	89	412	89	413	89	414	89
415	89	416	53	417	53	418	51	419	51	420	51
421	51	422	51	423	51	424	51	425	89	426	89
427	89	428	89	429	99	430	99	431	99	432	99
433	99	434	99	435	99	436	99	437	99	438	99
439	99	440	15	441	15	442	15	443	15	444	15*
445	13	446	13	447	13	448	13	449	99	450	99
451	99	452	99	453	99	454	99	455	99	456	99
457	99	458	99	459	99	460	99	461	99	462	99
463	99	464	99	465	99	466	99	467	99	468	39
469	39	470	39	471	39	472	39	473	39*	474	37
475	37	476	37	477	37	478	31	479	31	480	31*
481	29	482	29	483	29	484	29	485	29	486	17
487	17	488	17	489	17	490	17	491	17	492	17
493	17	494	17	495	17	496	17	497	17	498	17

An Asterisk (*) indicates a change that became effective 4/2001

Continued Next Page

Social Security Chart 3 *Continued* – Highest Group Issued Table as of May 1, 2001

Area #s	Group #s	Area #s	Group #s	Area #s	Group #s	Area #s	Group #s	Area #s	Group #s	Area #s	Group #s
499	15	500	15	501	27	502	27*	503	31	504	31
505	43	506	43	507	41	508	41	509	19	510	19
511	19	512	19	513	19	514	17	515	17	516	35
517	35	518	61	519	59	520	43	521	99	522	99
523	99	524	99	525	99	526	99	527	99	528	99
529	99	530	99	531	47	532	47	533	47	534	47*
535	45	536	45	537	45	538	45	539	45	540	59
541	59	542	59	543	59	544	57	545	99	546	99
547	99	548	99	549	99	550	99	551	99	552	99
553	99	554	99	555	99	556	99	557	99	558	99
559	99	560	99	561	99	562	99	563	99	564	99
565	99	566	99	567	99	568	99	569	99	570	99
571	99	572	99	573	99	574	33	575	89	576	89
577	33	578	31	579	31	580	33	581	99	582	99
583	99	584	99	585	99	586	45	587	87	589	99
590	99	591	99	592	99	593	99	594	99	595	99
596	66	597	66	598	66	599	64	600	99	601	99
602	25	603	25	604	25	605	25	606	25	607	25
608	25	609	25	610	25*	611	25*	612	25*	613	25*
614	25*	615	25*	616	23	617	23	618	23	619	23
620	23	621	23	622	23	623	23	624	23	625	23
626	23	627	76	628	76	629	76*	630	76*	631	76*
632	74	633	74	634	74	635	74	636	74	637	74
638	74	639	74	640	74	641	74	642	74	643	74
644	74	645	74	646	58	647	56	648	24	649	22
650	18	651	18*	652	16	653	16	654	10	655	10
656	09	657	09	658	09	659	03	660	03	661	03
662	03	663	03*	664	01	665	01	667	12*	668	10

An Asterisk (*) indicates a change that became effective 4/2001

Continued Next Page

Social Security Chart 3 *Continued* – Highest Group Issued Table as of May 1, 2001

Area #s	Group #s	Area #s	Group #s	Area #s	Group #s	Area #s	Group #s	Area #s	Group #s	Area #s	Group #s
669	10	670	10	671	10	672	10	673	10	674	10
675	10*	676	01	677	01*	680	30*	700	18	701	18
702	18	703	18	704	18	705	18	706	18	707	18
708	18	709	18	710	18	711	18	712	18	713	18
714	18	715	18	716	18	717	18	718	18	719	18
720	18	721	18	722	18	723	18	724	28	725	18
726	18	727	10	728	14	764	09	765	07	766	01
767	01*	768	01*	769	01*	770	01*	771	01*		

An Asterisk (*) indicates a change that became effective 4/2001

Appendix II - The Social Security Number Check

Sample Social Security Activity Report

```
NAME:                              MARY SMITH
SOCIAL SECURITY NUMBER:            111-11-1111
STATE OF ISSUE:                    PENNSYLVANIA
YEAR OF ISSUE:                     1960
```

Social Security Number - Cross-checking with resume, application, and other sources Required!

```
SOCIAL SECURITY NUMBER VERIFICATION:

03-94:   MARY A. SMITH, 1 MAIN ST., PATERSON, NJ 07513
12-93:   MARY B. SMITH, 1 MAIN ST., PATERSON, NJ 07513
01-93:   MARY SMITH, 2 FIRST ST., GARFIELD, NJ 07026
09-92:   MARY A. JONES, 3 MAPLE ST., GARFIELD, NJ 07026
03-91:   MARY A. SMITH, 3 MAPLE ST., GARFIELD, NJ 07026
03-91:   C. SMITH, 3 MAPLE ST., GARFIELD, NJ  07026
09-90:   MARY JONES, 4 CEDAR ST., PASSAIC, NJ 07055
03-90:   MARY JONES, 5 PALM COURT, BOCA RATON, FL
08-89:   MARY JONES, 6 OCEAN VIEW WAY, FT. LAUDERDALE, FL

AKA LISTED AS:  MARY JONES
EMPLOYER LISTED IN 01-93:   ABC COMPANY, NJ
EMPLOYER LISTED IN 03-90:   DEF COMPANY, FLORIDA
YEAR OF BIRTH LISTED AS:    1945
AGE LISTED AS:  49
MIDDLE INITIAL LISTED AS:   A and B
SPOUSE INITIAL LISTED AS:   C
```

Check Against Date of Birth on Application and Resume

```
SUBJECT'S NUMBER WAS ALSO USED ONCE IN 03-91 BY A C. SMITH.
INVESTIGATION REVEALS THAT THIS APPEARS TO BE THE SUBJECT'S
SPOUSE.

SUBJECT IS ALSO LISTED AS USING SOCIAL SECURITY NUMBER
222-22-2222. INVESTIGATION REVEALS THAT THIS NUMBER APPEARS TO
BELONG TO HER SPOUSE, C. SMITH.

SUBJECT IS ALSO LISTED AS USING SOCIAL SECURITY NUMBER
333-33-3333 IN 03-90 AND 09-90. THE ONLY INFORMATION FOUND IN
CONNECTION WITH THIS NUMBER INVOLVES THIS SUBJECT. INFORMATION
FOLLOWS:

09-90:   MARY JONES, 4 CEDAR ST., PASSAIC, NJ 07055

03-90:   MARY JONES, 5 PALM COURT, BOCA RATON, FL
```

How to Verify Social Security Numbers Free Through the Social Security Administration

The Social Security Administration (SSA) Enumeration Verification Services (EVS) is a free service that permits employers to match names and SSNs before submitting W-2 Forms (Wage and Tax Statements). This service is also available to third-party submitters— accountants, service bureaus, etc.

💡 **KEY POINT:** This form of Social Security Number verification through the Social Security Administration can only be done after an employee is hired.

Making sure names and SSNs entered on the W-2 match Social Security's records is important because unmatched records can result in additional processing costs for the employer and uncredited earnings for employees. Uncredited earnings can affect future eligibility to (and amounts paid under) Social Security's retirement, disability and survivors program.

How to Use EVS

EVS is easy to use. Employers must complete the registration form, sign the appropriate privacy act statement, then mail or fax the forms to SSA. Soon after, SSA issues a requester identification code to the employee who can then submit a data file or paper listing for verification.

EVS is ideal for verifying an entire payroll database or when hiring more than 50 workers at a time. Requests for verification can be submitted year around and generally take 30 days or less to process.

Employers with less than 50 Requests

To verify less than 50 names and SSNs, you do not need to use Social Security's EVS or register ahead of time. By calling the toll-free number for employers, 1-800-772-6270, or SSA's general toll-free number, 1-800-772-1213, employers receive verification for up to 5 names/SSNs over the telephone. Include first name, last name, middle initial, date of birth, sex, and SSN. Both telephone numbers are open for service weekdays from 7:00 AM to 7:00 PM Eastern Time.

To verify 6 to 50 names and SSNs, contact a local Social Security office. There are over 1,300 local offices.

Registration Instructions for Employers and Third-Party Submitters

For more information, visit the SSA's home page at www.ssa.gov.

Appendix II - The Social Security Number Check

Appendix III
Employer Forms

Feel free to use these forms as templates for your company's own custom forms. Not all of the forms included in this book will be useful to every business. A few alterations might make the forms work even better. However, be mindful not to add questions that expose the company to discrimination claims.

Not all positions within a company perform the same function. Rather, one company may have a varied work force, ranging from drivers to clerks to professionals. As such, one generic application for all positions is typically insufficient and is not recommended. Employers should consider using applications that are tailored to individual positions or "job families." The extra effort and minor expense of producing tailor-made applications is more than offset by the long-range savings of time and getting only the specific information you need.

All forms used in this book are freely available for use. You can download them from www.brbpub.com/forms.htm.

Appendix III - Employer Forms

Name of Form	Page Number In Lesson	Page Number In Appendix
Applicant/Resume Evaluation	39 & 125	271
Applicant Waiver	33	272
Basic Application, page 1	25	273
Basic Application, page 2	25	274
Basic Application, page 3	25	275
Confidentiality Agreement	135	276
Criminal Background Check Release	36	277
Employee Data Sheet	131	278
Employment Eligibility Verification (I-9)	32	279
Exit Interview Report, page 1	211	280
Exit Interview Report, page 2	211	281
General Release Form	34	282
Induction Form	133	283
Local Police Information Request	79	284
Military Records Request, front	87	285
Military Records Request, reverse	88	286
New Employee Record Chart	132	287
New Hire Reporting Form	147	288
Non-Compete Agreement	136	289
Performance Review, page 1	177	290
Performance Review, page 2	178	291
Pre-Employment Check by Phone	68	292
Rejection Letter Sample	141	293
Request For Education Verification	82	294
Request For Information	70	295
Substance Abuse Screening Test Consent	222	296
Workers' Compensation Release	224	297

Applicant/Resume Evaluation

APPLICANT/RESUME EVALUATION

Completion of this form assists compliance with non-discrimination guidelines and ensures the basis for hire and reject decisions are documented and job related.

Name of Applicant: _____

Date Application/Resume Received: _____

Position Available: _____

Will Applicant be Interviewed: _____ Yes   Date of Interview: _____

                               _____ No   Reason for Rejection: _____
                                                                 Code Number(s)

Will Job be extended: _____ Yes Title: _____ Salary: _____

                        _____ No

Job-Related Reason Applicant is Best Qualified: _____

_____

If No, Reason for Rejection: _____
                          Code Number(s)

_____
Signature Interviewer/Evaluator   Position/Department   Date

You have the right to hire qualified individuals and to reject unqualified individuals. Selection and rejection decisions must be based on valid job-related criteria that are consistently applied to all applicants. The following are acceptable reasons for rejection provided the same statement could not be applied to the selected candidate. If numbers 1-8 do not apply, please complete 9 with a job-related reason.

1. *Does not meet minimum job requirements*
2. *Meets minimum requirements but not best qualified*
3. *Cannot work required hours/schedule*
4. *Cannot perform physical requirements of job*
5. *Prior experience unrelated*
6. *Less related experience than person selected*
7. *Less related education/training than person selected*
8. *Lower skill level than person selected*
9. *Other (specify)* _____

Appendix III - Employer Forms

Applicant Waiver

Applicant Waiver Form

(To be signed by all job applicants along with application form.)

1. I agree and understand that all the information and statements on my application are correct and no attempt has been made to conceal or withhold pertinent information. I agree that any omission, falsification, or misrepresentation is cause for my immediate termination at any time during my employment.
2. In connection with this request, I authorize all corporations, companies, credit agencies, persons, educational institutions, law enforcement agencies and former employers to release information they may have about me, and release them from any liability and responsibility from doing so; further, I authorize the procurement of an investigative consumer report and understand that such report may contain information as to my background, mode of living, character and personal reputation. This authorization, in original and copy form, shall be valid for this and any future reports that may be requested. Further information may be made available upon written request from _____.
3. I hereby authorize investigation of all statements at this time with no liability arising therefrom.

_____   _____
Signature   Date

_____   _____
Signature of Company Representative   Date

        * * *

STATE of: _____

COUNTY of: _____

My commission will expire:

_____

This Instrument was acknowledged before me

this _____ day of _____, 20____,

by _____ AS WITTNESS.

_____
Notary Public   No.

Basic Application (page 1)

Application must be filled in completely or it will not be processed. If a box does not pertain to you, indicate with **N/A** in that space.

_____ is an equal opportunity employer whose policy is to select the most qualified candidates without regard to race, religion, color, sex, age, marital or military status, history of disability or national origin.

Date_____   Social Security #

Drivers License #_____ State_____
    (only if you will be operating a company vehicle)

Last Name   First Name   Initial

Street Address   City   State   Zip
Home Phone #_____ Work Phone #_____
Have you ever worked or attended school under another name? ( ) yes ( ) no
    If yes, state dates: _____
Position applying for: 1._____ 2._____ Salary desired _____
How did you contact _____
    ( ) Newspaper   ( ) Employee Referral   ( ) Employment Agency   ( ) Other
Please specify: _____

Have you ever worked for _____ ( ) yes ( ) no
    When? _____ Where? _____
Do you have any relatives employed by _____ ( ) yes ( ) no
    If yes, Name:_____ Where?_____
Are you a citizen of the USA. or a lawfully admitted resident alien? ( ) yes ( ) no If yes, Alien Reg. # _____
Have you ever been convicted of a crime or offense other than for minor traffic violations?   ( ) yes   ( ) no
If "Yes," explain _____
Conviction of a crime is not an automatic disqualification for employment. All factors will be considered.
Have you ever served in the Armed Forces? ( ) yes ( ) no   Military occupation _____
Date of duty, from _____ to _____ Branch _____ Serial # _____
              Month Day Year   Month Day Year

EDUCATION	NAME & ADDRESS	No. YEARS ATTENDED	COURSE, MAJOR or DEGREE
High School			
College			
Post Graduate			
Business or Trade			
Other			

Appendix III - Employer Forms

Basic Application (page 2)

Other experience(s) skills you would like to mention: _____
_____
_____
_____

At least (2) two Personal References:
Name: _____ Phone #: _____
Address: _____ Years Known: _____
Name: _____ Phone #: _____
Address: _____ Years Known: _____

In case of emergency notify: _____
Phone numbers: _____
Address: _____
Relationship: _____

Print Name: _____ S.S. #_____

I AGREE AND UNDERSTAND THAT ALL THE STATEMENTS AND INFORMATION ON MY APPLICATION ARE CORRECT AND NO ATTEMPT HAS BEEN MADE TO CONCEAL OR WITHHOLD PERTINENT INFORMATION. I AGREE THAT ANY OMISSION, FALSIFICATION, OR MISREPRESENTATION IS CAUSE FOR IMMEDIATE TERMINATION AT ANY TIME DURING MY EMPLOYMENT.

I HEREBY AUTHORIZE INVESTIGATION OF ALL STATEMENTS AT THIS TIME WITH NO LIABILITY ARISING THEREFROM _____.

I WILL ABIDE BY ALL RULES, REGULATIONS AND POLICIES OF _____.

AT THE OPTION OF THE COMPANY, I AGREE TO PHYSICAL EXAMINATION BY A PHYSICIAN CHOSEN BY _____ WITH THE UNDERSTANDING THAT MY EMPLOYMENT AT _____ DEPENDS UPON MY PASSING THE PHYSICAL.

I UNDERSTAND THAT A 90 WORKING PROBATIONARY PERIOD WILL BE IN EFFECT IN THE EVENT EMPLOYMENT IS OFFERED.

DATE _____   SIGNATURE _____

Basic Application (page 3)

Other experience(s) skills you would like to mention: _____
_____
_____
_____

At least (2) two Personal References:
Name: _____ Phone #: _____
Address: _____ Years Known: _____

Name: _____ Phone #: _____
Address: _____ Years Known: _____

In cases of emergency notify: _____
Phone numbers: _____
Address: _____
Relationship:_____

Print Name: _____ S.S. #: _____

I AGREE AND UNDERSTAND THAT ALL THE STATEMENTS AND INFORMATION ON MY APPLICATION ARE CORRECT AND NO ATTEMPT HAS BEEN MADE TO CONCEAL OR WITHHOLD PERTINENT INFORMATION. I AGREE THAT ANY OMISSION, FALSIFICATION, OR MISREPRESENTATION IS CAUSE FOR IMMEDIATE TERMINATION AT ANY TIME DURING MY EMPLOYMENT.

I HEREBY AUTHORIZE INVESTIGATION OF ALL STATEMENTS AT THIS TIME WITH NO LIABILITY ARISING THEREFROM _____.

I WILL ABIDE BY ALL RULES, REGULATIONS AND POLICIES OF _____
_____.

AT THE OPTION OF THE COMPANY, I AGREE TO PHYSICAL EXAMINATION BY A PHYSICIAN CHOSEN BY _____ WITH THE UNDERSTANDING THAT MY EMPLOYMENT AT _____
DEPENDS UPON MY PASSING THE PHYSICAL.

I UNDERSTAND THAT A 90 WORKING PROBATIONARY PERIOD WILL BE IN EFFECT IN THE EVENT EMPLOYMENT IS OFFERED.

DATE _____   SIGNATURE _____

Confidentiality Agreement

CONFIDENTIALITY AGREEMENT

In consideration of being employed by _____ (Company), the undersigned hereby agrees and acknowledges:

1. That during the course of my employ there may be disclosed to me certain trade secrets of the Company; said trade secrets consisting of:

   a) Technical information: Methods, processes, formulae, compositions, inventions, machines, computer programs, and research projects.

   b) Business information: Customer lists, pricing data, sources of supply, and marketing, production, or merchandising systems or plans.

2. I shall not during, or at any time after the termination of my employment with the Company, use for myself or others, or disclose or divulge to others any trade secrets, confidential information, or any other data of the Company in violation of this agreement.

3. That upon the termination of my employ from the Company:

   a) I shall return to the Company all documents relating to the Company, including but not necessarily limited to: drawings, blueprints, reports, manuals, correspondence, consumer lists, computer programs, and all other materials and all copies thereof relating in any way to the Company's business, or in any way obtained by me during the course of my employ. I further agree that I shall not retain any copies of the forgoing.

   b) The Company may notify any future or prospective employer of the existence of this agreement.

   c) This agreement shall be binding upon me and my personal representatives and successors in interest, and shall inure to the benefit of the Company, its successors, and assigns.

   d) The enforceability of any provision to this agreement shall not impair or affect any other provision.

   e) In the event of any breach of this agreement, the Company shall have full rights to injunctive relief, in addition to any other existing rights, without requirement of posting bond.

_____   _____
SIGNATURE   DATE

Criminal Background Check Release

Criminal Background Check
Release Form

NAME_____
        Last   First   Middle   Maiden

ADDRESS_____
        Street   City   State

ALIASES OR OTHER NAMES USED _____

DATE OF BIRTH _____ AGE ___ RACE _____ SEX ___

SOCIAL SECURITY # _____

DRIVER'S LICENSE # _____ STATE _____

* * *

I hereby authorize _____ of _____
                Name   Name of Company

_____
Company Address/City/State/Zip

to conduct a criminal background check on myself through the

_____ .
Name of State and Police Agency

X_____
Applicant Signature

* * *

STATE of:_____ This Instrument was acknowledged before me this ___ day of
COUNTY of:_____ _____, 20 ____, by _____
My commission will expire: _____AS WITNESS.

_____

_____
    Notary Public   No.

Appendix III - Employer Forms

Employee Data Sheet

EMPLOYEE DATA SHEET

THE FOLLOWING INFORMATION IS NECESSARY TO MAINTAIN COMPANY RECORDS ON ALL OUR EMPLOYEES

EMPLOYEE #:_____ DEPARTMENT:_____ DATE OF HIRE: _____

NAME: _____

ADDRESS:_____

HOME TELEPHONE NUMBER: _____

SOCIAL SECURITY #: _____ DATE OF BIRTH: _____

RACE (PLEASE CIRCLE):

WHITE   BLACK   HISPANIC   ASIAN   AMERICAN INDIAN   OTHER _____

ARE YOU A CITIZEN OF THE UNITED STATES?   _____ YES   _____ NO

ALIEN REGISTRATION #: _____

MARITAL STATUS: ____ SINGLE   ____ MARRIED   ____ DIVORCED

              ____ LEGALLY SEPARATED   ____ WIDOWED

DATE OF MARRIAGE: _____ SPOUSE'S NAME: _____

SPOUSE'S SS#: _____ SPOUSE'S DATE OF BIRTH: _____

CHILDREN:

NAME	DATE OF BIRTH	AGE	SEX
NAME	DATE OF BIRTH	AGE	SEX
NAME	DATE OF BIRTH	AGE	SEX
NAME	DATE OF BIRTH	AGE	SEX

WHO WOULD YOU LIKE US TO NOTIFY IN CASE OF EMERGENCY?

NAME: _____ RELATIONSHIP: _____

ADDRESS: _____

TELEPHONE NUMBER: _____

Employment Eligibility Verification (I-9)

EMPLOYMENT ELIGIBILITY VERIFICATION (I-9)

SECTION I. EMPLOYEE INFORMATION AND VERIFICATION: (To be completed and signed by employee)

NAME: _____
       Last   First   Middle   Maiden

ADDRESS: _____
      Street number and name   City   State   Zip

DATE OF BIRTH: _____ SOCIAL SECURITY NUMBER: _____

I attest, under penalty of perjury, that I am (check one):
- _____ A citizen or national of the United States
- _____ An alien lawfully admitted for permanent residence (Alien #A_____).
- _____ An alien authorized by the Immigration and Naturalization Service to work in the U.S.(Alien #A_____). or Admission Number _____. Expiration of employment authorization, if any _____).

I attest, under penalty of perjury, the documents that I have presented as evidence of identity and employment eligibility are genuine and relate to me. I am aware that federal law provides for imprisonment and/or fine for any false statement or use of false documents in connection with this certificate.

SIGNATURE: _____ DATE: _____

PREPARER/TRANSLATOR CERTIFICATION (if prepared by other than the individual). I attest, under penalty of perjury, that the above was prepared by me at the request of the named individual and is based on all information of which I have any knowledge.

SIGNATURE: _____ NAME (print or type): _____
ADDRESS: _____
      Street number and name   City   State   Zip

****

SECTION II. EMPLOYER REVIEW AND VERIFICATION: (To be completed and signed by employer)
Examine one document from those in List A and check the correct box, *or* examine one document from List B *and* one from List C and check the correct boxes. Provide the *Document Identification Number* and *Expiration Date*, for the document checked in that column.

List A	List B	List C
Identity and Employment Eligibility	Identity	and Employment
____ United States Passport	____ A State issued drivers license or I.D. card with a photograph, or information, including name, sex, date of birth, height, weight, and color of eyes.	____ Original Social Security Number Card (other than a card stating it is not valid for employment)
____ Certificate of U.S. Citizenship		____ A birth certificate issued by State, county, or municipal authority bearing a seal or other certification
____ Certificate of Naturalization		
____ Unexpired foreign passport with attached Employment Authorization	____ U.S. Military Card	
____ Alien registration Card with photograph	____ Other (Specify document and issuing authority)	____ Unexpired INS Employment Authorization. Specify form.
Document I.D.# _____	Document I.D.# _____	Document I.D.# _____
Exp. Date _____	Exp. Date _____	Exp. Date _____

CERTIFICATION: I attest, under penalty of perjury, that I have examined the documents presented by the above individual, that they appear to be genuine, relate to the individual named, and that the individual, to the best of my knowledge, is authorized to work in the United States.

SIGNATURE: _____ NAME (print of type): _____ TITLE: _____

EMPLOYER: _____
       Name   Address   Date

Exit Interview Report (page 1)

EXIT INTERVIEW REPORT

ALL ANSWERS ARE HELD STRICTLY CONFIDENTIAL

Employee's Name: _____ Employee #: _____

Department: _____ Position: _____

Dates of Employment: From _____ To _____

Supervisor: _____

Reason for leaving Company: _____

Return of:

_____ keys	_____ company documents	_____ uniform
_____ I.D. card	_____ safety equipment	_____ tools
_____ credit card	_____ other company property	_____ company auto

Employee informed of restriction on:

_____ trade secrets	_____ employment with competitor (if applicable)
_____ patents	_____ removing company documents
_____ other data	_____ other _____

Employee exit questions:

1. Did management adequately recognize employee contributions? _____
   _____

2. Do you feel that you have had the support of management on the job? _____
   _____

3. Were you adequately trained for your job? _____
   _____

4. Did you find your work rewarding? _____
   _____

(Continued)

Exit Interview Report (page 2)

EXIT INTERVIEW REPORT PAGE 2

5. Do you feel you were fairly treated by the company? _____

6. Were you paid an adequate salary for the work you did? _____

7. Were you content with your working conditions? _____

8. Do you feel your supervision was adequate? _____

9. Did you understand company policies and the reasons for them? _____

10. Have you observed incidences of theft of company property? _____

11. How can the company improve security? _____

12. How can the company improve working conditions? _____

13. What are the company's strengths? _____

14. What are the company's weaknesses? _____

15. Other comments: _____

USE ADDITIONAL SHEETS FOR FURTHER COMMENTS

Appendix III - Employer Forms

General Release Form

General Release Form

In connection with my application for employment (including contract for service) with you, I understand that investigative inquiries are to be made on myself including consumer credit, criminal convictions, motor vehicle, and other reports. These reports will include information as to my character, work, habits, performance and experience along with reasons for termination of past employment from previous employers. Further, I understand that you will be requesting information from various Federal, State, and other agencies that maintain records concerning my past activities relating to my driving, credit, criminal, civil, education, and other experiences.

I authorize without reservation any party or agency contacted by this employer to furnish the above-mentioned information.

I hereby consent to your obtaining the above information from _____ _____ and/or any of their licensed agents. I understand to aid in the proper identification of my file or records, the following personal identifiers, as well as other information, is necessary.

Print Name _____

Social Security Number _____-____-_____

Date of Birth _____ Sex _____ Race _____

Current Address _____

City/State/Zip Code+4 _____

Former Address _____

Applicant Signature _____ Date _____

Prospective Employer _____

Induction Form

INDUCTION FORM

NAME: _____ SS#: _____

CLOCK #: _____ STARTING DATE: _____

JOB TITLE: _____

DEPT: _____ SUPERVISOR: _____

COMPANY BENEFITS AND RULES

1. HOURS: _____ AM/PM until _____ AM/PM a _____ lunch, and two _____ minute rest breaks, one at _____ and one at _____. The regular work week is _____ to _____.

2. TIME RECORDS: Punch only your own time card and in case of a mistake, take your card IMMEDIATELY to the office. After seven minutes, employees are docked 15 minutes for being late and repeated lateness is cause for discipline. If you are unable to come to work, call (___) ___-____ before the start of your shift.

3. HOLIDAYS: New Years Day, Good Friday, Memorial Day, 4th of July, Labor Day, Thanksgiving, Friday after Thanksgiving, and Christmas Day.

4. VACATIONS: You will earn _____ of vacation for each _____ of employment prior to _____ up to a maximum of _____ days. _____ weeks after _____ years of service and _____ weeks after _____ years.

5. INSURANCE: The company provides _____ insurance for all employees after _____ of service. If you wish coverage for your eligible dependents, this can be arranged through payroll deduction. After _____ months, the company provide $ _____ of life insurance and a weekly sick and accident insurance program that pays a maximum of $ _____ for 26 weeks after the first day of an accident and after the eighth day of illness.

If you have any questions at any time regarding your pay, benefits or job assignment, please discuss it with your supervisor.

I have read and understand the information above.

_____   _____
DATE   EMPLOYEE'S SIGNATURE

Witness:

_____   _____
Date   Signature

Appendix III - Employer Forms

Local Police Information Request

TO BE PRINTED ON YOUR LETTERHEAD

(DATE)

(NAME OF POLICE DEPARTMENT)
Att: Records
(STREET ADDRESS)
CITY, STATE, ZIP)

Re: (NAME OF EMPLOYEE)

Dear Sir/Madam:

Our medical facility is conducting a background check on the above-captioned prospective employee. I am writing to obtain local criminal history and/or character information from your Department. Enclosed please find a consent form with original signature, which has been notarized, authorizing the release of this information. Please indicate on the form the results of your record check, or lack thereof, and return it to us in the self-addressed stamped envelope provided.

Please advise us if there are any additional requirements, fees, etc. necessary to obtain this information.

Thank you for your assistance in this matter.

Sincerely,

(NAME - TYPED)
(TITLE - TYPED)

Appendix III - Employer Forms

Military Records Request (front)

Also available online at: www.nara.gov/regional/mprsf180.html.

Standard Form 180 (Rev. 4-96) (EG)
Prescribed by NARA (36 CFR 1228.162(a))

NSN 7540-00-142-9360

OMB No. 3095-0029 Expires 9/30/98

REQUEST PERTAINING TO MILITARY RECORDS

To ensure the best possible service, please thoroughly review the instructions at the bottom before filling out this form. Please print clearly or type. If you need more space, use plain paper.

SECTION I - INFORMATION NEEDED TO LOCATE RECORDS (Furnish as much as possible.)

1. NAME USED DURING SERVICE (Last, first, and middle)
2. SOCIAL SECURITY NO.
3. DATE OF BIRTH
4. PLACE OF BIRTH

5. SERVICE, PAST AND PRESENT (For an effective records search, it is important that ALL service be shown below.)

BRANCH OF SERVICE	DATES OF SERVICE		CHECK ONE		SERVICE NUMBER DURING THIS PERIOD (If unknown, please write "unknown.")
	DATE ENTERED	DATE RELEASED	OFFICER	ENLISTED	
a. ACTIVE SERVICE					
b. RESERVE SERVICE					
c. NATIONAL GUARD					

6. IS THIS PERSON DECEASED? ☐ NO ☐ YES   If "YES" enter the date of death. _____

7. IS (WAS) THIS PERSON RETIRED FROM MILITARY SERVICE? ☐ YES ☐ NO

SECTION II - INFORMATION AND/OR DOCUMENTS REQUESTED

1. **REPORT OF SEPARATION** (DD Form 214 or equivalent). This contains information normally needed to verify military service. It may be furnished to the veteran, the deceased veteran/s next of kin, or other persons or organizations if authorized in Section III, below. NOTE: If more than one period of service was performed, even in the same branch, there may be more than one Report of Separation. Be sure to show EACH year for which you need a copy.

    ☐ An UNDELETED Report of Separation is requested for the year(s) _____. This normally will be a copy of the full separation document including such sensitive items as the character of separation, authority for separation, reason for separation, reenlistment eligibility code, separation (SPD/SPN) code, and dates of time lost. An undeleted version is ordinarily required to determine eligibility for benefits.

    ☐ A DELETED Report of Separation is requested for the year(s) _____. The following information will be deleted from the copy sent: authority for separation, reason for separation, reenlistment eligibility code, separation (SPD/SPN) code, and for separations after June 30, 1979, character of separation and dates of time lost.

2. OTHER INFORMATION AND/OR DOCUMENTS REQUESTED _____

3. PURPOSE (OPTIONAL - An explanation of the purpose of the request is strictly voluntary. Such information may help the agency answering this request to provide the best possible response and will in no way be used to make a decision to deny the request.) _____

SECTION III - RETURN ADDRESS AND SIGNATURE

1. REQUESTER IS
    ☐ Military service member or veteran identified in Section I, above
    ☐ Legal guardian (must submit copy of court appointment)
    ☐ Next of kin of deceased veteran _____ (relation)
    ☐ Other (specify) _____

2. SEND INFORMATION/DOCUMENTS TO (Please print or type. See instruction 3, below.)

3. AUTHORIZATION SIGNATURE REQUIRED (See instruction 2, below.) I declare (or certify, verify, or state) under penalty of perjury under the laws of the United States of America that the information in this Section III is true and correct.

Name _____
Street _____ Apt. _____
City _____ State _____ ZIP Code _____

Signature of Requester (Please do not print.) _____
Date of this request _____   Daytime phone ( ) _____

Appendix III - Employer Forms

Military Records Request (reverse)

Also available online at: www.nara.gov/regional/mprsf180.html

STANDARD FORM 180 BACK (Rev. 4-96)

LOCATION OF MILITARY RECORDS

The various categories of military service records are described in the chart below. For each category there is a code number which indicates the address at the bottom of the page to which this request should be sent.

1. **Health and personnel records.** In most cases involving individuals no longer on active duty, the personnel record, the health record, or both can be obtained from the same location, as shown on the chart. However, some health records are available from the Department of Veterans Affairs (VA) Records Management Center (Code 11). A request for a copy of the health record should be sent to Code 11 if the person was discharged, retired, or released from active duty (separated) on or after the following dates: ARMY-- October 16, 1992; NAVY--January 31, 1994; AIR FORCE and MARINE CORPS--May 1, 1994. Health records of persons on active duty are generally kept at the local servicing clinic, and usually are available from Code 11 a week or two after the last day of active duty.

2. **Records at the National Personnel Records Center.** Note that it takes at least three months, and often six or seven, for the file to reach the National Personnel Records Center (Code 14) in St. Louis after the military obligation has ended (such as by discharge). If only a short time has passed, please send the inquiry to the address shown for active or current reserve members. Also, if the person has only been released from active duty but is still in a reserve status, the personnel record will stay at the location specified for reservists. A person can retain a reserve obligation for several years, even without attending meetings or receiving annual training.

3. **Definitions and abbreviations.** DISCHARGED--the individual has no current military status; HEALTH--Records of physical examinations, dental treatment, and outpatient medical treatment received while in a duty status (does not include records of treatment while hospitalized); TDRL--Temporary Disability Retired List

4. **Service completed before World War I (before 1929 for Coast Guard officers).** The oldest military service records are at the National Archives (Code 6). Send the request there if service was completed before the following dates: ARMY--enlisted, 11/1/1912, officer, 7/1/1917; NAVY--enlisted, 1/1/1886, officer, 1/1/1903; MARINE CORPS--1/1/1905; COAST GUARD--enlisted, 1/1/1915, officer, 1/1/1929.

BRANCH	CURRENT STATUS OF SERVICE MEMBER	WHERE TO WRITE ADDRESS CODE
AIR FORCE	Discharged, deceased, or retired with pay (See paragraph 1, above, if requesting health record.)	14
	Active (including National Guard on active duty in the Air Force), TDRL, or general officers retired with pay	1
	Reserve, retired reserve in nonpay status, current National Guard officers not on active duty in the Air Force, or National Guard released from active duty in the Air Force	2
	Current National Guard enlisted not on active duty in the Air Force	13
COAST GUARD	Discharged, deceased, or retired (See paragraph 1, above, if requesting health record.)	14
	Active, reserve, or TDRL	3
MARINE CORPS	Discharged, deceased, or retired (See paragraph 1, above, if requesting health record.)	14
	Individual Ready Reserve or Fleet Marine Corps Reserve	5
	Active, Selected Marine Corps Reserve, or TDRL	4
ARMY	Discharged, deceased, or retired (See paragraph 1, above, if requesting health record.)	14
	Reserve; or active duty records of current National Guard members who performed service in the U.S. Army before 7/1/72	7
	Active enlisted (including National Guard on active duty in the U.S. Army) or TDRL enlisted	9
	Active officers (including National Guard on active duty in the U.S. Army) or TDRL officers	8
	Current National Guard enlisted not on active duty in Army (including records of Army active duty performed after 6/30/72)	13
	Current National Guard officers not on active duty in Army (including records of Army active duty performed after 6/30/72)	12
NAVY	Discharged, deceased, or retired (See paragraph 1, above, if requesting health record.)	14
	Active, reserve, or TDRL	10

ADDRESS LIST OF CUSTODIANS (BY CODE NUMBERS SHOWN ABOVE) - where to write / send this form

1 Air Force Personnel Center
HQ AFPC/DPSRP
550 C Street West, Suite 19
Randolph AFB, TX 78150-4721

2 Air Reserve Personnel Center/DSMR
6760 E. Irvington Pl. #4600
Denver, CO 80280-4600

3 Commander CGPC-Adm-3
U.S. Coast Guard
2100 2nd Street, SW.
Washington, DC 20593-0001

4 Headquarters U.S. Marine Corps
Personnel Management Support Branch
(MMSB-10)
2008 Elliot Road
Quantico, VA 22134-5030

5 Marine Corps Reserve Support Command
(Code MMI)
15303 Andrews Road
Kansas City, MO 64147-1207

6 Archives I Textual Reference Branch
(NNR1), Room 13W
National Archives and
Records Administration

7 Commander
U.S. Army Reserve Personnel Center
ATTN: ARPC-VS
9700 Page Avenue
St. Louis, MO 63132-5200

8 U.S. Total Army Personnel
Command
200 Stovall Street
Alexandria, VA 22332-0400

9 Commander USAEREC
Attn: PCRE-F
8899 E. 56th St.
Indianapolis, IN 46249-5301

10 Bureau of Naval Personnel
Pers-313D
2 Navy Annex
Washington, DC 20370-3130

11 Department of Veterans Affairs
Records Management Center
P.O. Box 5020
St. Louis, MO 63115-5020

12 Army National Guard Readiness Center
NGB-ARP
111 S. George Mason Dr.
Arlington, VA 22204-1382

13 The Adjutant General
(of the appropriate state, DC,
or Puerto Rico)

14 National Personnel Records Center
(Military Personnel Records)
9700 Page Avenue
St. Louis, MO 63132-5100

Appendix III - Employer Forms

New Employee Record Chart

New Employee Record Chart

Employee _____ Position _____

Department _____ Date Employed _____

The above new employee must have checked item(s) in file.

Document	Required	Completed
Employment Application	_____	_____
Employee Data Sheet	_____	_____
W-4	_____	_____
I-9	_____	_____
Induction Form	_____	_____
New Hire Report	_____	_____
Applicant Waiver Releases	_____	_____
Substance Abuse Test Consent	_____	_____
Non-Compete Agreement	_____	_____
Confidentiality Agreement	_____	_____

_____

Supervisor

_____

Date

Appendix III - Employer Forms

New Hire Reporting

New Hire Reporting Form

Send Completed Form to: _____ Fax form to: _____
                                                                Agency fax
                       _____   or
                                                              _____
                       _____ For info, call: _____
                       Name & Address of New Hire State Contact   Agency phone

— EMPLOYER INFORMATION —

Federal Employer
Identification Number   _____

Employer Name   _____

Address   _____
                        (Please indicate the address where Income Withholding Order will be sent)

City/State/Zip+4   _____

— EMPLOYEE INFORMATION —

Social Security Number   _____ - ___ - _____

Employee Name   _____

Employee Address   _____

City/State/Zip Code+4   _____

— EMPLOYEE INFORMATION —

Social Security Number   _____ - ___ - _____

Employee Name   _____

Employee Address   _____

City/State/Zip Code+4   _____

Non-Compete Agreement

General Non-Compete Agreement

For good consideration and as an inducement for _____ (Company), to employ _____ (Employee), the undersigned employee hereby agrees not to directly or indirectly compete with the business of the Company during the period of _____ years following termination of employment and notwithstanding the cause of reason for termination.

The term "not to compete" as used herein shall mean that the Employee shall not own, operate, consult to, or be employed by any firm in a business substantially similar to or competitive with the present business of the Company or such business activity in which the Company may engage during the term of employment.

The Employee acknowledges that the Company shall or may in reliance of this agreement provide Employee access to trade secrets, customers, and other confidential data and that the provisions of this agreement are reasonably necessary to protect the Company.

This agreement shall be binding upon and inure to the benefit of the parties, their successors, assigns, and personal representatives.

Signed under seal this _____ day of _____, 20_____.

_____
Company

_____
Employee

Performance Review (page 1)

Performance Review

Employee Name

Reviewer Name

Job Title

Date of Review

	Circle One	*Reviewer Notes*
Availability Punctuality/Absence Time Awareness	Excellent Satisfactory Needs Improvement	
Job Awareness Accountabilities Sets Goals	Excellent Satisfactory Needs Improvement	
Behavior Interaction w/ others Manners/Neatness	Excellent Satisfactory Needs Improvement	
Complies w/ Policy Follows Procedures Safety Rules	Excellent Satisfactory Needs Improvement	
Dependability Performs assignments	Excellent Satisfactory Needs Improvement	
Initiative Develops Solutions Provides Ideas	Excellent Satisfactory Needs Improvement	
Independence Tracks Assignments Needs Supervision	Excellent Satisfactory Needs Improvement	
Productivity Quality / Accuracy Corrects Errors	Excellent Satisfactory Needs Improvement	

Continued

Performance Review (page 2)

Performance Review – Page 2

Employee Name _____

New and/or noteworthy accomplishments since last evaluation

_____
_____
_____
_____

Areas in need of improvement

_____
_____
_____
_____

Recommendations

_____
_____
_____
_____

Overall Performance Summary: Excellent
    (Circle one)   Satisfactory
        Needs Improvement

Employee Comments

_____
_____
_____
_____

_____   _____
Employee Signature   Reviewer Signature

_____   _____
Date   Date of Next Review

Pre-Employment Check by Phone

PRE-EMPLOYMENT REFERENCE CHECK BY TELEPHONE

Name of Applicant: _____

Name of Company Contacted: _____

Name and Title of Reference: _____ Telephone: _____

* *

INSTRUCTIONS:
Contact the reference, preferably the applicant's immediate supervisor. Identify yourself and state that you are "calling to verify some of the information given to_____
by _____ who we are considering for a position."

* *

What were the dates of his/her employment with you? From _____ To _____

What was the nature of his/her job? _____

What did you think of his/her work? _____

How would you describe his/her performance in comparison with other people? _____

What job progress did he/she make? _____

What were his/her earnings? _____ Bonus? _____

Why did he/she leave your Company? _____

Would you re-employ? _____

What are his/her strong points? _____

What are his/her limitations? _____

How did he/she get along with other people? _____

Could you comment on his/her:
(a) attendance
(b) dependability
(c) ability to take on responsibility
(d) potential for advancement
(e) degree of supervision needed
(f) overall attitude _____

Did he/she have any personal difficulties that interfered with his/her work? _____

Is there anything else of significance that we should know? _____

SIGNATURE: _____ DATE: _____

Rejection Letter Sample

(To be produced on your company letterhead)

(Insert date)

Dear *(insert name)*:

Thank you for your interest in working for our organization. Many talented and qualified people applied for this position, including you. After much consideration, we have hired another applicant.

Thank you for your time, and good luck in your job search.

Sincerely,

(Insert your signature and name here)

Request For Education Verification

Date_____

REQUEST FOR EDUCATION VERIFICATION

Registrar's Office:

The applicant identified below has applied for a position with our organization. He/she has claimed attendance, credits and/or degree as denoted herein. Would you kindly verify this information and return this form in the enclosed self addressed stamped envelope. Please note, the applicant has signed for the release of this request.

NAME OF FACILITY

ADDRESS   CITY   STATE   ZIP

ATTENDANCE: FROM_____ TO _____
                MO.   YR.   MO.   YR.

CREDITS
RECEIVED: _____   GRADUATE: YES NO _____
            TOTAL   AWARDS-LEVEL

DEGREE: YES NO _____ DATE _____
                    DEGREE RECEIVED

I hearby authorize the release to certify my records as stated above.

Signature _____

Name(print) _____

Address _____

City/State/Zip _____

Date of Birth _____

SS# _____

Appendix III - Employer Forms

Request For Information

DATE _____

REQUEST FOR INFORMATION

To Whom It May Concern:

Mr./Ms. _____ has applied for a position as a _____ and states that he/she was employed by you as a _____ from _____ to _____.

Will you kindly reply to this inquiry and return this sheet in the enclosed self-addressed envelope. Your reply will be held in strict confidence and will in no way involve you in any responsibility.

Sincerely,

Signature: _____

Name (print/type): _____   Title: _____

Company: _____   Telephone: _____

****

Is employment record correct as stated above?	Yes _____	No _____
What were this employee's duties? _____		
Did he/she have custody of money or valuables?	Yes _____	No _____
Were his accounts properly kept?	Yes _____	No _____
Was his/her conduct satisfactory?	Yes _____	No _____
Do you recommend him/her for rehire?	Yes _____	No _____

He/she was: Discharged _____   Laid Off _____   Resigned _____

Please list any Workers Compensation Claims: _____

	EXCELLENT	GOOD	FAIR	POOR
Quality of work	_____	_____	_____	_____
Cooperation	_____	_____	_____	_____
Safety Habits	_____	_____	_____	_____
Personal Habits	_____	_____	_____	_____
Attendance	_____	_____	_____	_____

REMARKS: _____

_____

Company Name: _____

Person Completing Form: _____   Title: _____

Date: _____

Substance Abuse Screening Test – Applicant Consent

SUBSTANCE ABUSE SCREENING TEST

APPLICANT CONSENT FORM

I, _____, understand and agree that the medical examination I am
    (Name)
about to receive includes a:
( ) Blood test for substance (drug/alcohol) abuse or chemical dependency.
( ) Urine test for substance (drug/alcohol) abuse or chemical dependency.

I understand that if I decline to sign this consent and thereby decline to take the test, the medical examination will not be completed. The Employee Relations Department will be so notified and my application for employment will be rejected.

I understand that if the test is confirmed as positive, the results will be reported to the Employee Relations Department. An exception will be made for the use of legally prescribed medications taken under the directions of a physician.

I have taken the following drugs or substances within the last 96 hours:

Identify Name and Amount

( ) Sleeping Pills_____
( ) Diet Pills _____
( ) Pain Relief Medication_____
( ) Cold Medication_____
( ) Anti-Malarial Drugs_____
( ) Any Other Medication or Substance_____

I hereby ( ) consent ( ) refuse to consent to the medical examination including the test(s) for substance (drug/alcohol) abuse and for the release of the test results to:

_____
(Name of Employer)

I hereby release_____
    (Name of Medical Facility)

the physicians, technicians, or employees of and the agents of all of the above-named parties, from any and all claims or causes of action resulting from this analysis and the release of the information regarding the results thereof.

_____
Signature of Applicant

    Date:_____
Witness:

_____
    Signature   Date

Appendix III - Employer Forms

Workers' Compensation Release Form

Workers' Compensation Release Form

From: Employer _____ Re: Employee _____
       Address _____   Address _____
                _____   Social Security # _____

--- EMPLOYEE AUTHORIZATION ---

I, _____, do hereby authorize certify that I received an offer
           Employee Name
of employment from _____
                              Employer Name and Address
on _____ and authorize the _____
         Date   Name of State & Workers' Compensation Agency
_____ to release all information from Bureau files.

I affirm the information I have provided herein is true. I understand that if I make any false statements which I do not believe to be true and thereby mislead the public servant to whom this request is directed in performing his/her official function, I may be subject to State Criminal Codes where provided.

_____   X_____
        Date   Employee Signature

--- EMPLOYER CERTIFICATION ---

I _____, _____, an employee of
          Name   Title with Employer
and acting as agent for _____ do hereby certify that
                                     Employer
_____ has extended an offer of employment to
                Employer
_____ on _____ and I agree that information
                Employee   Date
requested from the_____
                            State Workers' Compensation Agency
with regard to _____ will be used by _____
                       Employee   Employer
in conformance with both the Americans With Disabilities Act and _____
_____.
                   State and its Laws regarding Workers' Compensation

I affirm the information I have provided herein is true. I understand that if I make any false statements which I do not believe to be true and thereby mislead the public servant to whom this request is directed in performing his/her official function, I may be subject to State Criminal Codes where provided.

_____   X_____
        Date   Signature

                          _____
                                      Title

– Employer Forms

Appendix IV
Resources for Employment Management

We have accumulated a listing of many of the Recommended Resources from throughout the book.

The following four sub-sections list government and private web sites, as well as information on written materials and CDs.

Section One: The Hiring Process

Government Web Sites

http://www.eeoc.gov

> This is the web site is for the US Equal Employment Opportunity Commission, which administers many of the federal discrimination laws.

http://www.ftc.gov

> This web site is for the Federal Trade Commission, which oversees the Fair Credit Reporting Act. This site is filled with useful information about rights and compliance.

http://www.ssa.gov

> This is the web site for the Social Security Administration. Their fraud hotline number is 800-269-0271.

http://www.nara.gov/regional

> NARA offers US government records access services to the public from facilities throughout the United States. Download Form 180 for searching military records from the web site of the National Personnel Records Center in St. Louis, Missouri. Also, the agency offers a fax-on-demand service.

http://www.acf.dhhs.gov/programs/cse

> The Federal Office of Child Support Enforcement provides state agency contact phone numbers, frequently asked questions and policy requirements for the mandated New Hire Form.

Private Web Sites

http://csi.toolkit.cch.com

> This site provides an excellent array of downloadable checklists, model employment-related business plans, forms and other documents.

http://www.hrtools.com/frames.asp

> HRTOOLS.com is an excellent, comprehensive site that is focused on attracting, maintaining, and managing the workforce. Here are lots of good "tool kits" to browse.

http://www.looksmart.com

> This search engine gives excellent results if you search using these key words—recruitment articles for human resource professionals.

http://www.tsbj.com/editorial/03030407.htm

> This site contains an excellent article entitled *Recruiting Employees Can Be A Difficult Task* written by Gary M. Brown

http:// www.amanet.org

> The American Management Association is a worldwide leader in management development. With over 7,000 corporate and 225,000 individual members, their web page has many materials oriented toward recruitment.

http://www.wave.net/upg/immigration/dot_index.html

> The National Academy of Sciences, Committee on Occupational Classification and Analysis has created the *Dictionary of Occupational Titles* (DOT). Job Descriptions for everything from an abalone diver to a wrong-address clerk are included. Thankfully, the full text of the DOT is available on the Web. By visiting this site, one can access the full-text of the dictionary at no cost and download a searchable version.

http://www.brbpub.com/forms

> From this site you can download all of the forms shown in this book.

http://www.e-zlegal.com

> Look for their book entitled *Personnel Director*. It contains over 100 useful personnel forms.

Appendix IV - Resources for Employment Management

http://www.nolo.com

    Nolo Press is a leading publisher of legal "self-help" books. Their site is filled with great information regarding employment law and compliance.

http://www.publicrecordsources.com

    This site profiles over 200 of the nation's leading pre-employment screening agencies. Many firms listed have links to their home pages, some filled with screening tips.

http://www.shrm.org

    The Society for Human Resource Management (SHRM) is the world's largest human resource management association. SHRM provides education and information services, conferences and seminars, government and media representation, online services and publications to more than 160,000 professional and student members throughout the world. The web site is filled with articles and resources that can help in all phases of employee management.

http://www.studentclearinghouse.com

    The National Student Clearinghouse will perform educational verifications for a moderate fee. This can be accomplished over the Internet.

http://www.publicrecordsources.com

    Lists vendors who specialize in educational verification (under the Search Firms button). There are also over 200 pre-employment screening firms profiled under the Screening Forms button. Also, this site presents links of state and county sites offering free access via the Internet.

http://www.drugfreeworkplace.org

    The Institute for a Drug-Free Workplace is an independent, self-sustaining coalition of businesses, organizations and individuals dedicated to preserving the rights of employers and employees in drug-abuse prevention programs.

http://www.health.org/wpkit

    Making Your Workplace Drug Free: A Kit for Employers. This site is geared toward helping employees establish a drug free work environment. Both employee and employer fact sheets are included.

These four sites provide computer-assisted employment products and services:

    http://www.pstc.com

    http://www.aspentree.com

    http://www.telserve.com

    http://www.wonderlic.com

The three sites provide psychological or aptitude testing direct on the Internet:

http://www.employeeselect.com

http://www.saterfiel.com

http://www.test.com

http://www.pcmusa.com/CBI/index.htm

Competency-Based Interviewing®, part of SmartHire, is designed to enhance a company's interviewing skills and selection process. Check out the articles.

http://onlinestore.cch.com/default.asp?ProductID=1092

This site is from CCH and deals with shared learning, interviewing, and hiring practices. The online multi-media training program allows access to the course 24 hours a day, seven days a week.

http://www.hrtools.com

This site allows you to compare your organization's interviewing practice to other organizations. It offers a user poll and user input on the interviewing process.

http://www.hrtools.com/frames.asp

Click on the "New Hires" button for articles and reference. This will also lead you to a map with state links to web pages where you may download the above-mentioned form.

http://jobsearchtech.about.com/careers/jobsearchtech/mbody.htm

This site is an excellent resource for an array of sample rejection letters. Applicable letters are shown for various stages in the selection process.

Written Material

Winning the Talent Wars, by Bruce Tulgan

A great book if you are looking to change your recruitment methods. Mr. Tulgan offers a myriad of innovative techniques that can be applied almost immediately at little or no cost.

Competing for Talent: Key Recruitment and Retention Strategies for Becoming an Employer of Choice, by Nancy S. Ahlrichs

Ms. Ahlrichs advocates becoming an Employer of Choice, or EOC, which charts "new strategic directions that put people in the profit equation." Interesting reading.

The *National Directory of Public Record Vendors*, by BRB Publications, 800-929-3811

An entire section dedicated to screening companies and also provides an excellent source for finding specialty vendors.

Appendix IV - Resources for Employment Management

The MVR Book and *The MVR Decoder Digest*, by BRB Publications, 800-929-3811

    These annual references will tell you everything you need to know about driving records, including access procedures, privacy restrictions and regulation

The Criminal Records Book, by Derek Hinton, Facts on Demand Press, 800-929-3764

    The ultimate reference on criminal records, written for employers. Covers laws, regulations, access procedures, and privacy restrictions.

CD

The *Public Record Research System* by BRB Publications

    Many HR departments and screening vendors use this CD as a source of information for 26,000 government and private agencies dealing with public records. The system is also available as a web subscription at www.publicrecordsources.com. The book version, printed annually, is *The Sourcebook to Public Record Information*.

Section Two: Bringing The New Employee On Board

Government Web Sites

http://www.irs.ustreas.gov

    The IRS web site has extensive information about the differences between employees and independent contractors (subcontractors). Look for IRS Publication 15-A.

Private Web Sites

These three web sites have either software available or offer assistance to the orientation process:

    http://www.deliverthepromise.com

    http://www.intechnic.com

    http://www.hrnext.com

http://www.canmummery.com

    This site provides a table of contents for constructing your own handbook and has other products.

Appendix IV - Resources for Employment Management

http://www.employer-employee.com

This site hosts many related products from handbooks to job descriptions.

http://www.knowledgepoint.com

This site is another excellent source of products and self help tools.

http://www.fuba.org/fuba/letter/0009

This site contains an article in a recent newsletter by the Florida United Businesses Association. The article discusses the differences in worker's compensation issues between subcontractors and employees.

http://www.meaningfulworkplace.com

This web site is maintained by Tom Terez, the author of *22 Keys To Creating a Meaningful Workplace*. The book is filled with many ideas on how to strengthen your workplaces, and ways to motivate and treat employees. His web site summarizes much of the text of the book.

http://www.benefitslink.com

BenefitsLink has provided free compliance information and tools for employee benefit plan sponsors, service-providers and participants.

http://humanresources.about.com/careers/humanresources

Human Resources.com is a great source for articles on benefits, compensation, morale and motivations.

http://www.shrm.org/channels/

The Society for Human Resource Management site has some excellent free access articles. Click on the Benefits and Compensation channels.

http://www.hrtools.com/frames.asp

This site has many performance tool and checklists under the "training and performance" button. You will have to register.

http://www.business-marketing.com/store/appraisals.html

Business Training media has a variety of tools and products devoted to employee appraisals and performance reviews. Check out the helpful articles available online.

http://www.office.com

At this site, do a search for their multi-paged article entitled "Conducting Performance Reviews."

Written Material

HR Magazine, June 2001 Edition

The Society for Human Resource Management has an excellent article in the June 2001 edition of HR Magazine. Titled *A Tough Target: Employee or Independent Contractor*, it reviews this classification dilemma. The article may also be read at their web site, www.shrm.org.

Section Three: When Problems Arise

Government Web Sites

http://www.dol.gov/dol/asp/public/programs/drugs/employer.htm

Entitled *An Employer's Guide to Dealing With Substance Abuse*, this is an excellent site presented by the National Clearinghouse for Alcohol and Drug Information.

http://www.dol.gov/dol/esa/public/regs/statutes/owcp/stwclaw/stwclaw.htm

This site, from the U.S. Dept. of Labor, is contains overviews of individual state workers' compensation laws including their benefit tables.

Private Web Sites

http://www.lectlaw.com/files/emp03.htm

From the 'Lectric Law Library, an excellent article entitled *An Employer's Guide To Dealing With Substance Abuse*.

http://humanresources.about.com/careers/humanresources

Click on the "Performance Management" heading; there's lots of good reading and ideas here.

http://www.healthwellexchange.com/nfm-online/nfm_backs/Jun_99/grievances.cfm

This is a well-written article entitled Working Through Employee Grievances, by Carolee Colter.

http://www.shrm.org/channels

The Society for Human Resource Management site has some excellent free access articles. Click on the Employee Relations Channel.

Appendix IV - Resources for Employment Management 306

http://www.cwce.com

> CWCE Magazine For The Workplace Community. This magazine is a great source of articles dealing with workers' compensation issues.

http://laborsafety.about.com/industry/laborsafety/mbody.htm

> This site, part of the About The Human Internet, has great reading material regarding workers' compensation issues.

http://www.workinjury.com

> Although this site is heavily oriented towards California related workers' compensation laws and procedures, there is plenty of useful information for everyone.

http://sanantonio.bcentral.com/sanantonio/stories/1998/05/04/smallb4.html

> This is an excellent article on exit interviews that appeared in an edition of the San Antonio Business Journal.

http://www.ewin.com/articles/exit.htm

> This article, *How and Why to Conduct Exit Interviews*, is posted by Winning Associates. It is well written and ends with a useful checklist.

http://sanantonio.bcentral.com/sanantonio/stories/1998/05/04/smallb4.html

> This is an excellent article on exit interviews that appeared in an edition of the San Antonio Business Journal.

http://www.ewin.com/articles/exit.htm

> This article, *How and Why to Conduct Exit Interviews*, is posted by Winning Associates. It is well written and ends with a useful checklist.

Written Material

CWCE Magazine For The Workplace Community. This magazine is a great source of articles dealing with workers' compensation issues.

Section Four: Abiding By The Law

Government Web Sites

http://www.eeoc.gov

>US Equal Employment Opportunity Commission oversees a number of the laws mentioned in this book, including the Civil Rights Act and Americans With Disabilities Act. Their Publications Center can be reached at 1-800-669-3362.

http://www.ftc.gov

>The Federal Trade Commission oversees the Fair Credit Reporting Act. Go to www.ftc.gov/os/statutes/fcrajump.htm to view the act and notices.

http://www.nlrb.gov

>The National Labor Relations Board oversees employers involved in unions and interstate commerce.

http://www.dol.gov

>The US Department of Labor is responsible for the administration and enforcement of over 180 federal statues dealing with workplace activities.

Private Web Sites

http://www.employmentlawcentral.com

>This site does an excellent job of disseminating employment law. There are many pages and links to recent laws, opinions, and court cases. A great site!

http://www.icle.org

>The Institute of Continuing Legal Education offers an impressive Internet site of educational and legal resource materials, including an Employment Law Central link.

http://guide.lp.findlaw.com/11stategov

>Findlaw.com is a great resource of legal information including the federal government. The URL listed above provides a gateway to every state's "cases, codes and regulations."

http://www.hrtools.com

>Do a search under "workers comp" and this site will provide a wealth of information about state worker's compensation laws.

http://www.references-ect.com/main.html

> This company has an terrific page of state employment laws. Find your way to www.references-ect.com/state_employment_statues.html.

http://www.employmentlawcentral.com

> This site does an excellent job of disseminating employment law. There are many pages and links to recent laws, opinions, and court cases. A great site!

http://www.nolo.com

> Nolo Press is a leading publisher of legal "self-help" books. Their site is filled with great information regarding employment law and compliance.
>
> including the federal government.

http://www.shrm.org/channels

> The Society for Human Resource Management site has some excellent free access articles. Click on the Employee Relations Channel.

http://www.aidsfund.org/bossguide.htm

> The National Aids Funds provides a great deal of terrific information for employers and managers on how to deal with aids in the workplace. Highly recommended.

http:// www.amanet.org

> The American Management Association is a worldwide leader in management development. With over 7,000 corporate and 225,000 individual members, their web page is an excellent starting point for learning programs including e-learning and self-study courses.

http:// www.msec.org

> The Mountain States Employers Council is a non-profit organization that provides assistance with human resource matters, employment law, and training needs.

Appendix V
State Agency Public Record Restrictions Table

Codes

O   Open to Public
R   Some Access Restrictions (Requesters Screened)
N/A   Not Available to the Public
F   Special Form Needed
S   Severe Access Restrictions (Signed Authorization, etc.)
L   Available only at Local Level

State	Criminal Records	Worker's Comp	Driver Records [i]
Alabama	S	S	S
Alaska	R	R	S
Arizona	S	S	S
Arkansas	S	O	S
California	N/A,L	R	S
Colorado	R	S	S
Connecticut	O	S	S
Delaware	S	S	S
Dist. of Columbia	S,F	S	S
Florida	O	S	S
Georgia	S	S	S
Hawaii	O	S	S
Idaho	R	S	S
Illinois	S,F	O	S
Indiana	S,F	S	S
Iowa	O	O	S
Kansas	R,F	R	S
Kentucky	S	R	S
Louisiana	S	R	S
Maine	O	R	S
Maryland	S	O	S

Appendix V - State Agency Public Records Restrictions Table

State	Criminal Records	Worker's Comp	Driver Records [i]
Massachusetts	R	R	S
Michigan	O	R	S
Minnesota	R	S	S
Mississippi	N/A,L	R	S
Missouri	O	R	S
Montana	O	S	S
Nebraska	O	O	S
Nevada	S	S	S
New Hampshire	S	S	S
New Jersey	S,F	O,F	S
New Mexico	S	S	S
New York	L	S	S
North Carolina	N/A,L	S	S
North Dakota	S	S	S
Ohio	S,F	O	S
Oklahoma	O	O	S
Oregon	O	S	S
Pennsylvania	R,F	S	S
Rhode Island	S,L	S	S
South Carolina	O	S	S
South Dakota	S,F	S	S
Tennessee	N/A,L	S	S
Texas	O	S,F	S
Utah	N/A,L	S	S
Vermont	N/A,L	S	S
Virginia	S,F	S	S
Washington	O	S	S
West Virginia	S,F	S	S
Wisconsin	O	S	S
Wyoming	S,F	S	S

[i] Driver Records -- indicate restriction codes based on the assumption that the requester is "the general public" or an "employer." All employers must obtain a signed release from the applicant before accessing records. In general, these records are open ("O") or restricted ("R") to the insurance industry and other permissible users as defined by DPPA.

Facts on Demand Press

Find It Online

Get the information you need as quickly and easily as a professional researcher. *Find it Online* is a practical, how-to-guide written by a non-techno geek and developed for real people. Learn the difference between search engines and search directories, find people online, cut through government red tape and access the vast amounts of information now available on the Internet.

Alan M. Schlein • 1-889150-20-7 • Revised 2001 • 512 pgs • $19.95

Online Competitive Intelligence

Competitive intelligence on the Internet . . . it's not the wave of the future . . . it's here now! The latest information to keep ahead of the competition is literally at your fingertips. *If* you know where to find it. *Online Competitive Intelligence*, a new title by the nation's leading information professional — Helen P. Burwell, empowers you to find the latest information that major corporations spend thousands of research dollars for — from your own computer.

Helen P. Burwell • 1-889150-08-8 • Revised 2000 • 464 pgs. • $25.95

Public Records Online

How can someone determine which records are available online — who has them and what is available for "free or fee" — without spending time searching endless sources? Use *Public Records Online*. As the only "Master Guide" to online public record searching, *Public Records Online's* second edition details thousands of sites, both government agencies and private sources. This new edition is 80 pages larger, easier to use, and contains:

Michael Sankey • 1-889150-21-5 • Revised 2001 • 460 pgs • $20.95

Available at Your Local Bookstore!

1-800-929-3811 • Facts on Demand Press • www.brbpub.com

Facts on Demand Press

The Accountability Revolution

The Accountability Revolution is the "Emperor's New Clothes" for those who want to achieve and maintain dynamic, results oriented leadership. Samuel pulls no punches in revealing the flaws in today's accepted business thinking. He provides powerful strategies and practical tools that increase morale & productivity, reduce team conflicts, decrease turnover, increase performance ratings, and earn greater profits. *The Accountability Revolution* puts you and your company on the fast track to breakthrough results and greater success.

Mark Samuel • 1-889150-27-4 • Pub. Date 2001 • 248 pgs • $17.95

Organizing the Good Life

Organizing The Good Life is packed with tips on achieving a successful business and home life. It's a welcome source of support for the emotional drains of disorganization, work addiction and the nagging self-doubt that occurs when you forget you are in charge of creating the life you want. Celia's philosophy is truly unique. It's a workplace simplicity message for those who have too much to do — yet don't want to give up the good parts of "having it all."

Celia Rocks • 1-889150-26-6 • Pub. Date 2001 • 170 pgs. • $12.95

Criminal Records Book

Criminal records provide essential information used for employment screening, locating people, fraud detection and other investigative purposes. This book is the complete guide to accessing and utilizing criminal records housed at the federal, state and county level. Learn how to:

- determine where criminal records are stored.
- obtain records at each jurisdiction level.
- select a record vendor.
- legally access criminal records.

Coming March, 2002!

Derek Hinton • 1-889150-27-4 • Pub. Date 2002 • 320 pgs • $19.95

Available at Your Local Bookstore!

1-800-929-3811 • Facts on Demand Press • www.brbpub.com